Demands on Rural Lands

About the Book and Editors

Planning for the use of rural lands in the developed countries of the world has become an increasingly contentious process as resources become more limited and conflicting needs grow stronger. The critical questions are "Which is more important—agriculture, livestock production, recreation, industry, or urban housing?" and "Who decides priorities and responsibilities for use?" The capacity of the land to meet all of the demands placed upon it, without serious environmental disruption, has become a major concern for all. Recognizing the exigencies of the situation, the contributors define and evaluate the theoretical and methodological frameworks within which rural land-use problems can be analyzed. In Part 1, the discussions focus on the identification and characterization of resources and competing users of rural lands, stressing that a careful articulation of the problem is essential to effective planning. Part 2 is aimed at developing appropriate information bases useful in planning for the problems related to the management of these rural lands. The discussion of policy options for rural resource use in Part 3 builds upon the material in the previous two sections to provide a framework for an analysis of rural resource use.

Chris Cocklin teaches in the Department of Geography, University of Auckland, New Zealand. **Barry Smit** is professor of geography, University of Guelph, Canada. **Tom Johnston** is a doctoral fellow, Department of Geography, University of Waterloo, Canada.

Demands on Rural Lands

Planning for Resource Use

edited by
**Chris Cocklin, Barry Smit,
and Tom Johnston**

Westview Press / Boulder and London

Westview Special Studies in Natural Resources and Energy Management

Published in 1987 in the United States of America by Westview Press, Inc.; Frederick A. Praeger, Publisher; 5500 Central Avenue, Boulder, Colorado 80301

Library of Congress Catalog Card Number: 87-50751
ISBN: 0-8133-7361-1

Composition for this book was provided by the editors.
This book was produced without formal editing by the publisher.

Printed and bound in the United States of America

CONTENTS

TABLES

FIGURES

PREFACE

This book evolved from an international conference on the Management of Rural Resources held in Guelph, Ontario, Canada in 1985. The meeting, which included a major theme relating to demands on rural land, provided the basis for selecting contributions to this volume. The conference was jointly organized by the rural study groups of the Canadian Association of Geographers, the Institute of British Geographers, and the International Geographical Union.

Rural areas provide many of the goods and services essential for modern societies, but the ability of the land base to meet the increasing demands placed upon it, without environmental disruption, is being questioned. Competition for the use of rural land resources has become actively debated. This book draws upon the expertise of scholars and practitioners to provide a range of perspectives on this debate. The objectives in compiling this volume are:

1. to identify and characterize rural land-use planning issues,
2. to describe developments in resource information systems and evaluate their ability to assist rural land-use planning, and
3. to present several analytical frameworks and assess their potential contribution to planning the use of rural lands.

The manuscript was prepared at the University of Guelph with production supported by the Land Evaluation Group and the Department of Geography. We are particularly thankful to Deborah Bond who efficiently coordinated the production, and Marie Puddister, for cartographic assistance. We gratefully acknowledge the Social

Sciences and Humanities Research Council of Canada for a grant in
support of this publication. We are also indebted to the authors of
the papers for providing the ideas and experiences upon which this
book is based.

Chris Cocklin, Auckland, New Zealand
Barry Smit, Guelph, Ontario
Tom Johnston, Waterloo, Ontario

PART 1
INTRODUCTION

1

RURAL LAND-USE ANALYSIS AND PLANNING: AN OVERVIEW
Chris Cocklin, Barry Smit and Tom Johnston

INTRODUCTION

Planning for the use of rural resources has emerged as a contentious issue in recent years. A matter of particular concern is the way in which society uses its land resources since, with only minor exceptions, the amount of land available is unalterably finite. From this stock resource a diverse set of products and services are provided, including food and fibre, minerals, timber, recreation and open space. As human populations have grown so too has the demand for those items which the land resource yields. Consequently, the ability of the land base to meet these requirements without causing major environmental disruption has been increasingly questioned. Widespread statement of concern over the exploitation of rural land resources is therefore hardly surprising. Concomitantly, extensive debate has taken place with respect to the appropriate mechanisms that should be invoked in order that conflicts over use are resolved in a satisfactory manner.

There is little doubt that in order to address effectively the questions raised in this debate at least the following must be accomplished:

1. a precise definition and characterization (both theoretically and empirically) of land-use issues,
2. the identification of the need for resource policy and planning,
3. assessments of the potential impacts of resource policies and plans, and
4. the evaluation of policy alternatives.

The essays presented in this volume address various elements of the broad research program implied in this set of requirements.

3

ISSUES IN THE USE OF RURAL LANDS

Accurate identification and characterization of rural land-use problems is an essential prerequisite to planning. Too often, governments have responded to land-use problems that are believed to exist, doing so in the absence of accurate information on the nature, magnitude and spatial extent of the perceived problems. Costs of intervention may be very high, particularly when the land-use problems are misinterpreted. In addition to policy development and administration, costs may be incurred by individuals, corporations, and society as a whole through forgone opportunities for economic development.

The issues themselves are diverse and multifaceted. Traditionally, that which has probably attracted the greatest interest is the conversion of agricultural land to urban uses. As cities continue to expand outward in order to accommodate increasing populations, land at the periphery is transferred from agricultural to urban-based activities. The spatial coincidence of human settlements and land well-suited to food production means that it is generally the agricultural land with highest productivity that is paved over.

There exists little consensus with respect to the seriousness of the problem posed by the conversion of agricultural land to urban uses. On the one hand, people point to the substantial areas of land that have been irreversibly removed from agriculture, the quality of this land for food production, and question the ability to adequately feed future generations (Briggs and Yurman, 1980; Centre for Agricultural Strategy, 1976; Platt, 1977; Plaut, 1980; Vining et al., 1977). In the absence of adequate information about the future, foodland preservationists often advocate a "better safe than sorry" policy. Other commentators question the need for farmland preservation measures, pointing out that the quantity of land converted is small in relation to the total available (Johnston and Smit, 1985) and that yield increases afforded by technological and management improvements have more than compensated for losses in production due to land conversion (Frankena and Scheffman, 1980). Whether such yield gains can be perpetuated is, of course, another issue for conjecture (Frink and Horsfall, 1980).

Although the agriculture-to-urban land conversion issue has held prominence for some time, other land-use issues have also been widely recognized. The implications of environmental degradation for food production capabilities, for example, is a subject about which much urgency exists. Soil erosion, pollution, and shortages of sufficient clean water for irrigation are all regarded as potential, if not existing, threats to meeting food requirements.

The conflicts relating to rural land use, whether existing or potential, are much more numerous than this, though. For example, there is the issue of reduced amenity value of rural areas as a consequence of food production activities. There are also issues associated with the reservation of land for recreational purposes in the face of demands for the land from other activities. Conflicts may also emerge between agriculture and forestry, mineral extraction and agriculture, forestry or amenity protection, and the growing of crops for energy versus food production, among many others.

It is worth noting that the issues associated with land allocation extend beyond those of production. Urban encroachment, for example, has been found to affect the social character of rural communities, and to contribute to the inflation of land prices, farm fragmentation, decreased agricultural investment, and to affect the quality and cost of rural servicing (Brown, 1977; Bryant and Russwurm, 1979; Rodd, 1976; Sinclair, 1967). The diversification of rural areas from agriculture to an increasing level of forestry development has also been seen to have implications for the character of rural society (Smith, 1981).

In all of these cases there is an important distinction to be made between that which is conjecture and that which is demonstrably true. It may prove to be most unfortunate that planning authorities have responded to the former in the absence of sufficient attention to corroboration. Suspicions of market failure and the hypothesized existence of land-use conflicts is not a sufficient basis for the institution of land-use policy.

The conversion of agricultural land to urban uses, for example, has stimulated policy responses in many jurisdictions (Furuseth and Pierce, 1982). The aforementioned observations with respect to the quantities of high quality land transferred out of agriculture can be held to account for such policy development in several contexts. All too often, however, studies that have documented the pattern of land loss fail to assess the implications in terms of the demands (present and future) for the products of the land. It makes little sense to suggest that land conversion represents a problem unless it can be reasonably demonstrated that such conversions will constrain society's ability to satisfy its goals, specifically in this context those goals relating to food production levels. The mere fact that land may be of high capability for food production does not provide agriculture with inalienable rights to the land. The same land may be well-suited to other uses, including urban, and the case for preservation for agriculture must be firmly established. As noted previously, unjustified intervention by the state in the land market may impose a host of unnecessary costs.

The essence of the analytical problem is revealed by Figure 1.1. Historically, both food production and the demands for food have risen over time and, at least in the developed world, supply has generally exceeded demand. It is reasonable to expect demand to continue to grow as population increases. The future trend in supply is however less certain, and two general scenarios are

6

FIGURE 1.1: THE SUPPLY OF AND DEMAND FOR FOOD

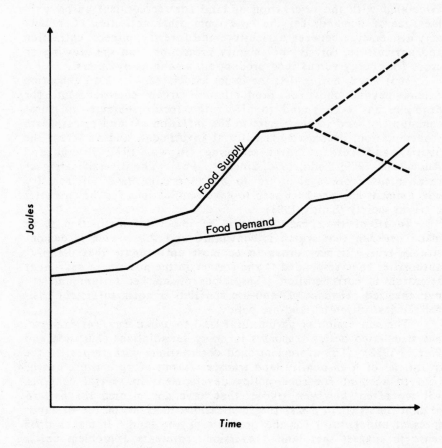

identified by the diverging dotted curves in Figure 1.1. One suggests continuing increases in supply as, perhaps, technology and management practices foster increases in yield. Alternatively, the rate of growth in supply begins to decline, as food producing capacity is constrained by land conversions, environmental degradation and so forth. Under such circumstances a point may ultimately be reached where demands exceed supply, leading to food shortages.

The most important analytical issue in this regard is to identify the extent to which supply and demand differ in quantity. A predicted large excess of supply would, in the absence of other concerns, suggest minimal intervention in the land market. Alternatively, a forecasted shortfall in supply might suggest some role for government, in order to preserve sufficient food producing capacity for future generations. While the analytical problem has been identified in relation to the urban versus agriculture land issue, a similar conceptual framework could be applied to the analysis of those other issues identified previously.

These observations have important implications for the procedures followed in the process of public policy formulation. Traditional models of the planning process suggest that at the first stage a problem is perceived, followed by the identification of policy objectives. In subsequent stages alternative strategies are identified and assessed, a preferred plan is implemented, and performance of the plan relative to the objectives is monitored. The major modification implied here is that an additional stage of analysis be considered following the perception of a land-use problem and prior to the formulation of the policy objectives. This step in the process would involve an empirical analysis of the nature, extent and magnitude of the perceived problem. Assuming that such an analysis suggests that the problem is of sufficient importance to warrant intervention, a set of policy objectives would then be formulated. Before proceeding, the objectives would be evaluated in terms of their consistency with the problem, as defined empirically. The rationale for these modifications to the public policy formulation process is explored in greater detail in Smit and Johnston (1983).

INFORMATION SYSTEMS AND ANALYSIS

The relatively recent interest in planning for resources from a rural perspective has meant that methodology development is in many respects still at an early stage. Increasingly, it has been recognized that methodologies developed to resolve urban-based problems may not be appropriate for the analysis of rural resource planning issues. In some cases existing analytical approaches can be modified, but in other cases new procedures must be devised. In this regard Cloke (1980, p. 202) stated "Thus, rural geography is presented with challenging opportunities for technical innovation, so that the essential processes of analysis, forecasting, and evaluation may be suitably carried out within the rural environment". An essential prerequisite to the types of analysis suggested by Cloke is the development of adequate data bases and appropriate systems for managing these. In the absence of adequate information it cannot be assumed that planning will achieve reasonable results.

In recent years significant advances have been witnessed in the realms of geographical information systems. These include the development of extensive data bases relevant to specific regional contexts, as well as the technical developments in data collection, handling and management. The latter affords analysts the capability to store large quantities of information and to retrieve this information in a variety of useful formats, including tabular, graphic and map output. Although in many respects still a relatively new field, significant progress has already been made.

Ultimately, though, for effective policy development the appropriate forms of analysis must be identified. Cloke (1980) accused rural studies of being hampered by both "conceptual famine" and "methodological plagiarism". Response to the former can come at least in part by way of the effective characterization of resource-use issues in the rural environment, as implied above. The plagiarising of methods may not in itself be unjustifiable, since as Kaplan (1964, p. 25) has noted in this respect, it is "not the question of whether everybody's doing it, but the very different question of whether anything gets done by it". Due largely to lack of experience, what is not known is the degree to which existing methodologies are suited to rural resource planning problems.

What is more certain, however, is that what has been a widespread reliance upon land capability or suitability measures as a basis for decision making with respect to land allocation is not justifiable. In this regard, the arguments have been explored in depth by Flaherty and Smit (1982). In short, the mere fact that land has a high capability to support a particular use is not adequate justification for the reservation of the land for that use.

A long tradition of applying more systematic procedures in the analysis of rural land-use problems has been established by Heady (Heady and Nicol, 1974; Heady and Spaulding, 1979; Heady and Timmons, 1975). More recently, the Land Evaluation Group at the University of Guelph, Canada, has developed analytical procedures for the evaluation of the land resource and investigating options for its use (Land Evaluation Group [LEG], 1984; Smit et al., 1984). Also, land allocation decisions with respect to forestry projects have been assisted through the utilization of multiobjective linear programming techniques (Dane et al., 1977; Dyer et al., 1979). These same programming techniques have been applied by McGrew (1975) in planning park developments, and by Cocklin et al. (1986) to assess options in resource use in relation to forest energy plantations.

In the context of evaluating alternative land-use developments, cost-benefit analysis has found application in the past (Peters, 1970), and more recently a case has been made for the application of this procedure in evaluating agricultural land preservation policies (Frankena and Scheffman, 1980). In recent years, then, a more widespread adoption of appropriate methodologies for rural land-use analysis and planning has been witnessed.

Often it will be the case that for particular problems new procedures may need to be developed, and this is clearly reflected in several of the papers contained within the final part of this volume. With increased experience, the array of techniques available for rural land-use analysis should improve in terms of both their utility and the selection available.

CONCLUSIONS

Particularly over the last twenty years, there has been increasing concern for ensuring the effective utilization of rural land resources. A limited resource base coupled with a diverse range of demands for products from the land suggests the potential for competition for what is available. Where competition does in fact exist, land allocation decisions must be made and appropriate mechanisms for facilitating such decisions need to be identified.

Effective management of rural resources demands the development and application of appropriate analytical frameworks with which to assess the need for resource policy, to identify the potential impacts of resource policies and plans, and for the evaluation of policy alternatives. In the absence of such information, inappropriate allocative mechanisms may be applied, for which society may ultimately pay a high cost.

Drawing upon the recent experiences of the respective authors, this volume presents a set of essays that make a timely contribution to the field of rural land-use planning. The second part of the book presents a selection of papers that are concerned specifically with the identification and characterization of land-use problems in the rural context. Contributions to Part 3 cover a range of information systems, including computer-based information systems and decision aids, agricultural land classification systems, and remote sensing techniques. These essays evaluate the utility of the various information systems specifically in terms of their potential contribution to rural land-use planning. In the fourth part of the book, the essays describe the development and application of methods of analysis within the context of rural land-use planning. The collection of essays presents a statement on both rural land-use planning issues and appropriate methods for analysis, therein providing a useful review of recent developments in this important and exciting field.

REFERENCES

Briggs, D. and E. Yurman, 1980, "Disappearing Farmland: A National Concern", Soil Conservation, 45 (6), pp. 4-7.

Brown, R., 1977, Exurban Development in Southwestern Ontario. Toronto: Economic Development Branch, Department of Treasury, Economics and Intergovernmental Affairs.

Bryant, C.R. and L.H. Russwurm, 1979, "The Impact of Non-Farm Development on Agriculture: A Synthesis", Plan Canada, 19 (2), pp. 122-140.

Centre for Agricultural Strategy, 1976, Land for Agriculture. Reading: University of Reading.

Cloke, P., 1980, "New Emphases for Applied Rural Geography", Progress in Human Geography, 4, pp. 181-217.

Cocklin, C., S. Lonergan and B. Smit, 1986, "Assessing Options in Resource Use for Renewable Energy Through Multiobjective Goal Programming", Environment and Planning A, 18, pp. 1323-1338.

Dane, C., N. Meador and J. White, 1977, "Goal Programming in Land Use Planning", Journal of Forestry, 6, pp. 325-329.

Dyer, A., J. Hof, J. Kelley, S. Crim and G. Alward, 1979, "Implications of Goal Programming in Forest Resource Allocation", Forest Science, 25 (4), pp. 535-543.

Flaherty, M. and B. Smit, 1982, "An Assessment of Land Classification Techniques in Planning for Agricultural Land Use", Journal of Environmental Management, 15, pp. 323-332.

Frankena, M.W. and D.T. Scheffman, 1980, Economic Analysis of Provincial Land Use Policies in Ontario. Toronto: University of Toronto Press.

Frink, C.R. and J.G. Horsfall, 1980, "The Farm Problem". In A Woodruff (ed.), The Farm and the City: Rivals or Allies. Englewood Cliffs: Prentice-Hall Inc.

Furuseth, D. and J. Pierce, 1982, Agricultural Land in an Urban Society. Washington: Association of American Geographers.

Heady, E. and K. Nicol, 1974, "Models and Projected Results of Soil Loss Restraints for Environmental Improvement Through U.S. Agriculture", Agriculture and Environment, 1 (4), pp. 355-371.

Heady, E. and B. Spaulding, 1979, "Implications of Alternative Land Use Policies in the North Central Region", Regional Science Perspectives, 9 (1), pp. 18-29.

Heady, E. and J. Timmons, 1975, "Land Needs for Meeting Food and Fibre Demands", Journal of Soil and Water Conservation, 30 (1), pp. 15-22.

Johnston, T. and B. Smit, 1985, "An Evaluation of the Rationale for Farmland Preservation Policy in Ontario", Land Use Policy, pp. 225-237.

Kaplan, A., 1964, The Conduct of Inquiry. Pennsylvania: Chandler Publishing Co.

LEG, 1984, Analysis of the Production Possibilities of Ontario Agriculture: Prospects for Growth in Ontario's Agri-Food Sector Under Alternative Conditions of Supply and Demand. Guelph: Publication No. LEG-18, University School of Rural Planning and Development, University of Guelph.

McGrew, J., 1975, Goal Programming and Complex Problem Solving in Geography. University Park: Papers in Geography 12, University of Pennsylvania.

Peters, G., 1970, "Land Use Studies in Britain: A Review of the Literature with Special Reference to Applications of Cost-Benefit Analysis", Journal of Agricultural Economics, 21, pp. 171-214.

Platt, R., 1977, "The Loss of Farmland: Evolution of Public Response", Geographical Review, 67 (1), pp. 93-101.

Plaut, T., 1980, "Urban Expansion and the Loss of Farmland in the United States: Implications for the Future", American Journal of Agricultural Economics, 62 (3), pp. 159-170.

Rodd, R.S., 1976, "The Crisis of Agricultural Land in the Ontario Countryside", Plan Canada, 16/3 (4), pp. 159-170.

Sinclair, R., 1967, "Von Thunen and Urban Sprawl", Annals of the Association of American Geographers, 57, pp. 72-87.

Smit, B. and T. Johnston, 1983, "Public Policy Assessment: Evaluating Objectives of Resource Policies", The Professional Geographer, 35 (2), pp. 172-178.

Smit, B., M. Brklacich, J. Dumanski, K.B. MacDonald and M.H. Miller, 1984, "Integral Land Evaluation and Its Application to Policy", Canadian Journal of Soil Science, 64, pp. 467-479.

Smith, B., 1981, "Forestry and Rural Social Change in New Zealand", Town Planning Quarterly, 63, pp. 27-29.

Vining, D., T. Plaut and K. Beri, 1977, "Urban Encroachment on Prime Agricultural Land in the United States", International Regional Science Review, 2 (2), pp. 143-156.

2
SOME CHOICES IN RURAL RESOURCE MANAGEMENT
Andrew Dawson

INTRODUCTION

There is great concern about the countryside. As the human race exerts pressures upon it dramatic changes are resulting. The rural domain is smaller than it was and variety within it is being lost - variety of landscape and of species. Some types of countryside are disappearing. Plants and animals have become extinct. And still the demands which people are making on the rural areas of the world are growing.

But is this a serious and widespread problem? Are not the land areas beyond the cities large, and their natural endowment of soils and vegetation likewise? Is not the great wealth and comfort created for millions of people by their exploitation of the rural environment sufficient justification for the changes which are being wrought within it? And, if there is a consequential tendency towards uniformity and impoverishment of that environment, is that any more than a marginal, aesthetic loss?

The perception of rural resource problems is not the same in all societies and even within particular societies perspectives often differ widely. The purpose of this paper is to outline briefly in a general sense some of the alternative views.

THE NATURE OF RURAL RESOURCES

It is widely believed that the stock of rural resources is fixed. The area of the earth's surface is strictly determined and similarly the biomass potential is constrained. Once destroyed or impoverished, soils may never reform, and if they do, the process may involve hundreds, if not thousands, of years. In other words, once the stock of rural resources is depleted it cannot be restored. Therefore, it might be suggested that it is irresponsible to farm, mine,

13

deforest or develop in any way which will reduce still further those resources which have been inherited.

However, such a view would be simplistic, for some resources are renewable, and within relatively short periods of time. In many temperate latitudes, for example, clear-felled forests regenerate and achieve the same variety of species composition and biomass as their predecessors. Similarly, fish stocks can recover even after heavy over-fishing. In short, some resources are not stocks but flows. Responsible management of them requires the maintenance of the maximum possible rate of flow, rather than some outright ban upon their exploitation.

Of course, there are resources which cannot be described as flows. Good agricultural land once used for building cannot, except at enormous expense, be restored to its former quality, and the quantity of such land is fixed. However, the ability to use it is not. Growing knowledge of the relationships between crops and the soil, improved methods of cultivation and advances in crop breeding all mean that soil productivity may rise and that such increases may be sustainable. Thus, reductions in stock resources may be justifiable if they are at a rate which is not faster than that at which the knowledge of how to use them is increasing.

MARKET FAILURE

Part of the problem associated with rural resources lies in the fact that, whether as flows or stocks, it may pay owners to use them in ways which do not reflect their value to society as a whole. Individuals who are faced with a need to make a living, or firms which are under pressure to make profits, may well consider that conversion of farmland they own to housing, industry or roads, the destruction of rare marshland habitats or woodland in pursuit of larger outputs from their farms, or the mutilation of beautiful scenery through the extraction of minerals is unfortunate, but inevitable. Moreover, any individual or firm may argue that their actions are so small that they will make little difference to the total stock of agricultural, scenic or other resources.

Society as a whole, however, may view the matter differently. If the growth of population will eventually require the use of every suitable piece of land for food production, or if science will need the knowledge which can be obtained only from the study of unique wildlife habitats, no further conversion of, or damage to, such resources can be permitted by society in the interests of future generations. In other words, the time horizon of society is very long, and communities cannot allow that which is irreplaceable to be consumed by the present generation if the effect is to reduce the options which will be available to later ones. Alternatively, it may be said that the resource costs involved in the use of these assets are much greater than the money costs which are paid by the users in the market. The market, therefore, fails to put the true value upon some rural resources.

Rural resources are also put at risk because of spillovers or externalities. Much land is used not only by its owners but also by others who have no formal property rights to it. Where these unformalized uses occur without the permission of the landowners or recompense to them, or in circumstances in which they cannot collect an appropriate payment, the market has failed. Thus, when electricity generating companies pollute the atmosphere and cause damage to forests and the death of fish by acid rain, or when toxic industrial waste is dumped into inadequately prepared landfill sites or rivers, producers and individuals are getting rid of their rubbish at little or no cost to themselves. The owners of the affected areas are obliged to accept the damage or to remedy it at their own expense. If such externally-imposed costs are the consequence of the actions of a large number of individuals and firms, each of whose contributions to the total is small, it may not be worth the while of those who have suffered to seek direct redress through the courts. Similarly, there may be cases where the general public enjoys, for example, the appearance of the countryside and demands that farmers be restrained from altering it as the technology of their industry develops. The farmers, though, cannot effectively charge the public for looking at their land and thus, market mechanisms are inadequate.

A further problem arises where it is generally agreed that some minimum provision of amenities and services should be made. This arises from the recognition that the distribution of income is such that many people would be excluded from the benefits of some resources if their availability were to be determined by the market. For instance, rural recreational sites, such as country and wildlife parks, have been provided privately and subject to entrance charges in many countries. They have also been provided by government with free or subsidized entry charges in places where it has been argued that such provision should be universally, or at least more widely, available.

THE MANAGEMENT OF RURAL RESOURCES

The question therefore arises as to how rural resources are to be managed, if problems of the types alluded to above are to be avoided. One answer is the nationalization of all such resources. If resources are natural, and not of humanity's making, then their ownership by individuals or limited groups is inappropriate, for they are the inheritance of the whole community. Furthermore, if they are an inheritance not from humanity, but from nature, they should be handed down to succeeding generations. Public ownership is, therefore, the most appropriate form in which such resources should be held, allowing the fullest possible regulation of those who are chosen to make use of them.

Something similar to this, though not quite in its fullest form, occurs in the centrally-planned, socialist societies of the USSR, Eastern Europe, China and some other countries, where it used to be assumed that resource abuse was a peculiarly capitalist problem, and could not occur under socialism. However, the balance which has been struck between the consumption and the preservation of agricultural land, clean air and water, scenery and forests, to name but a few resources, in many socialist countries seems to have been tilted even more in favour of economic development and resource consumption than in some market economies. Between 1961 and 1979, a larger proportion of Poland's agricultural land was transferred to other uses than in Britain. Atmospheric pollution in recent decades in parts of Czechoslovakia, East Germany and Poland has been as severe as anything in Western Europe, and the USSR has allowed gross pollution of the unique aquatic environment of Lake Baikal by industry for many years. It is unlikely that such a tipping of the scales against the maintenance of rural resources would have been permitted by the public in the western democracies, nor in Eastern Europe either, if Solidarity's efforts to close down industrial plants in Poland during the early 1980s were representative of public opinion there.

A second answer - and one which has proved to be increasingly popular during the twentieth century in market economies - has been to regulate the consumption of resources and to discipline their owners and polluters through the power of government. Zoning, land-use planning, pollution control and the designation of national parks, sites of special scientific interest and wilderness areas have all restrained the workings of the market, and have removed some resources from its decisions altogether. In substituting administrative for market decisions the door has been opened to all those individuals and groups who previously were barred, because of their lack of ownership, from influencing the way in which resources are used. This form of management, however, has frequently failed to satisfy the resource owners, who claim that they are not fully compensated for the restrictions which are placed upon them. Neither has it satisfied the environmental protection groups. They allege that owners are often able to make secret deals with administrators in order to achieve their ends.

Thirdly, there exists the possibility of improving the working of the market. The purchase of agricultural land at its current-use value by the state, followed by its sale to developers at development value, the regular charging of polluters for the costs of cleaning up their mess, and the requirement that opencast mining companies restore land to its previous state are all examples of the way in which the market can be made to provide a more accurate signal about value to users.

CONCLUSION

Thus, the management of rural resources is not a simple matter. In many cases the full nature or true cost of resource consumption is not known, and whether it is too rapid cannot be said. Nor is it necessarily known which of the three broad groups of management strategies outlined above will prove most effective. Many of the papers in this volume proceed from the assumption that there is a problem: that the rate at which developed market economies, at least, are using resources is not sustainable; and most seek controls within the framework of the institutions of democracies of the western type. As such they represent but a selection of the range of views and approaches to rural resource management. Nevertheless, within that context they offer much that is highly relevant.

PART 2
ISSUES IN THE USE OF RURAL LANDS

A wide range of trends and problems in relation to the use of rural lands have prompted policy responses in most countries. As the role of the public sector in this area has evolved, the need for timely and sound information has been increasingly recognized. One way to ensure that misinformed policy is not implemented or that required measures are not prematurely dismantled is to promote clear understanding of concerns relating to resource use. Faithful articulation of resource management issues is a prerequisite to action.

The choices open to government in terms of the nature of involvement in land-use allocation are varied. At one extreme is the nationalization of resources, while at the other the government might elect to allow the market to allocate resources among uses.

The range of issues relating to the use of rural resources is broad. Competition for land exists as, for example, between urban development and agriculture, mineral extraction and agriculture, and habitat protection and "productive" land uses, among many others. Other issues relate to land ownership and tenure, land degradation and the effects of environmental changes on resource use. Manning provides an overview of these and other specific issues within the context of a conceptual framework for land resource analysis. The need to increase both the breadth and depth of analysis, as well as to extend the timeframe for analysis, are recognized as important elements of the research agenda. Central to the discussion is the stated need for analysis to proceed in such a way that ultimately it will enhance understanding of land resource issues and promote appropriate policy responses.

The conceptual framework outlined by Manning provides a general outline for analysis of rural resource issues, and suggests the need for specificity with respect to particular issues. Munton achieves the latter in an analysis of conflict between conservation of the natural environment and agricultural activities. The expressed need for broad-based investigation, considering macro-level economic and political changes, farm organization, and social and environmental changes, reflects a more comprehensive approach than most traditional analysis.

The provision of land for recreation poses some particularly difficult problems for land-use planners. It is often difficult to provide justification for the reservation of land for recreation activities in the presence of demands for the same land from forestry, agriculture or mining. Pigram discusses possibilities for multipurpose use of rural land resources, wherein recreation opportunities are integrated with other land uses. The concept appears to have had some success in several national contexts, and would seem to offer the opportunity to circumvent potential land-use conflicts.

Environmental degradation in the form of pollution or resource depletion is also widely recognized as potentially having significant impacts on land use. Declines in productivity are likely to result and increased capital inputs may be required in order to maintain output levels. In some cases it may be necessary to adopt alternative land-use practices. Changes in management techniques and the adoption of alternative crop varieties are documented by Nellis as responses to the depletion of water resources in the mid-western United States.

One of the most controversial land-use issues has been the conversion of rural land to urban development. Williams and Pohl argue that in the face of uncertainty about the future, concerted efforts must be made to preserve foodland in anticipation of future shortages. The need to direct policy towards the protection of agricultural land is not universally accepted however. McDonald and Rickson suggest that in Australia urban encroachment onto farmland is not a major national policy issue. In that context, and elsewhere, poor management practices, environmental degradation and resource shortages (e.g., water) may pose greater threats to production capacity than land transferral.

The suitability of policy instruments, where they are applied, will depend expressly upon the circumstances at hand. Of concern here are the objectives to which policy is directed, the specific problem under consideration, the degree of uncertainty involved, institutional arrangements, and a host of other factors. Classifying management strategies as either risk-averse or optimal, Pierce assesses their suitability in the presence of uncertainty, particularly in relation to policies directed at land protection and soil loss control. The need to identify and correctly respond to uncertainty will have an important influence on the success of policy.

The range of topics addressed here is not exhaustive. Several of the more important topics are considered though, and the ways in which they are analyzed provide useful guidance in the important tasks of conceptualizing and describing land-use issues. In addition to providing unique insights into some fascinating questions, these chapters are offered as examples of the ways in which important and pressing questions can be elucidated.

3

SUSTAINABLE USE OF CANADA'S RURAL LAND RESOURCES: RELATING RESEARCH TO REALITY

Edward W. Manning

INTRODUCTION

At first glance, in terms of both land and environment, Canada would seem to be very rich - the last place on earth where one might imagine conflicts with respect to the amount of land and how it is used. Canada has been one of the last frontiers, although the limits are becoming apparent. Even now, there are some areas where initial settlement is taking place, where the land is first being tilled and where virgin forests can still be found; but Canadians are gradually coming to understand that even their environment has real limits. Their land resource, like that of other nations, is indeed exhaustible and provides real limits to what is practical in terms of sustainable development. Canadians are also coming to realize that they depend directly upon the land resource base for their national welfare. Forty per cent of Canada's gross national product and 25 per cent of its jobs are directly related to the land resource. The land base is the common denominator where the resource demands encounter the constraints of the environment. The sustainable development of the nation's resources is contingent upon a clear understanding of the land base and its limits.

This paper focusses on applied research concerned directly with the utilization of the nation's land resource base for sustainable economic development. Sustainable economic development is defined as the economic use of the resource base which maintains its capability and renewable productivity on a perpetual basis. Sustainable development is where economics meets the environment. It is a way of ensuring continued productivity, while maintaining those characteristics of the environment necessary to human welfare and well-being in the longer term. Implementation of sustainable development depends upon research to evaluate the use of the environment as the source of production. The land is the synthesis of the environmental and resource qualities of space. It can be the

23

focus of analysis to identify current and potential problems, and to devise applicable solutions to problems which threaten sustainable use.

This paper focusses on a comprehensive model of land research and how it relates to contemporary rural land issues in Canada. The objective of the model is to identify research opportunities which can be of the greatest use in the long-term conservation or wise management of the nation's resource base.

FROM EXPLORATION TO EXPLANATION

The first explorers - Champlain, La Verendrye and MacKenzie- made the initial contributions to knowledge of Canadian land resources. Their role was to find out what was there. The charting of Canada by the Hudson Bay Company and the fur traders enhanced the general knowledge of the extent and resource base of the nation. The first scholars in Canada to look significantly at land as a resource were economists and geographers who continued the focus on description. In fact, the bulk of Canadian geography until the mid-twentieth century was essentially descriptive, refining the regional descriptions of particular areas of Canada in terms of their economic activity, their physical resources and their human-land relationships. The comprehensive inventories undertaken in the 1960s continued this trend, with complete coverage of the agricultural, forest and wildlife resources of the Canadian ecumene. This was largely undertaken under the Canada Land Inventory, producing maps at a scale of 1:250,000, digital output, tabulations and specific sector reports. Taken together, these maps and analyses can be seen as the basis of an environmental inventory, related directly to the land resource base. Northern land-use mapping, focussing on the northern territories, continues and is scheduled for completion in 1988. The northern parts of the provinces, except Ontario and Alberta, have still not been comprehensively inventoried for renewable resource capability.

The approaches to Canada's land have therefore been ones necessary and appropriate to a nation which has indeed been a frontier. The very first questions to be answered have been: how much is there? where is it? what are its limits? and for what is it good? These have necessitated a great deal of exploration, of description and of inventory to simply establish the pool of information which will allow for a better understanding of the physical base and its use. It greatly surprised many Canadians when, in the 1970s, the Canada Land Inventory revealed that less than one-half of 1 per cent of Canada's agricultural land could be considered Class 1, or without limitations for agriculture, and that in fact only approximately 11 per cent of the total land area of the nation could support any form of sustained agricultural production (Lands Directorate, 1976). Similar figures can also be calculated for forest potential or wildlife habitat. For example, only 14.9 per cent of the inventoried area was found to have high capability (Classes 1-3) for forestry (Rump, 1983).

Certainly the bulk of research effort in Canada by resource or environmental scholars has been in the field of classification or documentation. It has often been focussed specifically on the documentation of land capable of particular uses or on the tracing of historical trends in land occupance and use and the relationship of these to land capability. These efforts have certainly been valuable and constitute the base required to address land resource issues.

When Canada was first settled, land was often viewed as a free good. Land was available for very low prices, or in some cases was available for the taking. If a farmer or forester exploited their own land to the point where it was no longer productive, they had only to go over the hill to find another area equally productive which could then be claimed as their own.

That era has passed. One of the main products of the resource inventories has been to show that the land now in use is the best land available to Canadians. In most areas the economic limits of agriculture or of forestry have been reached and a retrenchment is taking place (Figure 3.1). That land not specifically allocated is, in almost all cases, less desirable, more fragmented, more climatically risky, or physically disadvantaged relative to that land now in production (Bentley, 1982). The person who goes over the hill to find new land to exploit is likely to meet someone coming the other way. The realization that the limits have been approached has forced Canadians to reassess their land resource. It is now known what is and what isn't there: the question is "How is it to be allocated and how is it to be managed?" (Manning, 1980).

There is a growing realization that the land is the basic resource, or, looking at it from another perspective, the fundamental environmental variable which allows the synthesis of a wide variety of different factors in addressing society's wants and needs. From this common base society demands food, fibre, space for residence, work, transportation and recreation, as well as a source for water and the maintenance of biotic resources. Land problems are multi-sectoral, multidisciplinary and spatial. They therefore provide an ideal focus for many disciplines; providing they build on each other's strengths. But not without an expansion out of traditional, more narrow concerns. Reuben Nelson (1984), a Canadian futurist, has noted that there is an increased realization that problems are not limited. He has identified a need to assess problems from an enlarged perspective in three different dimensions. He notes:

FIGURE 3.1: CHANGE IN CANADIAN FARMLAND AREA, 1961-1976

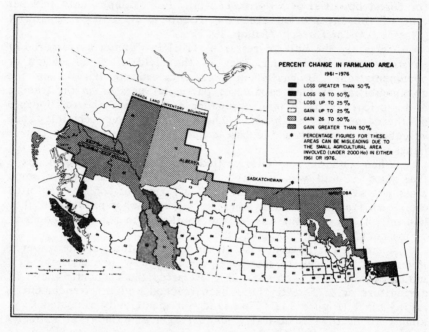

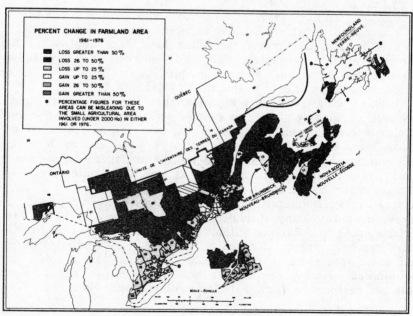

1. the need to broaden research to take in factors which are outside traditional limits. The trend towards cross-impact analysis, environmental assessment, or social impact assessment can be seen as evidence of this dimension,

2. a need to look further ahead or to lengthen timeframes, and

3. a need to look deeper, particularly through causal linkages, involving not only immediate causation but longer causal trains, involving the querying of the root assumptions of theory on society, economy or environment.

Research to address problems regarding the allocation and use of Canadian land resources has followed to some extent these themes, but the progress has been uneven.

Broadening the View

The broadening of land resource research to address concerns regarding the misallocation and mismanagement of resources has occurred over the past two decades; exploring increasingly interfaces between disciplines such as geography, economics, sociology and the physical and biological sciences, and applying techniques derived from all of these. Research into land concerns has looked at economic causes, social and behavioural measures as well as the more traditional environmental influences. But such broadening of the research base has remained limited relative to the wide number of interesting and real problems with respect to land resources which can be identified.

Lengthening the Perspective

There have been some successes in lengthening timeframes, generally through the adoption of increased quantification, although time series data is often difficult to obtain. Yet researchers have often left looking to the future to those who identify themselves as planners. Longer timeframes in looking at problems, of course, demand better techniques and more sophisticated techniques of dealing with data, something which has not always been handled very well by resource researchers, particularly those who allow their mathematical zeal to exceed the limits and quality of their data. Yet some of the most interesting phenomena are apparent only if spatial and temporal variation can be viewed simultaneously (McCuaig and Manning, 1982).

Deepening the Causal Analysis

It is the third dimension that gives the most concern. Coming from the very descriptive background of exploration and of inventory, scholars of land resources have often had considerable difficulty in expanding their concerns beyond these levels. Yet the type of problem with respect to the land resource, often involves not only knowing what the resource is, but also where it is, how much is there, and how it relates spatially. Increasingly, the analysis also involves the relationship of the land resource to societal needs, and indeed to the values that society itself places on the land resource. From an applied perspective, the ultimate objective is to rectify changes which are seen to be negative from a societal point of view; in other words to find direct solutions to real problems and to find means to apply them.

A WAY OF LOOKING AT LAND RESEARCH

Given these concerns for broadening and applying research to the real and growing problems of who is to get to use Canada's land and how they are to manage that land once they have it, a conceptual framework has been developed to assist in evaluating land research in Canada. It is a pyramidal structure which establishes as a goal at the top to understand and influence use of the land resource (Figure 3.2). Based upon management by objectives and logical framework analysis techniques (Practical Concepts Inc. and United States Agency for International Development [USAID], 1973), this pyramidal structure shows the logical steps necessary to address land resource concerns. The structure is conceived of from the top down, is built in steps from the bottom up, but in practical terms is most usually approached from the centre, where problems are identified. From the point of view of applied research, the existence of a problem is the reason for initial interest, the justification for research, and in practical terms is the means to obtain resources to address the problem.

In moving up, then down the pyramid there are six distinct levels. The base level (F) is data collection. In the centre of the lowest level are specific measures regarding the dependent variable - the land itself. At the corners are data sets relating to the socio-economic and biophysical information necessary both to modify understanding of land and to look at the relationships of land to society's goals. The second pyramid level (E) is the analysis of facts and trends. Researchers have traditionally concentrated much of their effort at this level. Most spatial theoretical developments, from von Thünen and Christaller to the application of quantitative methods, have been focussed on these bottom two levels.

FIGURE 3.2: A CONCEPTUAL STRUCTURE FOR LAND RESOURCE ANALYSIS

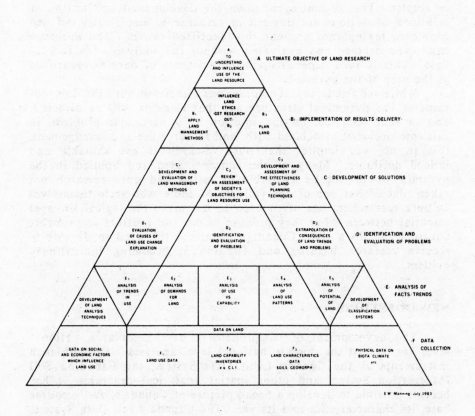

EW Manning July 1983

There is a marked paucity of work on higher levels of the pyramid. The remaining levels of the pyramid focus on the identification and evaluation of real problems, their causes and consequences (D), the development of solutions (C), and the implementation of these solutions (B) in support of a specific and defined objective (A). The logic of the pyramid, coming back down, is that the ultimate objective can be obtained through implementation of the solutions or results. This is contingent upon the development and testing of solutions. Solutions are devised in response to empirically defined problems, taking into account the identified causes. The problems cannot be defined and evaluated without the analysis of a factual base. This in turn depends upon the existence of data as identified at the base of the pyramid.

While the fundamental assumptions associated with the development of the pyramidal structure are that research will be directed, and in fact focussed, on the solution of a particular problem, in this case problems associated with land resource use and management, this in no way implies that pure research is not valuable and indeed desirable. Many of the concepts used and applied in the pyramid would not be available or tested had pure research not taken place. But one of the failures of those who style themselves as pure researchers has often been to not make the logical linkages essential between what they propose to do, and possible or probable future uses. In a tight Canadian economy, the need to do this to receive research backing and funding is becoming increasingly evident.

NEW QUESTIONS

The development of comprehensive data bases at a national level has opened the door to national level analyses. Through such instruments as the Canada Land Data System, the Canadian Soil Information System and other spatial analytical programs, it has become possible to develop a broad picture of Canada's land resource base, its characteristics and its use. The Canada Land Data System, housed in Environment Canada, is the largest land data base in the world and has overlay capabilities for these data. The data and analytical capabilities provide a vital base for land research. This is a fundamental step in addressing the key economic and environmental questions of the allocation of land between sectors and the management of that land by its users. It is now possible to build on this base, and to identify new research potential.

At this point, an example may be illustrative; a new spatial analytical product in the form of national maps, produced by the Rural Land Analysis Program of Environment Canada's Lands

Directorate. These maps illustrate some of the new dimensions which are now opening up for research into Canadian resource and environmental issues. The Rural Land Analysis Program is designed to synthesize data from many sources, like the Canada Land Data System, the Census, and climatic information, to allow:

1. preparation of national overviews,
2. correlation analysis at the county level of environmental, social and economic variables,
3. identification of national/regional level hypotheses regarding resource use/change, and
4. identification of anomalies, areas of interest for more detailed regional investigation.

The maps which follow are examples of the output of this analytical system which is in use in Environment Canada. It has helped to identify many questions worthy of further investigation. For example, a major westward trend in agricultural land use has become apparent. Large areas of land have been abandoned from agriculture in the east, the destination uses not yet documented. That remaining in use has often undergone significant intensification. Advance of the agricultural frontier in the west (Figure 3.3) is taking over large areas of forested land and disturbing wildlife habitat, but the implications of this at the local and national scale have not yet been studied comprehensively. In many parts of Canada, land use exceeds the theoretical carrying capacity of the land resource, threatening sustainability (Figure 3.4). The current level of analytical work, much of it targeted towards contemporary problems such as urbanization of prime lands, land degradation due to inadequate agricultural or forestry management practices, or growing non-resident land ownership, gives only a foretaste of what remains to be learned. Not enough is known about these and similar problems. There is inadequate data, too few and scattered analyses, little basic research on key problems of land allocation relative to supply, sustainable carrying capacity or demand, inadequate understanding of the economic and environmental implications of these trends and problems, and a very limited effort in the definition and evaluation of the effectiveness of remedial measures.

AGENDA FOR FURTHER EFFORT

With reference to the conceptual structure defined earlier in this paper, it is evident that many opportunities for further research exist at all levels of the pyramid (Figure 3.2). The management of Canada's environmental resource in terms of the demands of all

FIGURE 3.3: THE AGRICULTURAL ZONES OF CANADA

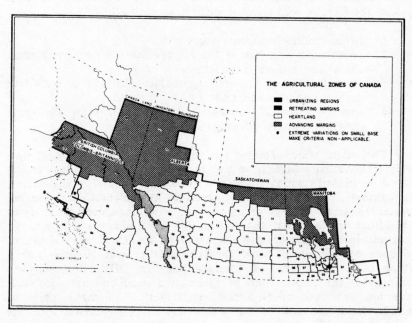

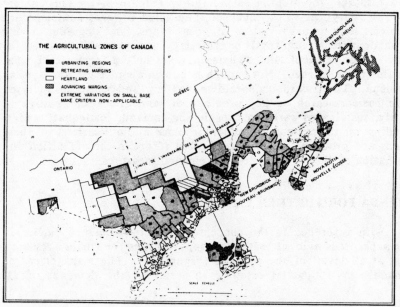

FIGURE 3.4: RELATIONSHIP OF LAND IN IMPROVED AGRICULTURE TO LAND WITH DEFINED CROPPING CAPABILITY

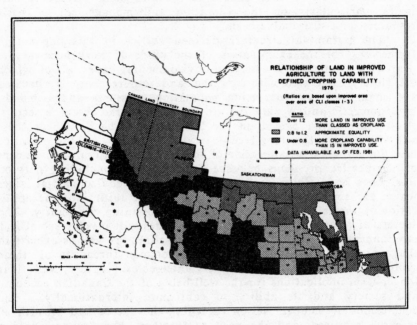

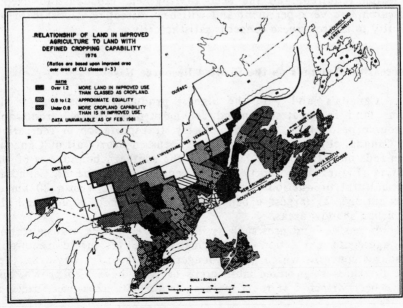

users will depend upon success in providing the knowledge and
tools required. While much of the research needs identified can be
styled as applied, work in the basic areas is also fundamental to
the needs. Such research should be focussed on key resource base
issues, particularly on the allocation and management of basic
resources on a sustainable basis.

The pyramidal structure defined earlier in this paper is a
framework for the examination of the kinds of work necessary to
deal with a number of emerging environmental issues, all of which
are closely associated with how the land resource base is allocated
and managed. As increasing population pressures and demands,
both domestic and worldwide, are focussed on the resource sectors,
stresses are being placed on the land resource base. Where these
stresses exceed the long-term carrying capacity of the resource
base due either to misallocation of the land or due to mismanagement
of it, specific problems or issues result. The concluding part of
this paper is a catalogue of some of the major environmental issues
which are emerging and which provide opportunities for the application of the talents of the academic and planning community. The
successful resolution of many of these issues will involve social and
environmental scientists from many disciplines, as well as experts in
the applications of solutions. But a common thread to all these
problems is their complexity, their intersectoral nature, and their
longer-term implications for the well-being of the Canadian economy
and society and its ability to contribute internationally. The
conclusions of Reuben Nelson regarding the nature and breadth of
research required, and the need to lengthen, broaden and deepen
research, are very pertinent and will bear direct relationship to the
ability to address these concerns satisfactorily.

Increasing Demands on the Limited Resource Base

Canada's land with the highest productive capability is the
same land in greatest demand for most uses, be they renewable
resource production, housing, industry, transportation or recreation.
In Canada, climate and history have focussed nearly all of Canada's
demands on a few prized lands near the southern boundaries of the
nation (Figure 3.5). Forty-six per cent of the value of Canadian
agricultural production came in 1981 from areas within 80 km of
the nation's 23 largest urban centres - from their commutersheds,
or urban shadow areas.

Intensive land uses such as industry, residences, transportation
or aggregate extraction are normally able to outbid renewable
resource concerns which have a longer timeframe for pay-offs. Yet
the pressures to produce more crops or trees have also grown, and
have been directed at the remaining lands. Direct consequences of

FIGURE 3.5: URBANIZATION OF THE NIAGARA FRUIT BELT

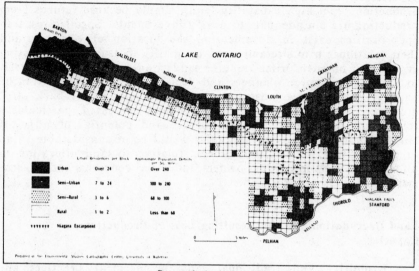

Degree of urbanization, 1965.

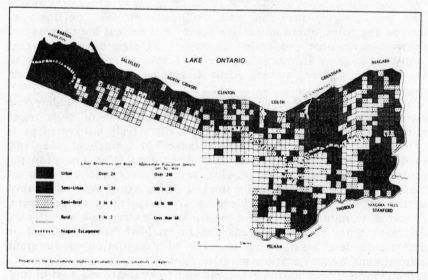

Degree of urbanization, 1975.

Source: Krueger (1978)

this have been pressures to over-intensify the use of land, resulting in degradation and overall rising land prices. In a recent study of the Okanagan Valley, fruitlands were found selling for over $40,000 per hectare. Urban-related pressures may exclude renewable resource production from high capability lands, simply because returns from production are not adequate to justify investments. Specific research opportunities exist in documenting the location of demands and their relationship to site and resource quality measures. A focussing of research on such prime resource lands would be of direct benefit to Canadian resource planners and decision makers. The siting of undesirable land uses, waste sites, and other "not in my back-yard" uses are also inadequately documented and evaluated, particularly relative to their impacts upon the use and potential of adjacent lands. Similarly, behavioural studies would be of considerable value in documenting the decision process relative to land allocation to different uses by individual owners, industrial concerns, and governments.

Land Degradation and the Resulting Loss of Productive Capacity

Exploitive and traditional land management practices are reducing the quality of the soil resource in many areas of Canada. The great risk is that the land resource itself will be degraded beyond the point where mitigative action will be feasible to maintain renewable resource production capacity. In simple terms, owners and users of land are exceeding the sustainable carrying capacity of the resource, and not making adequate management inputs to ensure that it is maintained in a useable condition (Bentley, 1982; Sparrow, 1984). Some specific symptoms of this are widespread salinization, erosion, acidification and compaction of soils, most notably on the Canadian Prairies and in intensively cultivated parts of southern Ontario and Quebec (Figure 3.6). Much of the land used for forestry is also mismanaged, in that it is not properly reforested and there is a growing reservoir of productive forest land which is not satisfactorily stocked. Disposal of wastes, notably toxins, is increasingly a problem, as are the effects of acid rain. Research is required to document the area, extent and severity of different types of land degradation, to establish broad regional or nationwide data bases, to relate levels of degradation to different management and allocation practices, to develop and examine the effectiveness of mitigating measures and to evaluate the spatial and economic impacts of specific mitigating measures in addressing these concerns. Work is also required to project the long-term implications of these resource use concerns for the economy, society and environmental maintenance of Canada.

FIGURE 3.6: SALT-AFFECTED SOILS AND RELATIVE RISK OF SOIL SALINIZATION

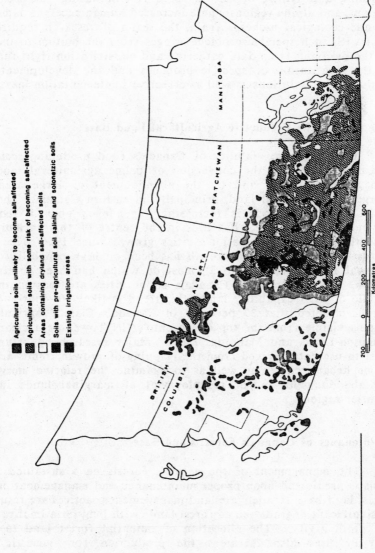

- Agricultural soils unlikely to become salt-affected
- Agricultural soils with some risk of becoming salt-affected
- Areas containing dryland salt-affected soils
- Soils with pre-agricultural soil salinity and solonetzic soils
- Existing irrigation areas

Source: Coote et al. (1981)

Ecosystem Maintenance

The advance of human economic activity, in particular extensive monoculture, is threatening the diversity and stability of many of Canada's unique ecosystems. Some specific examples include filling and draining of wetlands which function both as wildlife habitat and as water retention areas, prairie grasslands where very few natural grasslands remain, peatlands where extraction of peat or draining and filling of natural bogs is eliminating vast peatland regions, and alpine regions where increased human access is damaging unique ecological niches. Again, the realm of research required to deal with such specific problems ranges from the bottom to the top of the pyramid; from data gathering and classification right through to the localization of specific problems and the development and evaluation of solutions as well as effective implementation measures.

The Loss of the Productive Agricultural Land Base

The long-term viability of Canada's food producing sector is threatened both by the conversion of prime agricultural lands to nonagricultural uses and by the abandonment of large areas of marginal agricultural land, principally in eastern Canada. The net result of these trends is increasing dependence upon a reduced agricultural land base. But it is in the centre of this agricultural base that most of the nation's cities grow. Since 1966, over two-thirds of Canada's urban growth has been on high capability agricultural land (Classes 1 to 3), most of which had been producing farms. Because most of Canada's major cities are located in the middle of high capability lands, this trend is likely to continue. It has been noted that 37 per cent of Canada's Class 1 agricultural land is visible from the top of Toronto's CN Tower on a clear day (Simpson-Lewis and Manning, 1981). Major research opportunities exist to use data derived from the mapping of growth trends around major urban centres as well as to examine the relative merits of the abandonment and/or redeployment of marginal lands in the frontier regions.

Maintenance of Canada's Forest Land Base

The management of the nation's forests on a sustained yield basis is predicated upon proper maintenance and management of the forest land base. Inadequate land management practices are resulting in significant degradation of forest lands with long-term implications for productivity. The allocation of potential forest land to non-forestry uses also threatens the production for domestic and international markets and reduces the area of high capability forest open to sustained management. Failure to reforest has left huge areas of potentially productive forest land unstocked (Figure 3.7). Pressures towards multiple use of forests has reduced the ability of forest managers to manage. Present ownership patterns and management practices mean that there is little incentive to reforest and resources are sold to those who will use them at far below replacement cost.

Because the forest industry is principally on Crown lands or managed by large forest companies, there has been little standardized inventory and no consistent nationwide measure exists to locate productive forests or to permit an analysis of the state of their maintenance, although through the Forests Program of the Canadian Forestry Service some standardized data is now emerging. A major effort, ranging from the mapping on a consistent basis through to the measurement of changes, the analysis of the implications of different management practices, the relationship of ownership to management, and the economics of different management practices are essential just to establish the supply base. The opportunity for major industrial location studies is also present and serious questions exist with respect to the continuing supply of forest products to existing mills and to potential ones.

Habitat Loss

Virtually all human actions tend to influence wildlife habitat. Clear-cutting of forests, drainage of land for agricultural or other purposes, the management of agricultural lands, or the establishment of transportation routes can all remove or alter natural habitat. The key requirements are the identification, evaluation, designation and preservation or maintenance of that habitat critical to the nation's wildlife species. Too little is known regarding the function, quality or distribution of habitat. While inventory maps exist of wetlands and of ungulate capability, little work has occurred to relate these to the specific requirements of individual species. Except for the Ontario Wetland Habitat Evaluation System, criteria have not yet been adequately developed to allow an understanding of which habitats are most important for which species, and what types of trade-offs must be taken if habitat enhancement is undertaken to aid one species, perhaps at the expense of another. From a broader social or environmental science point of view, criteria have not yet been established regarding what population levels of species are critical, from which one could derive questions of adequate habitat. Once these are established, methods of habitat management and methods of encouraging owners and users of habitat to maintain and preserve particular qualities will need to be adequately

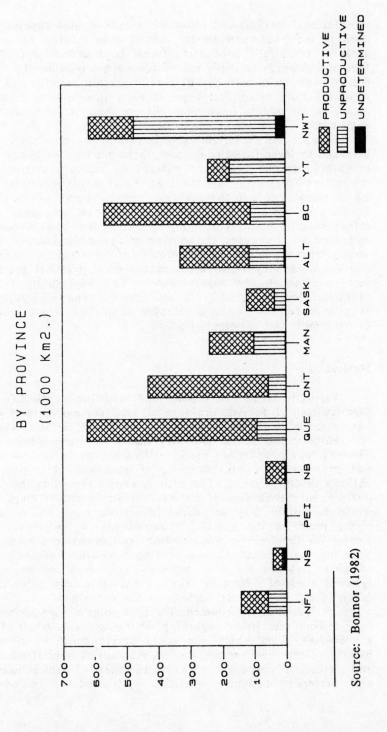

FIGURE 3.7: FOREST LAND PRODUCTIVITY

BY PROVINCE
(1000 Km2.)

Source: Bonnor (1982)

researched. Similarly, few effective planning instruments have been developed, short of purchase and direct management, to allow governments to effectively ensure that prime habitat areas are adequately maintained. Where adequate techniques have been developed, the political will to implement them is often lacking.

Energy and Mineral Land Management and Exploitation

With growing demands for fossil fuels, for minerals and for industrial aggregates, large parts of Canada are being identified as potential sources for these substances. Much of the land identified as having fuel or mineral potential lies underneath lands with other potentials. Thus, a great likelihood exits for conflict between land resource users. The specific concerns current in Canada include the growing demands for aggregates near major cities (most of these aggregate sources lie under good agricultural land); the growing demand for open pit and strip mining, notably for coal; the location of pipelines and transmission corridors relative to other land uses; the flooding of valleys for hydro-electric power development; the disposal of tailings on top of land which has other resource capabilities; and the rehabilitation of extractive sites. Many of these concerns are quite site-specific, although again the distribution and relative importance is not adequately known yet to permit an overall national perspective to be developed (Marshall, 1982). Research requirements, apart from data base development, lie in the development and evaluation of rehabilitation techniques and work dealing with the economic side of the equation, to allow rational decisions to be made regarding land allocation from, perhaps, a cost-benefit framework. But it is increasingly realized that normal cost-benefit procedures have been inadequate to address the question of renewable versus non-renewable resources or to incorporate the longer-term costs associated with site rehabilitation and the eventual harvest of renewable resource products. A needed focus is on the spatial element - the trade-offs being made between different sites and different site potentials and the opportunity costs associated with different sites and their alternatives.

Coastal Zone Conflicts

To a great extent the coastal zone conflicts in Canada are a microcosm of all of the previous land allocation and management problems described to this point. The management of coastal zones is a complex problem requiring an integrated approach in order to reflect adequately the interplay of the physiographic, biotic, marine, lacustrine, and climatic systems relative to the social and economic demands being placed upon them. The principal land issue is related to who is to get to use particularly favoured parts of the coastal zone and what their impacts are likely to be on their neighbours and on the quality of the coastal zone environment. While work has been underway for some time to document the ecological characteristics and uses of the Canadian coastal zone, and a broad level inventory exists for most inhabited coastal zones, the integrated planning and management schemes and methods necessary to allow significant problems to be dealt with are not yet in place. This may be a key area where experience of other nations could be of considerable use to Canada in terms of applicable methods to deal with the satisfaction of all demands simultaneously, or methods of choosing between such demands. This issue is becoming increasingly pressing, given growing recreation demands for seashores in their by-and-large natural state, and increasing development of offshore resources, whose shore facilities must often focus in the same areas.

Increasing Impact on the North

Rapid massive development is taking place in Canada's northern environment, an area which is poorly understood and yet highly vulnerable to the activities of industrial development, notably mining and petroleum. Northern landscapes and renewable resources are fragile and many areas are incompatible with human access or use. To a great extent, the original reconnaissance of resources, potentials and human uses is only now underway and will not be completed for some years. Thus, original work which is descriptive or only exploratory continues to be of value. But there are also many opportunities to advance the analysis of the relationship of humans and environment in the north, particularly associated with the rapid economic development and cultural change forecast for the region. Both the opportunity to plan ahead of development and the necessity to plan in the aftermath of development are presenting themselves with real challenges for environmental and resource scientists. The north presents a unique region for innovative solutions, perhaps derived from the kinds of mistakes that may have been made in other parts of the world.

The Ownership and Tenure of Land

Major concerns exist in Canada regarding the ownership of land: whether it should be public or private, whether foreigners should be allowed to participate as equals as landowners and developers, whether Crown or private lands should be held in an unused state or exploited and developed, and whether native Canadians have prior rights over huge areas of Canada for which they need to be compensated. With increasing competition for prime resource lands, the question of ownership and control is intensifying and focussing on the degree of regulation desirable or necessary, and on the specific role of territories and provinces in the regulation of land resources. A further question of interest is whether or not property rights are to be entrenched in the Canadian Constitution, bringing with them specific limits on what governments can do without compensation. Because ownership is so closely related to the way in which the land is allocated and to the way in which it is managed by its owners, leasers, etc., analysis of ownership patterns is increasingly important. Data bases do exist which could be accessed to obtain data on a cadastral basis or through tax rolls. But these data exist in many forms in different provinces and municipalities and are not readily accessible on a consistent basis. The opportunity exists for data compilation, analysis, integration and many varied studies relating land ownership to other phenomena. Decisions as to who is to get to control vast areas of Canada's resource lands, particularly relating to native claims, can have significant impact on the spatial organization of Canada and resource development. All of these provide good opportunities for productive and interesting research.

Land for the Future

The trends evident in land allocation or management yield concerns for the sustainability of different resource development options. Can Canada develop its forest industry at the same time as it increases export of foodstuffs? Which lands will be critical to the resource supply or to the environmental concerns foreseen in the next century? What is the expected role of Canada's resource base from an international perspective; a source of resources, a nature preserve, a repository for waste? What if large areas continue to be degraded? What if there is a need for self-sufficiency? Work to address these types of questions has been underway at the University of Guelph through the Land Evaluation Group and some valuable insights into land supply constraints, trade-offs and development opportunities have resulted (Land Evaluation Group [LEG], 1984; Smit et al., 1981 and 1984). Even so, this type of work, integrating foreseen demands with known resource and environmental opportunities and constraints is in its infancy. The Guelph model is operational at this time only for Ontario, and is restricted primarily to trade-offs between agricultural commodities and other demands on cropland. While progress is being made to model other sector demands and constraints and to build a national level integrated capability, progress is constrained by a general lack of research and lack of basic resource data. But with the nationwide coverage of the Canada Land Data System and the development of productivity indices for major renewable resource products, this provides a good, but not yet realized opportunity to develop the national land modelling central to sound land decisions. At the very least, the application of resource-base information to the planning process requires the development of better techniques and their application to real problems.

Applying Results to Reality

The final issue, and perhaps the most important one, relates to the top levels of the research pyramid (Figure 3.2) - getting the decision makers to use the results of the research and to apply them to their resource or environmental decisions. The existence of this as a serious issue is not the fault only of the decision makers; it is also the fault of the researchers. Too often, valuable research is rejected by decision makers because it is too complex or does not seem to address directly the questions they need answered. Yet no nation can afford to have decisions regarding its resource base taken in ignorance of the real constraints and of the longer-term implications of the decisions. In a complex society, it is essential to be able to deal rationally with the broader, longer-term and more fundamental aspects of issues, and this is particularly true in dealing with the land base as the source of sustained resource wealth and environmental health. There is no simple solution to this concern, only a challenge to the academic community to foster relevance to the maximum possible.

CONCLUSION

The overall objective of this paper has been to present a way of looking at land resource problems and research related to them in Canada. The application of Reuben Nelson's concepts to land resource concerns indicates a need for a much broader approach than most research in this field has traditionally been. This is true in terms of relationships to other sectors and to related disciplines, with respect to a temporal perspective, and with respect to the types of causal analyses which are only new to resource science. With the increasing demands placed upon the land resource base, Canada, like most of the rest of the world, is having to face decisions with respect to the use and management of this most basic resource. Some view the conflict as one between short-term economic demands and long-term environmental concerns, or as a zero-sum game between many different users or prospective users. This broad problem requires approaches involving the traditions of many disciplines to synthesize different demands and relate them in a spatial framework to the quality and constraints of the physical resource. Broadly-based, relevant research will be critical to decisions now being made with respect to the allocation and management of the rural resource base.

The conceptual pyramid shows the range of activities relevant to the land resource where researchers can become involved and indeed contribute. This has been used as a conceptual base to examine the present state of Canadian land research relative to the most pressing land related issues. There is enough to keep many times the number of land resource researchers now involved in Canada busy for the foreseeable future. Not only is there opportunity, but there is a pressing need for the kind of fundamental resource-related and environment-related research to feed into the decision processes now in place in the nation. Without this research and its direct application to the decision process, it is quite possible that decisions will be taken which do not respect the natural constraints of the resource base, and which will bring human, economic and environmental difficulties in future.

ACKNOWLEDGMENTS

I wish to acknowledge the help and suggestions of J. McCuaig, P. Rump, T. Pierce, N. Lavigne, P. Bircham and J. Pelton of the Lands Directorate, Environment Canada. Their input was of considerable value in the development of this paper.

This paper is based in part on the article "Canada's Land: Relating Research to Reality", in Zeitschrift-der-Gesellschaft-fur-Kanada-Studien, 1 (8), 1985, pp. 61-84.

REFERENCES

Bentley, C.F., 1982, Agricultural Land and Canada's Future. Ottawa: Klinck Lecture, 1981-1982, Agricultural Institute of Canada.

Bonnor, G.M., 1982, "Canada's Forest Inventory 1981". Ottawa: Canadian Forestry Service.

Coote, D.R., J. Dumanski and J.F. Ramsey, 1981, An Assessment of the Degradation of Agricultural Lands in Canada. Ottawa: LRRI Contribution No. 118, Research Branch, Agriculture Canada.

Krueger, R., 1978, "Urbanization of the Niagara Fruit Belt", The Canadian Geographer, 22 (3), pp. 179-194.

Lands Directorate, 1976, Land Capability for Agriculture. Ottawa: Canada Land Inventory Report No. 10, Environment Canada.

LEG, 1984, Analysis of Production Possibilities of Ontario Agriculture. Guelph: Publication No. LEG-18, University School of Rural Planning and Development, University of Guelph.

McCuaig, J.D. and E.W. Manning, 1982, Agricultural Land Use Change in Canada: Process and Consequences. Ottawa: Lands Directorate, Environment Canada.

Manning, E.W., 1980, Issues in Canadian Land Use. Ottawa: Lands Directorate, Environment Canada.

Manning, E.W., 1983, Agricultural Land Protection Mechanisms in Canada. Edmonton: Environment Council of Alberta.

Marshall, I., 1982, Mining, Land Use and the Environment. Ottawa: Lands Directorate, Environment Canada.

Nelson, R., 1984, Preparing for a Changing Future: A Catalogue and Analysis of "Futures Oriented" Work Undertaken by Canadian Governments. Ottawa: Square I Management.

Practical Concepts Inc. and USAID, 1973, Logical Framework Analysis. Washington: Practical Concepts Inc. and United States Agency for International Development.

Rump, P.C., 1983, "Land Inventories in Canada". In R. Louis Gentilcore (ed.), China in Canada: A Dialogue on Resources and Development, Proceedings of a Geography Conference, Canadian Association of Geographers and McMaster University, November 2-3, 1983.

Simpson-Lewis, W.L. and E.W. Manning, 1981, "Food for Thought: Can We Preserve Our Agricultural Land Resource", Alternatives, 10 (1), pp. 29-42.

Smit, B. and the Land Evaluation Project Team, 1981, Procedures for the Long-Term Evaluation of Rural Land. Guelph: Publication No. TSC-105, University School of Rural Planning and Development, University of Guelph.

Smit, B., M. Brklacich, J. Dumanski, K.B. MacDonald and M.H. Miller, 1984, "Integral Land Evaluation and Its Application to Policy", Canadian Journal of Soil Science, 64 (4), pp. 467-479.

Sparrow, H.O. (Chairman), 1984, Soil at Risk, Canada's Eroding Future. Ottawa: Standing Senate Committee on Agriculture, Fisheries and Forestry.

4

THE CONFLICT BETWEEN CONSERVATION AND FOOD PRODUCTION IN GREAT BRITAIN
Richard Munton

INTRODUCTION

Reliable evidence is now available to document the dramatic changes that modern farming practice has made to the appearance and wildlife value of Britain's countryside over the last 30 years. Public, professional and scientific opinion has become increasingly critical of these changes, and the dispute between farming and conservation interests reached a high point during the tortuous passage of the Wildlife and Countryside Act through the Houses of Parliament in 1981. During its passage an unprecedented 1,000 amendments were tabled and 200 hours spent in debate. Most contentious were the provisions which dealt with nature conservation, the countryside and National Parks, provisions that were intended to strike a balance between the needs of agriculture and those of the conservation of the semi-natural environment.

In retrospect it is easy to see that the Act represented no more than a milestone in a long process of adjustment to agricultural policy. The need to revise the objectives of West European agriculture, given growing food surpluses within the European Economic Community, is now clear, even if the state remains unsure of what role it should play in regulating agricultural development, and especially in managing the social and environmental consequences resulting from the continued substitution of labour and land by capital in the production process. And among academics too, there has only been modest progress in conceptualizing the relationship between environmental change and the social and economic forces responsible for it. In particular, there has been little research into the ways in which individual farmers adapt their businesses to meet changing economic conditions and family circumstances, and with what effects on the rural environment (Potter, 1986). It is towards a conceptualization of these questions that the second part of the paper is addressed. But first it is necessary to review the evidence on the nature and rate of environmental change in the farmed areas of the British countryside and to explain the form of the legislation that has been enacted so far.

THE NATURE AND RATE OF ENVIRONMENTAL CHANGE

Britain's countryside owes much of its variety to the actions of farmers. Change in its appearance and use is nothing new, and not for the first time in the nation's history many people disapprove of the alterations taking place. Evidence of widespread change has been accumulating for the last quarter of a century, indicating a substantial reduction in the area of all major wildlife habitats (Munton, 1983) and a significant loss of landscape features in all farming areas of lowland (Westmacott and Worthington, 1974 and 1984) and upland Britain (Countryside Commission, 1984). But, in spite of a decade of public consternation, losses continue even if the wholesale removal of landscape features by farmers has been replaced by the more insidious process of lack of upkeep and replacement (Westmacott and Worthington, 1984). Several studies even suggest a softening in the attitudes of farmers to the need for conservation. The problem is that these changes of heart regularly occur after the landscape has been modernized and farmers' attempts at landscape conservation can often be adjudged as cosmetic at best (Hamilton and Woolcock, 1984).

The main conclusions to be drawn from this very brief review are that losses of habitat and landscape features continue to occur as a result of modern farming methods, and that most new features are of lesser conservation interest than those they replace. Even a slow rate of loss can have major long-term consequences for the environment. Furthermore, significantly different environmental situations exist on neighbouring farms, as well as between different parts of the country, and in conservation terms the rich are getting richer (at least relatively) and the poor, poorer (Westmacott and Worthington, 1984). There is, therefore, more to an understanding of environmental change on farms than can be provided by an analysis of the structural conditions surrounding the farming industry alone. It is necessary to include an investigation of how individual farmers seek to cope with their particular business and family circumstances.

THE POLICY RESPONSE

For nearly two decades up until the mid-1970s agricultural interests argued that there was no real conflict between the management of farmland and the maintenance of an acceptable rural environment. They continued to express sentiments similar to those contained in the Scott Committee (1942) report in which it had been asserted that a prosperous farming industry was the best way of sustaining the social and environmental fabric of the countryside. This position, already weakened by growing evidence to the contrary, was fatally undermined in the late 1970s by a series of well-publicized conflicts between farmers and environmentalists, none of which portrayed farmers in a good light (Lowe, et al., 1986). The response of the agricultural lobby was to play down the general significance of these conflicts. Much more important, they said, were farmers' growing contribution to domestic food supply and improved business efficiency; and, it was suggested, most farmers and landowners were concerned about the environment and could be relied upon to remain the most effective and responsible stewards of wider interests in the countryside (National Farmers' Union [NFU] and CLA, 1977). All they needed was the right kind of financial support. Where conflict existed, it was the result of particular circumstances and in areas of special value to conservationists (Cox and Lowe, 1984).

During the 1970s farming interests managed to avoid any statutory legislation infringing upon their freedom to manage, and encouraged their members to participate in a voluntary approach towards limiting environmental change, accepting advice, grant aid and compensation in exchange for management agreements in the countryside. When the pressure for legislation became overwhelming, they concentrated their efforts on ensuring that the existing voluntary principle formed the basis of the Wildlife and Countryside Act (Cox and Lowe, 1983). From the point of view of the agricultural industry, the Act represents a classic damage-limitation exercise. The resulting legislation is limited in effect and extent. Farmers' and landowners' private property rights remain largely intact. Only within designated areas[1] are there additional controls on the giving of grants for agricultural improvement and an extension of the statutory notification system. In the case of Sites of Special Scientific Interest (SSSIs), for example, the new system requires the Nature Conservancy Council (NCC) to notify landowners as to the extent of the SSSIs which lie on their land and which management practices are prohibited, while owners have to give notice to the NCC that they propose carrying out damaging operations within their SSSIs in order to allow the NCC, if it so wishes, to enter into management agreements with them.

In effect, the Act seeks to deal with the conflict through limited action on the ground and at farm level, although the primary cause of agricultural intensification - the nature of agricultural policy - is determined elsewhere (Bowers and Cheshire, 1983). Recognition of this contradiction has grown since the Act was passed and it is now accepted that any long-term solution must address the goals set for the farming industry. The House of Commons Select Committee on the Environment, for example, has argued that the Ministry of Agriculture, Fisheries and Food (MAFF) should "fundamentally change its approach on financial structures so that resources are re-directed away from environmentally damaging operations and towards conservation-conscious methods" (House of Commons, 1985, p. xxiv). This recommendation follows criticisms made of agricultural policy by the House of Lords. They concluded: "As an element of the improvement of farming, care of the environment should have a comparable status with the production of food. Particularly with the current level of surpluses, the overriding importance of production, regardless of risks of damage to wildlife and landscape, has lessened" (House of Lords, 1984, p. xxxvi).

In spite of the Act, two important matters remain in dispute. Although major attempts can now be made to dissuade owners from carrying out damaging operations in designated areas, including the giving of advice, the with-holding of grant aid and the offer of a management agreement, the "voluntary approach means that the farmer cannot be *prohibited* from developing his land" (House of Commons, 1985, p. xv). In this respect the legislation does not go far enough in establishing the right balance between conservation and food production in the countryside, as implied by their "comparable status" in the House of Lords' report. Second, the principle upon which the payment of compensation is calculated for not carrying out an environmentally damaging operation is highly controversial (Department of Environment [DOE]/MAFF, 1983). It is "so arranged that a farmer is paid moneys in lieu of agricultural profits he would otherwise have made including agricultural profits he would have received" (House of Commons, 1985, p. xvi). In other words, the subsidy paid from one area of public spending (agricultural policy) inflates the level of compensation to be paid from another (environmental policy), a principle designed to ensure equity between owners. It has been roundly criticized as agricultural subsidies are presently contributing to the production of food surpluses of doubtful economic value. Moreover, the annual payments made to owners for loss of revenue can be substantial, as high as £500 per hectare per year in lowland England where wetland is being drained to permit the production of cereals (O'Riordan, 1985). It is questionable whether environmental agencies with their limited funds will be able to meet all the compensation claims made upon them (Adams, 1984).

Matters have not stood still since the Act was passed. At an institutional level the continuing debate has led the environmental and agricultural lobbies to draw closer together in arguing for revisions to agricultural policy; and one result has been a "greening" of the Common Agricultural Policy (CAP) with moneys being made available from this source to pay farmers for environmentally sensitive management practices (Baldock, 1986). Nevertheless, the agricultural community has been able to protect the essentials of its position, which are to avoid the introduction of wide-ranging controls over property rights, to keep attention focussed on designated areas and to ensure that levels of compensation for environmental protection do not leave its members any worse off (NFU, 1984). It can be argued, however, that this favourable outcome may prove short lived as the Act has:

> resulted in a marked shift in the terms of the debate. Whereas previously the onus had been on conservationists to demonstrate the deleterious effects of changing farming and forestry practices, the onus is now on the agricultural community and the Government to demonstrate that the Act is being effective in halting the destruction of wildlife habitats and landscapes [if further legislation is to be avoided] (Cox et al., 1985, p. 19).

It is imperative, therefore, to establish from field survey the extent to which farmers and landowners wish and feel able to comply with the spirit of the legislation. In spite of the generous compensation for those farming within designated areas, the public purse upon which they can draw is limited, and all farmers face an increasingly unstable market as concern over the cost of the CAP grows. Indeed, since the introduction of milk quotas in 1984 there has been a greater awareness among farmers that environmental degradation is only one consequence of increasing production. For the environmental lobbies there is the danger that the economic consequences arising out of any modification to the CAP will become the major area of concern for producers. Conservation planning and management agreements on individual farms may be even less enthusiastically received if quotas on production, reductions in grant aid and falls in the value of land occur. There is no guarantee that changes to the CAP, or to the wider workings of agricultural markets, will favour increased environmental concern among farmers and landowners. Those wishing to establish some degree of environmental stability must look beyond the environment to changes in the socio-economic structure of farming.

TWO FUNDAMENTAL PARADOXES

The continuing development of British agriculture contains several major paradoxes between the ideology expressed by farming interests and the way in which the industry operates. Two are of particular concern here. Both are encouraged implicitly or explicitly by public policy. The first is widely recognized, and is by no means restricted to Britain. It concerns, on the one hand, the consumption of large sums of public money by the farming industry, primarily in the form of price support, while the use, ownership and marketing of land, most of which is in private ownership, have minimal public controls imposed upon them. Collective public finance supports a selective concentration of private ownership over the means of production.

It is maintained, for example, that in 1979 financial support under the CAP alone was worth between £150 per hectare and £200 per hectare for every farmer in the United Kingdom (Bowers and Cheshire, 1983). On the other hand, well in excess of 95 per cent of farm businesses are privately owned, whether as proprietorships, partnerships or private companies, and about 90 per cent of all farmland is in private ownership (Northfield Committee, 1979). These monopoly rights thrive within a land market that is largely unconstrained by public regulation. There are no restrictions on who may purchase farmland, and purchasers do not have to demonstrate their farming competence. Today, the state holds almost no powers to enforce land redistribution, farmland is exempt from most planning controls except in certain environmentally designated areas, and it is accorded preferential capital taxation treatment as a business asset. This minimal degree of state interference is enhanced in England and Wales by the absence of a land register recording beneficial interests in land and which is open to public inspection.

This situation has been increasingly questioned in recent years if only because agricultural policy has encouraged over-production, promoted the substitution of capital for labour and land (capital has, in effect, been subsidized through capital grants and fiscal reliefs), and favoured the large farming business on high quality land more than the smaller concern on land unsuited to arable farming. More specifically, critical questions have been posed about:

1. the amount of public subsidy, derived from both the taxpayer and the consumer, being paid to farmers, even though the British government is committed to reducing public expenditure and encouraging market competition,
2. falling levels of farm employment, weakening the social and economic base of rural communities and reducing the scope for positive conservation work,
3. the smaller number of larger, full-time farm businesses, and
4. a farming industry that is increasingly intolerant of the multiple use of farmland.

The second paradox lies in the increasingly outmoded ideology of independence still articulated by many farmers. There is still considerable rhetoric expressed in favour of the small, independent family farm (Tranter, 1983) but without any explicit recognition by those making the case that within a capitalist economy this would mean the introduction of unwanted controls on the operation of credit supply and the land market. In practice, industrial and finance capitals have steadily increased their importance within the agricultural production process as farming has become a less significant element in the food chain (Smith, 1984; Wallace, 1985), placing the farmer on a technological treadmill in order to maintain profit margins (Dexter, 1977). The treadmill demands the increased use of manufactured inputs, ranging from chemicals to prepared animal feeds, and the production of better quality and more standardized products. Both these developments reflect the penetration of industrial capital into agriculture, while high land prices, the growing need for working capital and high interest rates have led to increased borrowing. As a result, various finance capitals, including both the clearing banks (see below) and other financial institutions (pension funds, insurance companies, etc.) have acquired a greater stake in the farming industry.

THE ANALYSIS OF CHANGE

The working out of these paradoxes is central to any inquiry into environmental change in the countryside. Environmental change forms an integral part of agricultural change, a process in which the state plays a crucial mediating role, and should not be viewed merely as a consequence of agricultural development.

In the United Kingdom the state has permitted as much internal competition within the industry as is socially acceptable. It has rejected farmers' demands to restrict the flow of nonagricultural capital into the industry (Northfield Committee, 1979), it has not constrained the operation of the land market, and it has adopted an approach to agricultural policy, despite rhetoric to the contrary, that favours the large, productive business at the expense of the small family unit (Marsden et al., 1986a). Since the early 1950s farm businesses have had to grow in order to survive and some have been better placed to achieve growth than others. Over most of this period, tensions within the farming industry, implicit in the differing abilities that individual businesses have to adapt, both between large and small producers and between the arable and livestock sectors, have been largely and effectively contained by the successful lobbying of the government by the NFU on behalf of the industry as a whole. The increasing inability of the union to represent the interests of all its members equally, given the polarizing trends inherent in agricultural development under capitalism, is reflected in the recent establishment of the Small

Farmers' Association and the Tenant Farmers' Association as separate interest groups.[2]

The present need is to develop a methodology capable of encompassing analysis of the structural processes outlined here and the responses farmers make to these within a single framework. The methodology needs to focus on the relations between structural forces and behavioural responses as neither provide a sufficient basis for an explanation of environmental change on their own.[3] Most previous analyses of change in British agriculture have either emphasized locality, community and family (Nalson, 1968; Williams, 1964) or the efficiency of farm production (Britton and Hill, 1975); but neither approach has provided an adequate basis for accommodating the wider macroeconomic and political forces which have been changing the nature of agricultural production.

The development of a political economy approach to agriculture can be viewed as a reaction to these weaknesses. Research in this tradition emphasizes a number of questions central to the previous analysis. It draws attention to the unique character of land in the agricultural production process, the transformation of the family farm under capitalism and the role of the state in agricultural development (Buttel, 1982; Marsden et al., 1986a). Of particular interest are the debates relating to the ability of non-farm capitals to penetrate agriculture and the persistence of the family-labour farm as the major form of production unit. These debates raise fundamental questions about the uneven nature of agricultural development, but they have yet to be explored fully in empirical terms. In particular, too much effort has been expended on establishing ideal forms of production and not enough on defining and explaining the processes that underlie change in the farm business.[4]

Family farms, for example, are continually adjusting their external production relations with the wider economy, and the distinction drawn between family and hired labour is too limiting to provide a full explanation of farm-level changes. For example, capitalist processes, particularly the substitution of labour by capital, have enabled some former "capitalist" farmers to return to "family-labour based production" while encouraging others to develop what Buttel (1982) terms "petty capitalist" businesses; and again, other family-based farming enterprises are being increasingly marginalized because of their inadequate access to capital or land, their occupiers leaving the industry or developing non-farming activities on their farms in order to retain their "names on the land" (Marsden et al., 1986b). At the level of occupation, all these variants represent family-managed businesses but more fundamentally they also reflect differing compromises with external capitals, compromises that may well weaken their managerial control. At the same time, the variety of compromises indicates that there is no single or uni-directional route to the development of farm businesses, even if certain broad tendencies can be established (Whatmore et al., 1987b). Thus, given that environmental change arises from the actions of individual farmers, it remains necessary to analyze changing production relations at the level of the individual business in a manner that allows for particular family circumstances, but to do so with a clear perspective on the structural conditions within which farmers take their decisions.

In summarizing this discussion three points can be made. First, the numerical dominance of family-based businesses and production belies an increasing penetration of the industry by non-farm industrial and finance capitals through such mechanisms as credit, partnerships, contract farming, direct landownership and technological dependence. Not only do these various mechanisms extract surplus value from the farm production process and transfer it to outside business interests, but they also reduce the effective independence of the farm family in its management control and ownership of capital. This development has been slowed by the peculiar and continuing dependence of agriculture on land as a means of production. Nevertheless, non-landed capitalists continue in their attempts to reduce this dependence by substituting industrial inputs for land in the production process and by capturing a growing share of the value added in the food chain through the processing of farm products. Similarly, finance capital, by way of the purchase of farmland, larger mortgages offered to farmers and, most importantly, increased credit for working capital, is acquiring a growing interest in the industry's assets. For example, a combination of increased capital requirements and high interest rates mean that the clearing banks, rather than private sources of credit, are now easily the single largest creditors to the United Kingdom's farming industry. Borrowing rose substantially during the 1970s so that by 1982 bank lending represented 32 per cent of the industry's working capital compared to only 16 per cent ten years previously (Agricultural Mortgage Corporation [AMC], 1982). Interest payments on commercial debts other than for land purchase are now equivalent to more than 25 per cent of farming income compared to 10 per cent in the first half of the 1970s (Burrell et al., 1984).

Second, the actions of the state are crucial. In Britain, not only has it safeguarded farmers from the full rigours of international competition but it has also retained unconstrained capital markets and protected private property. Agricultural policy favours large producers with ready access to capital and, in consequence, is sponsoring a particular transformation of the social and productive relations of family farms. Change is not expressed in the wholesale replacement of family-based farming but in the development of "petty capitalists", highly complex forms of land occupancy and ownership, and in the marginalization of small, full-time producers. Finally, the range of accumulation strategies farmers adopt means that agricultural development will be uneven, both between farms and between areas of the country. The analysis of macroeconomic processes needs to be combined with economic and ethnographic evidence from individual farms. In particular, evidence is required on farm histories, family development cycles and the strategies adopted by occupiers to ensure family continuity within the business (Marsden, 1984).

CONCLUSION

This paper is not concerned with the precise definitions that were employed or the detailed issues examined in a subsequent field survey of 265 farm businesses, although a clear indication of the matters raised with respondents is contained in Table 4.1. Neither does it contain a description of the farm sample.[5] The purpose has been to outline a conceptualization of the social and economic context of environmental change that incorporates an analysis of the major structural trends, contradictions and pressures for change in British agriculture. Unless these pressures are fully understood, policy will be misinformed.

If policy on the environment, as described, is to be altered, how should it be changed and at whom should the changes be directed? What advice, for example, should be given to farmers, land agents, conservation agencies, seed merchants, bank managers and the food industry? For although it is the farmed environment that is being altered, it is not enough merely to advise and direct the farming community, as has been the case so far. Agricultural change has to be viewed on a wider canvas incorporating the interests of other groups, financial, industrial and environmental, all of whom are involved in food production in their differing ways. The many roles of the state, especially those relating to property rights, fiscal legislation, the cost and flow of capital, and level of public expenditure, as well as the shaping of agricultural policy, create much of the context within which the farm family business operates. It is, however, the relations between these macro-political and economic issues and the historical development of the strategies for capital accumulation and continuity of land occupancy, as effected by individual producers and their families, that demand the greatest attention.

**TABLE 4.1: KEY COMPONENTS OF FARM
MANAGEMENT STRATEGIES**

1. DEGREE OF FAMILY CONTROL OVER PROPERTY ASSETS ON
THE FARM
   a) owner-occupation; with and without mortgage
   b) extent of non-family interest (e.g., trustees; partners, etc.)
   c) tenancy - security of lease; landlord's policy towards fixed
   improvements, etc.

2. DEGREE OF FAMILY CONTROL OVER BUSINESS MANAGE-
MENT AND CAPITAL OWNERSHIP
   a) credit and loan arrangements
   b) non-family ownership of business capital (e.g., company
   directors, landlord)
   c) advice, credit and contracting arrangements with industrial
   capitals
   d) employment of farm manager

3. ECONOMIC CENTRALITY OF THE FARM BUSINESS TO THE
FARM FAMILY
   a) proportion of family income obtained from farm business
   b) family agricultural interests off the farm
   c) family income from off-farm sources, including investment
   income and salaries

4. FAMILY REPRODUCTION: FAMILY WELFARE AND
CONTINUITY ON THE FARM
   a) family size and structure
   b) family association and continuity with the business
   c) aspirations over, and strategies for, achieving family
   succession

5. LABOUR RELATIONS ON THE FARM
   a) amount and proportions of family to hired labour
   b) proportion and skills of full-time to other categories of
   labour

58

NOTES

1. Most of the proposed changes relate to two kinds of area with an environmental designation. These are the ten National Parks in England and Wales (these extend to 1,360,000 ha or 9 per cent of the total area) and to the 4,048 Sites of Special Scientific Interest (in March 1983), which in total amount to 1,380,000 ha, some of which are located in the National Parks.

2. For an historical review of corporatism in British agriculture see Cox et al. (1986).

3. For an example of this approach see Whatmore et al. (1987a and 1987b).

4. For a current debate on these issues see Friedman (1986) and Goodman and Redclift (1985).

5. Interviews were conducted with 265 farm business principals and 31 landlords in three very different farming areas (West Dorset, Bedfordshire and London's urban fringe) during 1985 and 1986. Data on the development of farm businesses were collected for the period 1970-1985. Some results are to be found in Marsden et al. (1986b) and Whatmore et al. (1987b).

REFERENCES

Adams, W.M., 1984, "Sites of Special Scientific Interest and Habitat Protection: Implications of the Wildlife and Countryside Act 1981", Area, 16, pp. 273-280.

AMC, 1982, Farming Finance. London: Unpublished, Agricultural Mortgage Corporation.

Baldock, D., 1986, "Greening the CAP: A Progress Report", Ecos, 7, pp. 8-12.

Bowers, D. and P. Cheshire, 1983, Agriculture, The Countryside and Land Use. London: Methuen.

Britton, D. and B. Hill, 1975, Size and Efficiency in Farming. Farnborough: Saxon House.

Burrell, A., B. Hill and J. Medland, 1984, Statistical Handbook of UK Agriculture. London: Macmillan.

Buttel, F.H., 1982, "The Political Economy of Agriculture in Advanced Industrial Societies: Some Observations on Theory and Method", Current Perspectives in Social Theory, 3, pp. 27-55.

Countryside Commission, 1984, A Better Future for the Uplands. Cheltenham: CCP162, Countryside Commission.

Cox, G. and P. Lowe, 1983, "A Battle Not the War: The Politics of the Wildlife and Countryside Act". In A. Gilg (ed.), Countryside Planning Yearbook. Norwich: Volume 4, Geo Books, pp. 48-76.

Cox, G. and P. Lowe, 1984, "Agricultural Corporatism and Conservation Politics". In A. Bradley and P. Lowe (eds.), Locality and Rurality. Norwich: Volume 5, Geo Books, pp. 147-166.

Cox, G., P. Lowe and M. Winter, 1985, "Caught in the Act: The Agricultural Lobby and the Conservation Debate", Ecos, 6, pp. 18-23.

Cox, G., P. Lowe and M. Winter, 1986, "From State Direction to Self Regulation: The Historical Development of Corporatism in British Agriculture", Policy and Politics, 14, pp. 475-490.

Dexter, K., 1977, "The Impact of Technology on the Political Economy of Agriculture", Journal of Agricultural Economics, 28, pp. 211-221.

DOE/MAFF, 1983, Wildlife and Countryside Act 1981: Financial Guidelines for Management Agreements. London: Circular 4/83, Her Majesty's Stationery Office.

Friedmann, H., 1986, "Patriarchy and Property: A Reply to Goodman and Redclift", Sociologia Ruralis, 26 (2), pp. 186-193.

Goodman, D. and M. Redclift, 1985, "Capitalism, Petty Commodity Production and the Farm Enterprise", Sociologia Ruralis, 25, pp. 231-247.

Hamilton, P. and J. Woolcock, 1984, Agricultural Landscapes: An Approach to Their Improvement. Cheltenham: CCP 169, Countryside Commission.

House of Commons, 1985, Operation and Effectiveness of Part II of the Wildlife and Countryside Act. London: Volume 1, 1st Report, Environment Committee, Her Majesty's Stationery Office.

House of Lords, 1984, Agriculture and the Environment. London: 20th Report, Select Committee on the European Communities HL 247, Her Majesty's Stationery Office.

Lowe, P., G. Cox, M. MacEwen, T. O'Riordan and M. Winter, 1986, Countryside Conflicts: The Politics of Farming, Forestry and Conservation. Aldershot: Gower.

Marsden, T.K., 1984, "Capitalist Farming and the Farm Family: A Case Study", Sociology, 18, pp. 205-224.

Marsden, T.K., R. Munton, S. Whatmore and J. Little, 1986a, "Towards a Political Economy of Capitalist Agriculture: A British Perspective", International Journal of Urban and Regional Research, 10, pp. 498-521.

Marsden, T.K., S. Whatmore, R. Munton and J. Little, 1986b, "The Restructuring Process and Economic Centrality in Capitalist Agriculture", Journal of Rural Studies, 2, pp. 271-280.

Munton, R., 1983, "Agriculture and Conservation: What Room for Compromise?" In A. Warren and B. Goldsmith (eds.),

60

Conservation in Perspective. Chichester: Wiley, pp. 353-373.

Nalson, J.S., 1968, _Mobility of Farm Families_. Manchester: Manchester University Press.

NFU, 1984, _Policy Statement_. London: National Farmers' Union.

NFU and CLA, 1977, _Caring for the Countryside_. London: National Farmers' Union and CLA.

Northfield Committee, 1979, _Report of the Committee of Inquiry into the Acquisition and Occupancy of Agricultural Land_. London: Cmnd. 7599, Her Majesty's Stationery Office.

O'Riordan, T., 1985, "Halvergate Marshes: The Story So Far", _Ecos_, 6, pp. 24-31.

Potter, C., 1986, "Processes of Countryside Change in Lowland England", _Journal of Rural Studies_, 2, pp. 187-196.

Scott Committee, 1942, _Report of the Committee on Land Utilization in Rural Areas_. London: Cmnd. 6153, Her Majesty's Stationery Office.

Smith, W., 1984, "The "Vortex Model" and the Changing Agricultural Landscape of Quebec", _Canadian Geographer_, 28, pp. 358-372.

Tranter, R. (ed.), 1983, _Strategies for Family-Worked Farms in the UK_. Reading: CAS Paper 15, Centre for Agricultural Strategy, University of Reading.

Wallace, I., 1985, "Towards a Geography of Agribusiness", _Progress in Human Geography_, 9, pp. 491-514.

Westmacott, R. and T. Worthington, 1974, _New Agricultural Landscapes_. Cheltenham: CCP 76, Countryside Commission.

Westmacott, R. and T. Worthington, 1984, _Agricultural Landscapes: A Second Look_. Cheltenham: CCP 168, Countryside Commission.

Whatmore, S., R. Munton, J. Little and T.K. Marsden, 1987a, "Towards a Typology of Farm Businesses in Contemporary British Agriculture", _Sociologia Ruralis_, 27 (1), forthcoming.

Whatmore, S., R. Munton, T.K. Marsden and J. Little, 1987b, "Interpreting a Relational Typology of Farm Businesses in Southern England", _Sociologia Ruralis_, 27 (2), forthcoming.

Williams, W.M., 1964, _A West Country Village: Ashworthy_. London: Routledge and Kegan Paul.

5
COUNTRYSIDE PARKS AND MULTIPURPOSE USE OF RURAL RESOURCES
John J. Pigram

INTRODUCTION

In many parts of the industrialized world, rural resources are under pressure as various interests pursue their claims to the use of the countryside. In the face of competition from agriculture, forestry, mineral extraction, residential subdivision, energy projects, service corridors and land rights for indigenous people, the reservation of further areas of rural land for park and recreational purposes is becoming more difficult to justify.

In Australia, expansion of the parks system is under challenge from several quarters. Rural groups, in particular, are vocal in their condemnation of proposals to acquire more land for national parks. For many rural landholders, outdoor recreation is seen as being incompatible with other forms of land use and the establishment of parks and wilderness areas is perceived to be sterilization of otherwise productive land as enclaves, within which management practices leave much to be desired. Organizations such as Neighbours of National Parks and The Association for the Protection of Rural Australia have been especially critical of policies to create more parks on the North American model. Nor does this antipathy show much sign of abating. As recently as April 1985, a proposal to establish a new national park on the Northern Tablelands of New South Wales generated significant local opposition, partly on the grounds that such a move would alienate plans for a hydroelectric power station in the area.

At the same time, a good deal of questioning generally about the recreational role of national parks has emerged in Australia in recent years. The parks, which traditionally have formed a significant component of public recreation space, have tended to attach a high priority to management for environmental protection and nature conservation. As a consequence, other units in the parks system, such as State Recreational Areas, are being developed specifically to take recreational pressure off the national parks.

However, as with the parks themselves, the opportunities for adding to the stock of public resource-based recreation areas in this fashion are limited by a lack of land of suitable location and quality, especially in areas of greatest demand. Moreover, increasing competition for public funds along with budgetary restrictions on the agencies concerned are also working against the continuation of land acquisition programs as a practical means of broadening the array of park options available.

In these circumstances, it is perhaps surprising that relatively little attention has been given by park authorities in Australia to alternative approaches to creating opportunities for outdoor recreation in a rural setting. There are at least two options worth considering. The first of these involves making some privately held rural lands available for specified forms of public recreation. The second involves certain changes to the existing parks system in order to incorporate the multipurpose use concept. It is the purpose of this paper to discuss the merits of these proposals as practical means of creating additional rural recreation opportunities in Australia.

RECREATIONAL USE OF PRIVATE RURAL LAND

From the point of view of the government and the community, public use of private land represents a relatively cheap and sometimes free addition to the supply of recreation resources and thereby helps reduce pressure on public areas (Cullington, 1981). Private land, especially in agricultural use, provides variety in the recreation system for those who prefer human landscapes or whose activities are more suited to the settled countryside than to national parks or wilderness. It also forms a useful complement to publicly owned land in that it can cater to many linear forms of outdoor recreation, such as hiking, with minimal disruption to other uses of land. One way of extending community access to tracts of private rural land for outdoor recreation would be through the cooperation of land-holders in permitting and facilitating entry to their property.

In Britain, individuals and groups have long enjoyed at least *de jure* access to designated parts of the rural environment. Public pathways are part of the British heritage and an ancient network of long distance footpaths and bridleways covers much of the countryside. These "folk routes", often forgotten and overgrown, are gradually being redefined, marked and maintained to ensure a greater measure of *de facto* access to rural lands.

In New Zealand, a national walkway network is being established over public and private land as one way of bridging the gap between farmers and townsfolk. The goodwill of landholders is crucial to the system and the rights of property owners are fully protected with heavy penalties for offenses or damage by walkway users. The purpose of the scheme is to ensure "... that the people of New Zealand shall have safe, unimpeded foot access to the countryside for the benefit of physical recreation as well as for the enjoyment of the outdoor environment ..." (New Zealand Walkway Commission, 1979, p. 13).

In the United States, access to the countryside has been partially satisfied by making use of linear open space held in transportation and utility rights-of-way. Realization of the recreation potential of abandoned railroads, service corridors and canals eliminates the difficulty and expense of acquiring new land and permits more effective utilization of facilities whose original function has become redundant (United States Bureau of Outdoor Recreation, 1975). The United States Department of Agriculture has also funded a public access program in selected parts of rural America (Cullington, 1981).

Some landholders in North America and Britain see amenity agriculture as a paying proposition offering opportunities for supplementary income through commercial operation of hunting and fishing reserves, riding schools and campgrounds. Catering for tourists is also a successful economic activity in Britain where demonstration farms and open days are actively promoted by the Countryside Commission as a means of introducing visitors to the features and problems of modern agriculture.

In Australia, as in much of Canada, the lines seem fairly clearly drawn between town and country and the concept of inviolate rights of property ownership is widespread and generally accepted. In these circumstances, there appears to be little prospect of many landholders voluntarily diverting resources to recreational use (Cullington, 1981; Pigram, 1981). Public rights-of-way are rare and although access by consent can be arranged, such arrangements are by unwritten "handshake" agreement and usually on a short-term basis subject to abrupt cancellation. Typically, outdoor recreation is seen as incompatible with other land uses and landholders remain apprehensive of the consequences of negligence and vandalism by visitors.

In the more settled parts of eastern Canada, the attitude of some landholders is reflected in a submission to a study made by the Ontario Trails Council: "It is as reasonable to expect the country owner to allow the public use of his land as it would be to expect the urban owner to allow them to use his swimming pool and picnic on his lawn. The only reasonable place for public trails is publicly-owned land" (Cullington, 1981, p. 36). Similarly in Australia, most landholders perceive the disincentives to opening up access to rural land as outweighing any benefits. This pervasive attitude is typified by the following statement:

Access to private land for sport or recreation is a privilege and privilege is not a birthright but something that can be earned by good behaviour and responsibility. This Association will not consent to accept the entry upon private land, without the permission of owners or occupiers, or any persons who are not performing a statutory function, as other than trespass (Graziers Association of New South Wales, 1975, p. 3).

MULTIPURPOSE USE OF RURAL RESOURCES

Given the constraints on publicly sponsored programs to create additional park resources for rural recreation, and the apparent unwillingness of private landholders spontaneously to share their portion of the Australian countryside with others, it seems an opportune time to explore fresh approaches to expanding public access to rural lands.

Various methods of acquiring rural recreation space, short of outright purchase in fee simple, have been put forward (Howard and Crompton, 1980; Ontario Ministry of Natural Resources, 1977). These include differential property tax assessments, easements of different kinds, zoning, transfer of development rights, and national reserves. Of these, the last alternative, creation of national reserves, would appear to hold considerable promise for countries like Australia as an effective means of combining the economic and amenity functions of the countryside at low cost and with little disruption to rural interests.

National reserves are "living landscapes" where private ownership of land, existing communities and traditional resource uses are maintained. Established economic activities such as farming, forestry, mining and quarrying, transport networks, and settlements continue along with compatible recreational uses. By this means, coherent rural landscapes can be designated in which easements, zoning and incentives to protect ecological, scenic and cultural values, perhaps coupled with limited acquisition or donation of intensively used sites, ensure public access to high quality, functioning rural environments.

Kusler and Duddleson (1977) suggest that the national reserves concept holds several advantages. First, when compared with more traditional approaches, a wider spectrum of rural landscapes may be protected, ranging from historic fishing villages to farming communities. Second, a comprehensive approach can be taken to overall landscape planning and management, at lower cost of acquisition, operation and maintenance. Third, a mix of public and private lands helps maintain the economic viability of the areas and generates greater political and community support.

INTERNATIONAL APPLICATIONS OF THE NATIONAL
RESERVES CONCEPT OF MULTIPURPOSE USE

Despite some limitations and disadvantages, as well as initial opposition from landholders, versions of the national reserves concept have had wide application internationally. Although the policy was only embodied in United States law in 1978, some of the elements of the national reserves concept (known also as Greenline Parks in the United States) have been applied since 1961 with the establishment of Cape Cod National Seashore. Other areas in the United States in which the approach has been used include Adirondack Park in New York State, Cuyahoga Valley National Recreation Area in Ohio, and the Pine Barrens National Reserve in New Jersey. Adirondack Park, for example, contains 6 million acres (approximately 2.4 million ha), of which only 38 per cent is publicly owned. This situation may be contrasted with lands within the United States National Parks System where almost all land is publicly owned, uninhabited and undeveloped.

Other analogies can be found in Britain and Western Europe. In these older, more densely settled countries, few unaltered natural areas were left in which to set up national parks in the North American mould. Thus, in Britain when the first moves were made to establish national parks at the end of the Second World War, widespread acquisition of private lands would have been prohibitively expensive and politically unacceptable. The result is that the areas designated in England and Wales as national parks remain almost entirely in private ownership and productive use. In fact, all ten parks could more accurately be labelled national reserves, sharing many features with those in the United States. Agricultural holdings, fenced pastures, commercial forestry plantations, water storage reservoirs, quarries, transport routeways, and even villages and towns, are all found inside the park boundaries. Management plans administered by local committees endeavour to reconcile conflicting interests between landholders and recreationists. At the same time, attempts are made to maintain and enhance the resource base through controls over the location and nature of new facilities and proposals to alter existing structures.

Apart from Britain's ten National Parks, two definitive Regional Parks have now been established in the Lee Valley and Colne Valley near London. Both parks fit the national reserves concept with provision for outdoor recreation interwoven with all manner of urban fringe developments including industrial and housing estates, and in the case of Colne Valley, Heathrow Airport situated on the park boundary.

In the Netherlands, National Landscape Parks also have much in common with national reserves, as do the Regional Nature Parks in France and the *Naturparken* of West Germany. A report to the Netherlands Government describes National Landscape Parks as:

> areas of wild nature, water and/or woodland, *as well as* cultivated land and settlements, representing a great wealth of natural and landscape qualities and of cultural and historical values and forming a predominantly coherent and harmonious whole, in which government policy (based on a concept of planning, developing, managing and administering the area as a whole) is aimed at maintaining and developing the specific and differentiated character of the area, including making provision for recreation, but taking account of the social, cultural and economic needs of the population living and working there (Netherlands Ministry for Cultural Affairs, 1975, p. 19).

It should be noted that the Netherlands also has three national parks, where the emphasis is on nature conservation, and has plans to establish a further twenty. Clearly, however, in National Landscape Parks, the concern is not with purely natural areas, but with areas shaped by people and nature together over a long period of time. They include villages and towns, agricultural areas, typical architecture and other features of human activity characteristic of the Netherlands landscape. Embodied in the concept is the expectation that landholders, in addition to working their land, should assist in the management of the park and receive payment for activities concerned with its care as well as compensation for loss of income as a result of any limitations on land use. Thus farmers, for example, would no longer merely supply agricultural produce, but also provide the community with an attractive landscape. In the Netherlands, National Landscape Parks are seen as a complement to the National Parks System and an appropriate way of encouraging people living and working within rural areas to maintain the natural and cultural values of the countryside.

RECREATION AND MULTIPURPOSE USE OF RURAL RESOURCES IN AUSTRALIA

As noted above, a good deal of questioning of the role of national parks has emerged in Australia in recent years and already some elements of diversity are becoming evident within the parks system (Hibberd, 1981). However, to date, resource management agencies appear to have given little consideration to alternative means of expanding recreation opportunities along the lines of national reserves. Brisbane Forest Park, near the capital of the State of Queensland, is a step in this direction, although all land within the park, as in similar forest reserves, is publicly owned. In

New South Wales, the National Trust is sponsoring moves to declare certain parts of the Hunter Valley as Landscape Conservation Areas on the basis of their scenic, historic, cultural or scientific appeal (McDougall, 1982). These areas have some of the characteristics of the Areas of Outstanding Natural Beauty set aside in England and Wales and similar standards of development control are provided for under local environmental plans. However, the arrangement is largely voluntary and no specific provisions are made for public access.

In the State of Victoria, the Regional Strategy Plan proposed for the Upper Yarra Valley and Dandenong Ranges encompasses many of the features of the national reserves concept. Non-urban land in private ownership comprises 23 per cent (approximately 69,000 ha) of the total land area, with a further 3 per cent classified as urban. Approximately 105,000 people live within the region and the Strategy Plan provides for protection of the special features and rural character of the area, along with the maintenance of recreation opportunities on both public and private land (Upper Yarra Valley and Dandenong Ranges Authority, 1980). Similar planning policies are being applied on the Mornington Peninsula south of Melbourne and are under study for scenic zones in the Mt Lofty Ranges of Southern Australia, parts of the Darling Downs and Tamborine Mountain in Queensland, and in the far southwest of Western Australia (Mosley, 1978).

Apart from these initiatives, there has been a decided reluctance to depart from the existing national parks system (Johnson, 1978). Part of the reason for this lack of enthusiasm and even antagonism may be that the alternative is seen as a replacement for national parks, rather than a specialised application of the park concept and a useful additional unit within a broader parks system. However, establishment of a network of inhabited parks modelled on the national reserves in the United States would allow for the emergence of a dual system of countryside parks developed in tandem with traditional parks. The new style of park environment would encompass agricultural communities and rural settlements within distinctive scenic landscapes. The creation of multipurpose countryside parks in this way, along with continued endorsement of the existing parks system, should satisfy public recreation demand, park authorities, conservation-minded groups and private landholders.

MULTIPURPOSE COUNTRYSIDE PARKS - THE REALITY?

Given the prevailing negative attitude at official levels to the introduction of European-style national parks in Australia, coupled with growing resistance in rural areas to any further acquisition of parklands, progress towards establishment of multipurpose countryside parks is likely to be slow. At the outset, communities immediately affected will need to be convinced that traditional use of rural resources are not to be eliminated or threatened. If it can be shown, by successful pilot projects, that the economic and amenity functions of the countryside can be compatible, given certain management guidelines, then a range of park types can be created as and where appropriate.

An initial step in the process would be the tentative nomination of regions, preferably convenient to urban populations, with potential for designation as countryside parks. Surprisingly, as with some of the Landscape Conservation Areas in New South Wales, the initiative may well come from local groups with appreciation of, and concern for, what they see as special regional characteristics. Comprehensive inventory and appraisal of environmental resources, cultural elements, recreation potential, land use and other features of human activity would follow, directed towards delineation of coherent and distinctive rural landscapes and designation for multipurpose resource use.

Consultation and negotiation with landholders in order to explain the purpose and ramifications of the proposal are obviously vital. Boundaries would need to be established, easements secured and arrangements made for the purchase or donation of strategic parcels of land. Experience in the United States suggests that success is likely to be heavily dependent upon the qualities of the personnel charged with the task of park establishment and management. Obviously, cooperation is to be preferred to confrontation and legalistic, authoritarian decision making. A sensitive public relations program would be required to convince landholders of the feasibility of the multipurpose concept and to persuade them to surrender some of their rights of ownership in a mutually beneficial initiative to protect environmental resources and scenic values.

Considerable effort may also be needed to get landholders to accept the necessity for some restrictions on land use, such as retention and expansion of selected stands of vegetation, preservation of certain farm structures or features of the landscape and guaranteed access to specified recreation sites. They would need to be assured of minimal interference with independent farm decision making and of the reality of tangible government support by way of compensation for operating costs, maintenance and damage. In short, landholders would have to be convinced that disincentives are minimal and that they would in fact stand to gain by becoming part of an exciting new parkland concept. Apart from direct financial incentives, they should be freed from the problems and liabilities associated with indiscriminate trespassing. Many too, would undoubtedly gain a large degree of pleasure and personal satisfaction in finding that others appreciate the experience of sharing the countryside.

Education and interpretation programs, and sanctions, would also be essential for the community, so that visitors become aware of the privileges and responsibilities of recreational access and the need to observe certain restrictions at critical periods. The support of commercial enterprises, as well as local government agencies, would be an important factor in providing the necessary economic underpinning, infrastructure and facilities and services, and for the maintenance of traditional architecture and crafts in keeping with the functional concept of a countryside park and the distinctive character of its regional setting. If these were eliminated or allowed to decline, townscapes would deteriorate, a significant part of the historic and cultural heritage could be lost, and the integrity of the park landscape would be impaired.

CONCLUSION

For many years national parks in Australia have made a significant contribution to the recreation resource base in rural areas. Now, in many parts of the country, and for a variety of reasons, opportunities for further expansion of the National Park System are becoming limited. Indeed, it could be suggested that Australia is entering a mature phase of park development in which the initial stage of large-scale land acquisition is closing, to be replaced by careful appraisal, development and management of existing park resources. Henceforth, expansion of park use should come largely from within, by way of development of the parks system as it stands, refinements to the infrastructure and more efficient management of parkland already acquired. At the same time, consideration can be given to alternative means of expanding the recreation opportunities of urban populations by making available an array of different park options in accessible rural settings.

In a developed country like Australia, with all the pressures for greater output and more efficient production methods, the transition to large-scale stereotyped forms of land use is likely to be very rapid. Thus, there is some urgency regarding the implementation of an alternative approach to allocation of land to parks as the changing nature of agriculture and rural life acts as a disincentive for landholders to maintain the character and quality of the countryside in their keeping.

Despite scepticism and inevitably some opposition from several quarters, countryside parks, modelled on the concept of multipurpose use of rural resources, could play a useful role in Australia as an efficient, cost-effective means of making available recreation space, without the expense and disruption of outright public acquisition of additional parkland. Given time and enlightened management, such parks have the potential to demonstrate the benefits of sharing the countryside as a communal resource, both for economic purposes and outdoor recreation.

REFERENCES

Cullington, J., 1981, "Public Use of Private Land for Recreation". Waterloo: Unpublished M.A. Thesis, Department of Geography, University of Waterloo.

Graziers Association of New South Wales, 1975, Submission to Select Committee of the Legislative Assembly upon the Fishing Industry, Graziers Centre, Sydney.

Hibberd, J., 1981, "Nature Conservation Planning in Rural Areas - A National Parks and Wildlife Service Perspective", Presented to the 17th Conference, Institute of Australian Geographers, Bathurst.

Howard, D. and L. Crompton, 1980, Financing, Managing and Marketing Recreation and Park Resources. Dubuque: Brown.

Johnson, K., 1978, "National Parks - Australian Style", Victoria's Resources, 20, pp. 31-32.

Kusler, J. and W. Duddleson, 1977, Alternative Federal Strategies for Strengthening State and Local Urban Outdoor Recreation and Open Space Programs Including the Establishment of Greenline Parks. Washington, D.C.: National Urban Recreation Study, Volume 1, Technical Report No. 2, U.S. Government Printing Office.

McDougall, R., 1982, "Landscape as a Heritage Item", Presented to the 52nd ANZAAS Congress, Macquarie University, Sydney.

Mosley, J., 1978, "Regional Parks, National Parks and Wilderness Areas - A Framework for Recreation and Conservation", Presented to RAIPR Annual Conference, Burnie.

Netherlands Ministry for Cultural Affairs, 1975, Boen or Parkwachter (Farmer or Park-Keeper): Some Thoughts about National Landscape Parks. The Hague: Government Publishing House.

New Zealand Walkway Commission, 1979, "New Zealand's National Walkway Network", Parks, 4, pp. 13-14.

Ontario Ministry of Natural Resources, 1977, Alternative Methods for Securing Parkland. Toronto.

Pigram, J., 1981, "Outdoor Recreation and Access to Countryside-Focus on the Australian Experience", Natural Resources Journal, 21, pp. 107-123.

United States Bureau of Outdoor Recreation, 1975, Using Rights-of-Way for Recreation. Ann Arbor: Technical Assistance Bulletin No. 2, Department of the Interior.

Upper Yarra Valley and Dandenong Ranges Authority, 1980, Regional Strategy Plan. Melbourne: Government Printer.

6

LAND-USE ADJUSTMENTS TO AQUIFER DEPLETION IN WESTERN KANSAS
M. Duane Nellis

INTRODUCTION

Water resource projects, policies, and problems have long received close public scrutiny in the state of Kansas. Recent trends, associated with rapid development of irrigation land use and the resulting groundwater depletion in the Kansas High Plains (Figure 6.1), however, have resulted in an element of urgency and gravity not seen before in the state. This paper explores the human response to groundwater depletion due to irrigation in the Kansas High Plains. This is accomplished through an examination of the groundwater depletion problem, institutional response to resource depletion and land-use adjustments associated with significant reductions in groundwater availability.

THE AQUIFER SYSTEM

With limited surface water supplies and water deficits resulting from high levels of evaporation in relation to precipitation, the primary source of water for irrigation in the High Plains of Western Kansas is the Ogallala Aquifer; a massive underground water source, with an area of approximately 450,000 km^2, extending through eight states from South Dakota to Texas. The aquifer contains an estimated 4,000 billion m^3 of water and supplies 30 per cent of the groundwater used for irrigation in the United States. The groundwater system consists mainly of near-surface late Tertiary age sand and gravel deposits with saturated thickness levels up to 305 m. About 46 per cent of the aquifer has a saturated thickness of less than 30 m, whereas only 5 per cent has more than 180 m of saturated thickness (Weeks and Gutentag, 1984). Water quality is generally high throughout the aquifer system.

72

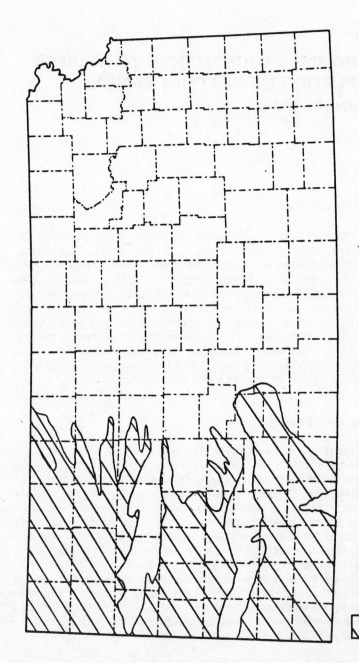

FIGURE 6.1: WESTERN KANSAS STUDY AREA

- THE KANSAS OGALLALA HIGH PLAINS REGION

GROWTH IN IRRIGATION

Although groundwater for irrigation in the High Plains of Western Kansas started in the late 1800s with the use of windmills, irrigation development was sporadic through the early 1950s. Only 101,000 ha of land were irrigated in Western Kansas as of 1951 (Fund, 1984). While the presence of an enormous amount of groundwater under Western Kansas was well known, the technological means and the institutional framework for intensive irrigation did not exist until the 1950s.

From 1950 through the mid-1970s, a variety of forces came together affecting farm structure and policy, and encouraging development of the groundwater resource for agriculture. Spurred by the discovery of natural gas in Southwest Kansas (providing an inexpensive energy source), tax policies favouring irrigation development, high land values, increasing credit availability, technological advances, non-farm income's entry into farming and a rising export market, the irrigated land area increased dramatically. By the early 1980s over half the market value of Kansas' agricultural production came from the counties with over 8,100 ha irrigated. By 1983, irrigated land area in Western Kansas reached 1.1 million ha. In addition, since 1950, crop yields have doubled, farm size doubled, and the region has experienced a greater concentration of ownership and power into the "super farm" (Kansas State Board of Agriculture, 1984). These were the years when the goal of Western Kansas' farmers became that of feeding the world by planting fence row to fence row and applying water with little thought of using a limited resource.

THE PROBLEM

The resulting impact of the dramatic growth in irrigated lands on groundwater is significant. As early as the 1930s Webb (1931) likened the Ogallala to a bank account of great size, maintained at a level by a balance of small deposits and small withdrawals. In essence, Western Kansas has been mining its groundwater resource, since water is being pumped from the Ogallala formation faster than the aquifer is recharging. Recharge, because of the region's low rainfall and depth to aquifer, is estimated to be approximately 6.4 mm annually. Withdrawals are 10 to 20 times the recharge rate (Kansas Water Office, 1984). The critical nature of long-term irrigation in Western Kansas is exemplified in Table 6.1, which shows that groundwater stores in the region of Southwestern Kansas, the region of most intensive irrigation development, will be depleted by the year 2017.

TABLE 6.1: AN ESTIMATE OF THE DURATION OF AQUIFER RESERVES IN THE HIGH PLAINS AREA OF KANSAS DATING FROM 1982

COUNTY	PRESENT WATER USE (1982) 000s M^3	NATURAL RECHARGE (Per Year) 000s M^3	NUMBER OF YEARS STORAGE WILL LAST	YEAR IN WHICH STORAGE WILL END
Finney	572358	18763	27.9	2012
Grant	327054	10906	34.0	2018
Greeley	54215	7036	23.0	2007
Hamilton	65536	6332	19.4	2003
Haskell	552395	11258	27.1	2011
Kearney	268759	12665	26.7	2011
Lane	40940	10085	35.4	2019
Morton	104774	12591	64.0	2043
Scott	160825	10555	17.8	2002
Seward	259699	10493	68.1	2052
Stanton	491138	13721	11.6	1996
Stevens	279090	12591	75.6	2060
Wichita	176253	11727	15.3	1999
TOTAL/ AVERAGE	3353036	148725	32.7	2017

Source: Kansas Water Office (1984)

In question then is the sustainability of the present irrigation-based systems of agriculture in Western Kansas. Currently, other resource variables provide additional pressure regarding the viability of agricultural land use. Declining land values, low commodity prices, over-production, declining export markets, and record debt levels contribute to a questioning of the attitude of short-term optional use of resources for the greatest economic benefit.

INSTITUTIONAL RESPONSE TO GROUNDWATER DEPLETION

Since 1945, the Kansas Water Appropriations Act has provided a framework for control over groundwater use. According to Shurtz (1967), the objectives of this Act are:

1. to govern the use of groundwater throughout the state,
2. to allow those already beneficially using water to continue such use as a vested right and to permit others to apply for appropriation rights, and
3. to grant right of beneficial use, not ownership of water.

Although the Chief Engineer of the Kansas State Board of Agriculture Division of Water Resources was, and is, entrusted to enforce the Act, no action has been taken to limit water use.

As a result of the lack of effective control of water depletion associated with irrigation development, concerns were raised in the early 1970s for a revised system of groundwater management. In order to conserve the groundwater resource, prevent economic deterioration, and stabilize agriculture, policy makers began exploring ways to implement tighter controls over the continued appropriation of water.

Acting to gain cooperation and enforcement over the management of groundwater resources, the Kansas State Legislature in 1972 passed the Groundwater Management Districts Act. The Act made possible formulation of regionally controlled groundwater management units with the authority to develop comprehensive management plans. Policies were implemented by the districts to provide for the orderly development of the Ogallala water reserves in order to extend the life of available water supplies. Districts were to be formed at the initiation of water users and landowners in an area, who would then prepare management plans tailored to fit area needs. Of the five resulting groundwater management districts, three overlie the Ogallala Aquifer. Management tools used in the districts include spacing of wells, limits on the number of wells, metering of water use, monitoring water quality, promotion of water conservation and modification of weather (cloud seeding). The main provision of the comprehensive management plans stipulate a maximum aquifer depletion rate of 40 per cent in 25 years. Well-drilling permits are recommended for approval to the Chief Engineer or rejected, depending on how closely the new well will impact on the depletion control goal (Kansas Groundwater Management Districts Association, 1980).

LAND-USE ADJUSTMENTS

Management Scenarios and Land-Use Projections

With institutional constraints associated with new well development and the associated increasing awareness by irrigators of a depleting water resource, it is reasonable to expect that changing land-use practices will be evident in Western Kansas. If institutional structure and associated management techniques are effective, statistics on land-use practices should demonstrate an increased movement in four major directions. First, a change from irrigated to dryland farming techniques; second, a change from high water consumptive crops to less water consumptive crops; third, improvements in irrigation efficiency; and, fourth, improvements in general management skills (Nellis, 1984).

According to Evans and Cant (1981), factors influencing the decision to adopt an irrigation farming system are based on an assessment of risk and uncertainty. This assessment involves perceived benefits of the irrigation farming system, perceived benefits from the use of water, perceived benefits from the on-site facilities, and perceived benefits from the availability of an alternative innovation.

Of particular importance to irrigators in Western Kansas would be their perceived benefits from the use of limited water and the availability of alternative innovations. Such decisions are strongly influenced by the management strategy put forth by the Groundwater Management District. In turn, then, it can be hypothesized that the district management strategy and associated groundwater depletion influences land use. Such a hypothesis can be accepted when one considers results of a land-use model developed by Buller (1982). Using 1977 as a baseline year and inputing various possible scenarios the model allowed for forecasts of land-use mix characteristics in the year 1985 and the year 2000. The five management scenarios considered were:

1. a management strategy based on currently authorized programs and available proven agricultural water management technologies,

2. a management strategy with aggressive regulatory water management through the adoption of advanced management and technology, with the aid of public policy to improve reduced rates or irrigation water use,

3. a management strategy of aggressive supply management through local water supply augmentation and weather modification, watershed management, and desalinization,

4. a management strategy to examine water supply augmentation by intrastate transfers of water from Eastern to Western Kansas, and

5. a management strategy of regional interstate importation of water to supply needs in Western Kansas.

The last three management strategies appear unrealistic for the Western Kansas region based upon past research, expense, and legal complications. Considering the first two management strategies, however, (one that is in place, and one that is more regulatory in nature) presents some interesting projections regarding land-use mix characteristics for the years 1985 and 2000. An analysis of land use in these two years allowed for an assessment of near and more long-term impacts of management approaches on land-use practices in the Western Kansas region.

Based on model forecasts that assume land-use practices using the current management strategy, irrigated corn, irrigated wheat and irrigated sorghum were all projected to either stabilize or decline significantly for both the near and long term (Table 6.2). Non-irrigated wheat, non-irrigated grain sorghum, irrigated soybeans and irrigated alfalfa were all projected to increase in land area from moderate to very high levels. The major projected impact of different management approaches on land-use practices relates most significantly to the rate of change to less water consumptive crops. A more stringent management strategy (Management Strategy 2) was projected to result in a more rapid increase in crops that are irrigated but use less water, such as soybeans, over the long term.

Recent Land-Use Trends

Modelled land-use trends are of particular interest when compared to actual land-use trends. Such a comparison may provide some indication of management effectiveness as hypothesized and projected with actual land-use dynamics. Actual trends were analyzed for Southwest Kansas since 1972, the year of implementation of the institutional forces acting to influence farmer decisions regarding land-use practices. Southwest Kansas contains 13 per cent of the state's area but greater than 50 per cent of the state's irrigated land area.

According to a recent survey of Southwest Kansas irrigators, 87 per cent of the irrigators responding to a question on their adjustments to groundwater depletion said that they had changed to less water intensive crops (Kromm and White, 1981). Using less irrigation water and the use of water conservation practices were also mentioned as adjustments by a majority of the irrigators responding. Given model forecasts, management structure and irrigation attitudes toward water conservation, it was of particular value to assess the actual level of adjustment as expressed through land-use practices. Adjustments were analyzed based on change from irrigated to dryland farming practices, and change from high water demand crops to moderate water demand crops.

Despite the growing awareness of the problems associated with groundwater depletion, land-use practices do not suggest that farmers are reverting to a greater intensity of dryland farming practices. In fact, the amount of dryland cropping associated with

TABLE 6.2: PER CENT FORECAST CHANGE IN LAND
USED FOR MAJOR CROPS BASED ON
CURRENT AND ALTERNATIVE MANAGE-
MENT STRATEGIES

	1985		2000	
	MGMT. 1[1]	MGMT. 2[2]	MGMT. 1	MGMT. 2
Corn, Irrigated	−20	−10	−80	−40
Wheat, Irrigated	0	−25	−50	−75
Wheat, Non-Irrigated	5	8	18	18
Sorghum, Irrigated	−40	−40	−80	−90
Sorghum, Non-Irrigated	400	450	650	700
Soybeans, Irrigated	119	103	532	762
Alfalfa, Irrigated	−2	−1	8	6

[1] Current management strategy
[2] Alternative management strategy

Modified from Buller (1982)

the region's two major dryland crops, wheat, and sorghum, has
actually decreased by 1.7 per cent since 1972 (Figure 6.2). Irrigators,
however, are shifting cropping practices from highly water consumptive crops to less water consumptive crops.

The amount of irrigated land has increased by 143 per cent
since 1972, although irrigated land area has decreased since 1977 by
5.5 per cent (Figure 6.3). What is significant about the dramatic
increase in irrigated land since 1972, however, is the dynamics
associated with type of crop irrigated. This is particularly evident
when comparing high water demand crops (e.g., corn) with more
moderate water demand crops (e.g., wheat). Corn, for example,
requires a much greater amount of moisture than wheat (38 per cent
more) to avoid crop stress during the critical stages of plant
development and maturation (Soil Conservation Service, 1985). The
resulting comparative advantage associated with total water use and
energy costs for pumping is reflected in the 255 per cent increase
in irrigated wheat since 1972 in contrast to the 11.3 per cent
decrease in land used for irrigated corn. In addition, since 1976,
the peak year for land planted to corn, the amount of land used
for irrigated corn has decreased by 44 per cent. Recent low corn

FIGURE 6.2: TRENDS IN DRYLAND AREA BY MAJOR CROP TYPE IN SOUTHWEST KANSAS, 1973-1984

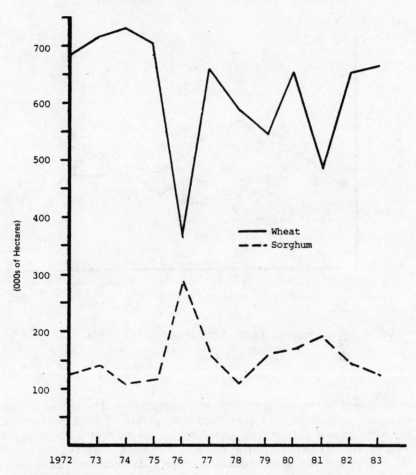

Source: Kansas State Board of Agriculture (1973-1984)

**FIGURE 6.3: TRENDS IN IRRIGATED AREA BY MAJOR
CROP TYPE IN SOUTHWEST KANSAS,
1973-1984**

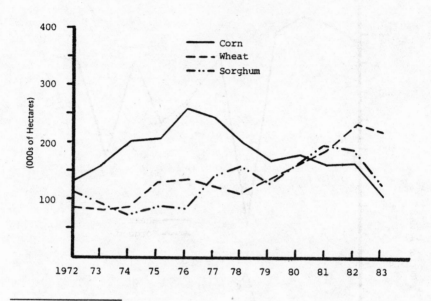

Source: Kansas State Board of Agriculture (1973-1984)

prices, which many analysts feel will remain low for the next few years, may contribute to a continued contraction of corn production.

Although of less overall significance, land devoted to irrigated soybeans and irrigated alfalfa has also increased dramatically since 1972, reflecting the more moderate water requirements. Land used for growing alfalfa has increased approximately two-fold while the land used for irrigating soybeans has increased by a magnitude of 15 times.

Land used for growing dryland sorghum, considered to be an important crop of the future based on model forecasts, has remained relatively stable in land area since 1972. The amount of dryland sorghum has actually decreased by 57 per cent since 1976. This decrease may reflect the comparative advantage, at least for the short term, of growing irrigated sorghum and other high return crops.

Other Land-Use Management Adjustments

The current overall efficiency of irrigation is estimated at an average of 35 to 50 per cent. By improving technology and management skills, it is estimated that efficiency can be improved to average around 80 per cent. Flood irrigation systems, for example, must now include tailwater pits for recycling. Efficiency is approximately 50 per cent without tailwater recycling. An estimated 20 per cent of the water applied runs off the field as tailwater. From 1978 to 1982 in Western Kansas, 1200 new tailwater pits were constructed (Fund, 1984).

Sprinkler systems with low pressure sprinkler heads (primarily associated with centre pivot systems) are increasing in popularity. Not only is the system adaptable to a greater range of terrain characteristics, but it is more flexible in water application. Although efficiency is approximately 75 to 80 per cent, during dry, windy weather the efficiency may be as low as 50 per cent.

When to apply water, how much, and when to shut it off are crucial elements to managing irrigation water. In the past, farmers turned the pumps on and let them run until they thought the field was well watered. Known as full irrigation, it often led to over-watering. Recent findings suggest that limited irrigation is producing nearly as much grain as full irrigation. Irrigators appear to be taking hold of this advice given response to recent surveys (Kromm and White, 1981).

CONCLUSIONS

Rapid depletion of the Ogallala Aquifer has resulted in several adjustments by resource managers in Western Kansas. Beyond the implementation of institutional forces associated with passage of the Groundwater Management District Act, farmers appear to be more aware of the long-term advantages of changing to more water efficient crops.

Despite growing awareness by State Officials and the farmers themselves of the groundwater depletion problem, it is highly unlikely that irrigation will be abandoned as a resource conserving technique. In fact, the area sown to dryland crops has decreased since 1972, whereas the amount of land used for irrigated crops has nearly doubled during this same period.

A comparison of actual land-use trends with model forecasts suggests that current policies, although a step in the right direction, may not be stringent enough to slow water depletion from the Ogallala Aquifer. It appears that model forecasts are rather optimistic about short-term benefit. When considering irrigation equipment investments, it is to the irrigators' economic advantage to switch to less water consumptive irrigated crops to meet district goals, rather than changing to dryland cropping techniques. Improvements in irrigation efficiency and management skills are stretching water supplies in the aquifer. It appears, however, that current management practices will, even if they are successfully implemented, simply prolong the eventual depletion of the Ogallala Aquifer, forcing irrigators to dryland farming practices over the long term. Although dryland farming techniques will also come with a more stringent approach, the gradual change in land-use practices would be more stabilizing to the region's economy and a wiser long-term resource management strategy.

REFERENCES

Buller, O., 1982, Ogallala Aquifer Study in Kansas: Linear Programming Model. Manhattan: Kansas State University Agricultural Experiment Station.

Evans, M. and G. Cant, 1981, "The Effect of Irrigation on Farm Production and Rural Settlement in Mid-Canterbury: A Comparison of the Irrigated and Dryland Farming Zones in the Lyndhurt-Pendarves Area, 1945-1976", New Zealand Geographer, 37 (2), p. 59.

Fund, M., 1984, Water in Kansas: A Primer. Whiting: Kansas Rural Center.

Kansas Groundwater Management Districts Association, 1980, Groundwater Management in Kansas. Topeka: Kansas Groundwater Management Districts Association.

Kansas State Board of Agriculture, 1973, Annual Report and Farm Facts. Topeka: Kansas Crop and Livestock Reporting Service.

Kansas State Board of Agriculture, 1974, Annual Report and Farm Facts. Topeka: Kansas Crop and Livestock Reporting Service.

Kansas State Board of Agriculture, 1975, Annual Report and Farm Facts. Topeka: Kansas Crop and Livestock Reporting Service.

Kansas State Board of Agriculture, 1976, Annual Report and Farm Facts. Topeka: Kansas Crop and Livestock Reporting Service.

Kansas State Board of Agriculture, 1977, Annual Report and Farm Facts. Topeka: Kansas Crop and Livestock Reporting Service.

Kansas State Board of Agriculture, 1978, Annual Report and Farm Facts. Topeka: Kansas Crop and Livestock Reporting Service.

Kansas State Board of Agriculture, 1979, Annual Report and Farm Facts. Topeka: Kansas Crop and Livestock Reporting Service.

Kansas State Board of Agriculture, 1980, Annual Report and Farm Facts. Topeka: Kansas Crop and Livestock Reporting Service.

Kansas State Board of Agriculture, 1981, Annual Report and Farm Facts. Topeka: Kansas Crop and Livestock Reporting Service.

Kansas State Board of Agriculture, 1982, <u>Annual Report and Farm Facts</u>. Topeka: Kansas Crop and Livestock Reporting Service.

Kansas State Board of Agriculture, 1983, <u>Annual Report and Farm Facts</u>. Topeka: Kansas Crop and Livestock Reporting Service.

Kansas State Board of Agriculture, 1984, <u>Annual Report and Farm Facts</u>. Topeka: Kansas Crop and Livestock Reporting Service.

Kansas Water Office, 1984, <u>Kansas Water Supply and Demand Estimates</u>. Topeka: Kansas Water Office.

Kromm, D. and S. White, 1981, <u>Public Perception of Groundwater Depletion in Southwestern Kansas</u>. Manhattan: The Kansas Water Resources Research Institute.

Nellis, M.D., 1984, "Land Use Related Adjustments to Aquifer Depletion in Southwestern Kansas", <u>The Geographical Bulletin</u>, 26, pp. 10-18.

Shurtz, E., 1967, <u>Kansas Water Law</u>. Topeka: Kansas Water Resources Board.

Soil Conservation Service, 1985, <u>Kansas Irrigation Guide</u>. Washington, D.C.: U.S. Department of Agriculture.

Webb, W.P., 1931, <u>The Great Plains</u>. Boston: Ginn and Company.

Weeks, J. and E. Gutentag, 1984, "The High Plains Regional Aquifer - Geohydrology". In G. Whetstone (ed.). <u>Proceedings of the Ogallala Aquifer Symposium II</u>. Lubbock: Texas Tech. University Water Resources Center, pp. 6-25.

7

"LET THEM EAT HOUSES!"
THE IMPLICATIONS OF URBAN
EXPANSION ONTO GOOD FARMLAND
Dan Williams and Ann Pohl

INTRODUCTION

In planning for land use in a region, projections of population and associated land requirements are commonly considered in determining future requirements for urban land. The same logical process could be applied to trends in population on a large scale, such as at the national or global level, to estimate the consequent food demands. Opinions as to whether the land base will have the capability to satisfy these demands differ. On the one hand, there are those who do not foresee severe food shortages in the western industrial nations and who believe that efficient resource allocations will be achieved via the market. Another view, and that expressed herein, is that population trends suggest that within the next few decades there may well be food shortages affecting the industrialized nations.

The particular concern here is the fact that present-day urban expansion is reducing the agricultural land base. This land transferral process will increase the likelihood that in industrialized countries it will not be possible to adequately feed future generations. Even before that happens, North America may find that it no longer has the capacity to respond to food demands from other parts of the world (Brown, 1981).

The province of Ontario, Canada provides an example of a jurisdiction where the irreplaceable high quality agricultural land resource base is being reduced at an alarming rate by urban expansion, even though there is within that jurisdiction an ample supply of land that has no potential for agriculture and that could be urbanized instead. This example is drawn upon here to make a case for more concerted efforts in the preservation of agricultural land. First, information is provided on the nature and extent of the agricultural land resource, with particular reference to Ontario.

Legislative efforts to plan for agricultural land preservation are then considered. Subsequently, selected case studies are discussed to illustrate the argument that current institutional arrangements within the province do not promote effective preservation efforts. The final section considers the need for more effective communication of information in the planning process, in the interests of promoting sound land-use planning.

THE LIMITED AGRICULTURAL LAND BASE

No more than 15 per cent of Canada is suitable for any agriculture, and this land is largely in the Prairie Provinces where the climatic constraints (short growing seasons and moisture limitations) are much more severe than in Southern Ontario. Ontario has less than one-tenth of Canada's farmland, but it represents a major part of Canada's agricultural land that is climatically best suited to agriculture and, hence, should be considered as a national resource. On the other hand, by far the largest part of this province's land is unsuitable for agriculture. For example, there are large areas of Canada Land Inventory (CLI)[1] class 7 land north and northwest of Kingston. These areas do not have an unduly harsh climate, they are almost ideally situated between the Toronto and Montreal markets, and they are close to the Great Lakes/St. Lawrence waterways, which would provide ready connections to the industrial heartland of northeastern North America and to Europe. Thus, when viewed at the provincial level, one can see ample alternatives to using land with good agricultural potential for urban development.

The historical pattern of development, however, has resulted in a situation where Canada's urban centres have occupied land that is of high capability for agricultural activities. Canada's larger urban centres occupy over 660,000 ha (Warren and Rump, 1981). Most of this land would otherwise have been good farmland and would have had the capacity to feed more than one and a half million people. In Ontario alone, the land occupied by urban uses would have the capability to provide food for three-quarters of a million people. The 660,000 ha of land occupied by urban centres in Canada in 1976 represented a 29 per cent increase from 1966, and 62 per cent of that increase occurred on high quality agricultural soils (CLI classes 1-3) (Warren and Rump, 1981).

In addition to soil characteristics, climatic factors also act to limit the spatial extent of agricultural activity in Canada. The agroclimatic resource index (ACRI), developed by Williams (1983), is a convenient method of quantifying the relationship between the climatic conditions and agricultural capability of an area. The measure is based upon the available frost-free period and is adjusted on a region-by-region basis to account for two other climatic restrictions; moisture deficits and insufficient accumulations of solar heat energy during the frost-free period. The values for the ACRI range from 1 (poorest for agriculture) to 3 (most suitable for agriculture). When the ACRI values are calculated and plotted on a map (Simpson-Lewis et al., 1979; Williams, 1983), the concentration of land which is climatically favourable for agriculture can be discerned. Approximately one-seventh of Canada's farmland has ACRI values of 2 or higher.

Urban development in Canada has tended to occupy the soils that have the highest capability for agriculture, and those areas that are climatically favourable (Williams, Pocock and Russwurm, 1978). More than one-half of the urban expansion occurring between 1971 and 1976 occurred in areas with ACRI values of 2 or higher (Figure 7.1). The ACRI averages 1.6 for Canadian farmland in general, but the average for land converted from rural to urban use between 1971 and 1976 was 2.

The large quantity of urban expansion recorded as having occupied regions with an ACRI rating of 1.6 seems anomalous at first glance (Figure 7.1), as if indicating that urban expansion concentrated on land with poorer agroclimates. In fact, the land in this category lies primarily around Edmonton and Calgary, Alberta, which have agroclimatic resources that are superior to those of the average prairie farmland.[2] Thus, even in that region, the pattern of developing land with the best agroclimate is evident.

THE MANAGEMENT OF FOODLAND RESOURCES

Programs of farmland preservation in North America have been grouped into four categories by Furuseth and Pierce (1982). They consider that the most effective type of program, which they call "comprehensive-mandatory", is that adopted in the Canadian provinces of British Columbia, Newfoundland and Quebec, and in the states of Hawaii and Oregon. Prince Edward Island, Canada and nine states in the northeastern and northcentral United States have programs that are not in the most effective category, but which are better than that adopted in Ontario. California, which, like Ontario, suffers from intense urban expansion pressures, has a program that is about as effective as those of Ontario, the Prairie Provinces, New Brunswick and Nova Scotia. In the United States, 36 of the 50 states have farmland preservation programs that are considered to be less effective than those of any of the Canadian provinces (Furuseth and Pierce, 1982).

Even the comprehensive-mandatory type of preservation program has not always proved to be effective in protecting valuable farmland resources. The loss of prime fruitlands in the Okanagan Valley of British Columbia due to urbanization, which has been extensively

FIGURE 7.1: FARMLAND LOSS AND CLIMATE

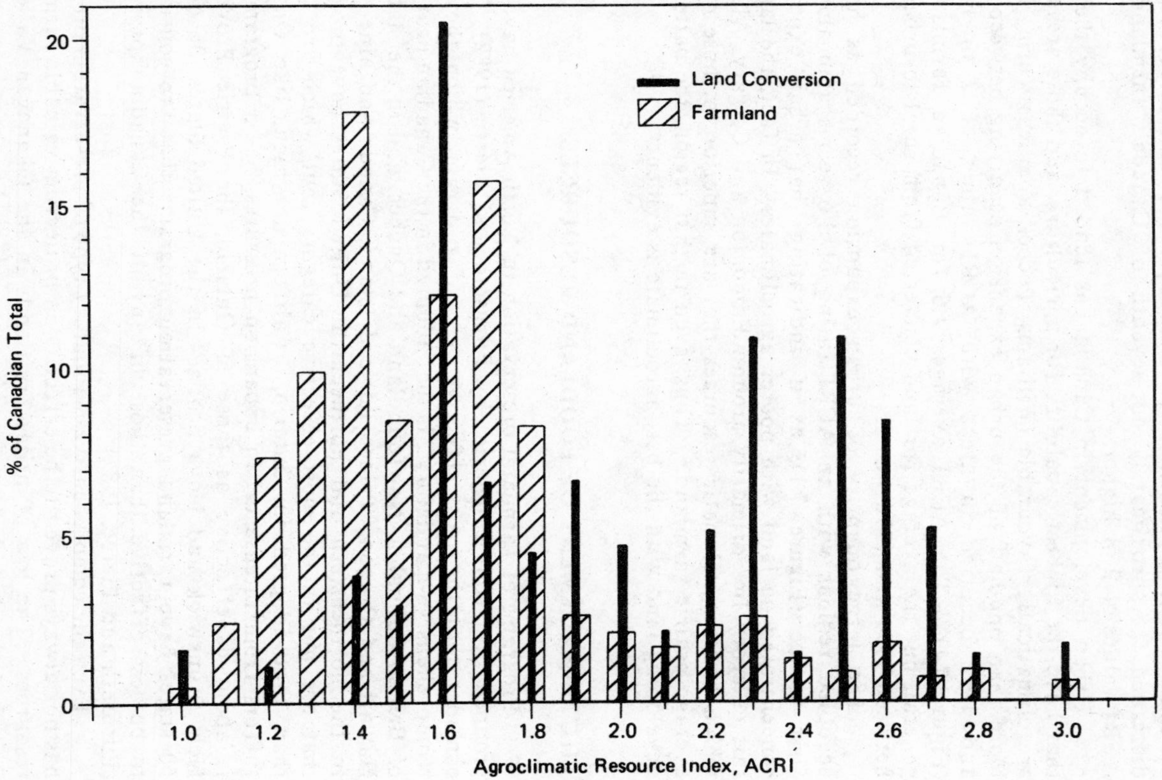

documented by Krueger and Maguire (1984), is a case in point.

Although in Canada prime agricultural land is recognized as a scarce national resource, the response to land loss has been highly fragmented. No protective legislation exists at the federal level (Troughton, 1981).

In Ontario, from 1970 to 1978, the provincial government promoted the Toronto Centred Region Concept (Gertler, 1976) in a series of policy documents which clearly stated that high quality agricultural land must remain agricultural. Three separate policy statements were issued over the period, while a task force dealt specifically with the Central Ontario Lakeshore Urban Complex (COLUC). In all of these planning activities, there was tremendous emphasis placed on the preservation of CLI class 1 soils and other highly productive agricultural areas.

Why, after all the effort and expense that were involved in developing these planning initiatives, does the issue then seem to have been neglected? When the country fell into an economic recession in the mid-seventies, the political reaction was one of encouraging growth, urban development and industrialization. Less and less regard was paid to the protection of natural resources, apparently because the policy makers feared that attempts to deal seriously with these matters would create impossible obstacles for the large corporations and thus worsen the poor economic conditions.

By 1977, the various agricultural land protection initiatives were in a period of neglect, without ever having been implemented in relation to foodland preservation. The next development was the release by the Ministry of Agriculture and Food of the Food Land Guidelines (Government of Ontario, 1978). These guidelines state "To help ensure a healthy and productive agricultural industry in the future, we must protect a land area which will be available on a long-term basis, and within which agricultural activity can occur with a minimum of disruption from competing or non-compatible land uses" (Government of Ontario, 1978, p. 4). It is further stated that "The Food Land Guidelines provide a method to incorporate agricultural considerations into local plans. The Guidelines outline ways to identify agricultural resource lands, locate lands of highest priority to agriculture, designate areas of agriculture, and implement these measures in municipal plans" (Government of Ontario, 1978, p. 3). However, the Food Land Guidelines, as their name implies, lack enforcement provisions. They are invoked on an inconsistent basis and seem to have had greatest effect in areas under the least pressure from urban expansion and with relatively less favourable soils and climates.

During the same time period, the province created regional municipalities. Each of these includes several municipalities, the aim being to provide a wider spatial context for priority setting and decision-making processes.

However, in most cases, even when a region has some land unsuitable for farming, urban development still tends to be permitted on higher capability agricultural land. Gayler (1982) draws attention to what he refers to as the "intransigence" of local municipalities. Instead of letting the planning staff get on with the job of determining urban area requirements according to specified needs and goals, "each local municipality has clamoured for as much land as possible" for urban and related development (Gayler, 1982, p. 169). This issue is discussed in more detail in the case histories described subsequently.

It has been suggested that "urban bias and failure to assign an equal priority to agricultural land" is characteristic of Ontario's response to the farmland loss problem (Furuseth and Pierce, 1982, p. 200). Similarly, Troughton (1981) commented that planning in Ontario has been oriented toward urban development, with the rural area considered as a "holding zone" for land for future urban expansion. This seems to be an echo of the concern expressed by Porenius (1972) in Sweden, who suggested that planning staffs tended to be dominated by technicians specialized in urban problems. There appears to be an anti-rural mind-set in relation to land-use matters. This is indicated at the highest level in Ontario by the fact that the decision-making process for rural land-use matters is administered by the Ontario Ministry of Municipal Affairs and Housing.

INSTITUTIONAL BARRIERS TO PRESERVATION: CASE HISTORIES

The institutional arrangements that currently exist in the province of Ontario do not work to promote the preservation of agricultural land. To illustrate this argument further, three examples of land-use decision-making are considered; the Niagara Region, the Peel Region, and the city of Barrie.

The Niagara Region has land with a uniquely favourable combination of climate and soils for tender fruit production that is not matched anywhere else in Canada, and indeed hardly matched anywhere in North America except in California (Krueger, 1977 and 1984). However, the official plan considered by the Niagara Regional Council in 1976 was essentially a composite of local municipal plans and would have permitted urban development on 3,000 ha of Niagara fruitlands. Concerted opposition by the Preservation of Agricultural Land Society (PALS), subsequent action by the provincial cabinet, and finally a two-year Ontario Municipal Board (OMB)[3] hearing process were needed to ensure a regional plan that recognized the need to preserve foodland for the future. The OMB acknowledged the public service rendered by the land-preservation efforts of PALS. But in spite of these efforts, 800 to 1,200 ha of the contested fruitlands were still incorporated in the urban boundaries (Krueger, 1984). At least one municipality immediately attempted to overturn parts of the decision by requesting that more land be made available for urban development.

Thus, it is clear that the creation of a region does not ensure good regional planning, as suggested previously. In fact, there are some blatant examples of disregard for such planning. In Peel, the area of Ontario which was recently the focus of the foodland preservation issue, twelve years after it was requested to produce an official plan, the regional municipality had still not done so.

In the absence of a regional plan, the OMB is expected to preside at the piecemeal dismantling and disposal of the agricultural land base, one municipality at a time. Peel's foodland is potentially more productive per hectare than the vast majority of Canadian farmland, but the OMB was asked to consider land-use issues in Mississauga, the southernmost and most urbanized of Peel's three municipalities, without reference to the concerns of the region, let alone the province. As a result of the OMB approval of the Mississauga Official Plan, 7,100 ha of farmland in Peel were lost, despite the efforts of the Association of Peel People Evaluating Agricultural Land (APPEAL) to save 4,500 ha.

When viewed from strictly the local municipal standpoint, the only choices for a city may be to restrict urban development to land already designated for such use, or to use high capability agricultural land for this development. Foodland is a provincial and national resource, but if decisions with respect to preserving the agricultural land base have to be made at the local municipal level, other local land requirements are often seen as having priority. Each municipality assumes that it can obtain agricultural products from elsewhere. Even though the OMB is an instrument of the province, in any particular hearing the emphasis is too often on local considerations within the municipality in question.

Under existing procedures, good farmland is subject to diversion to urban use despite the existence of viable alternatives. Such farmland was lost in Mississauga, although plentiful supplies of CLI class 7 land exist elsewhere in Southern Ontario and even though some relatively poor agricultural land is found in Caledon, the northernmost municipality of Peel Region. Later, in Caledon, attempts were made to designate good farmland for urban use in spite of the fact that there was poorer land, and some as yet undeveloped land already with an urban designation, elsewhere in the same municipality. There was also a request by the city of Brampton, which lies between Caledon and Mississauga, to divert

3,000 ha of prime farmland to urban use. Yet there exists extensive areas of undeveloped urban land in Brampton and other parts of Peel Region, as well as the lower quality land in Caledon. Brampton's agroclimate is among the best in the country, rating 2.4 on the ACRI scale. This places the farmland in Brampton in the top 5 per cent of Canada's farmland rated agroclimatically (Figure 7.1).

Some of the reasons for this unsatisfactory situation with respect to foodland preservation are evident. The need for agricultural land is constantly discounted. For example, the planning process never seems to include projections of food needs. Thus, if the land is currently not profitable in agricultural uses, it is usually considered not to be worth preserving for food production. But no effort is spared in seeking justification for allocating as much land as possible to urban uses, which are undeniably more profitable from the short-term economic standpoint.

Methods employed to estimate future urban land needs are usually based on population projections, which can be misleading. The population estimates used to project urban land needs in relation to the Niagara example are illustrative. Projections made with successive data sets since 1971 show a general decline in the size of the projected population of Niagara for 1996; for example, an estimate of 468,000 with 1975 data, 454,000 or 415,000 with 1977 data and 390,000 with 1981 data (Gayler, 1982). If the most recent estimate is taken as the most accurate, the 1975 example is 20 per cent too high. St. Catharine's, a municipality which received a major share of the land assigned for future urban expansion in the Niagara region, has experienced practically zero population growth in the 1980s.

The Peel example also illustrates some of the problems with the application of population projections to planning for a local municipality. Growth trends from the mid-seventies, a period of rapid growth spurred by programs to assist new homeowners, were used to argue that a 1,600 ha block of high quality agricultural land would be needed to accommodate anticipated urban and industrial growth in Brampton. A similar urban development elsewhere on class 7 land would avoid adverse effects on the agricultural industry and the land base.

Another process which contributes ultimately to rural to urban land conversion is action by a higher level of government that results in farmland being placed inside an urban boundary. For example, the city of Barrie, some 80 km north of Toronto, has annexed parts of several neighbouring townships; most recently, an Ontario legislative committee concluded that the city could annex a further 900 ha. The farmland in the area annexed would be among the climatically best 9 per cent of Canada's farmland. Provincial actions to expand urban boundaries by annexation or to create urban-oriented municipalities that include areas of good farmland have serious implications for food producing capabilities.

THE NEED FOR IMPROVED INFORMATION

Information and education are vital tools in the campaign for positive action. The land cannot speak for itself. The planning process is, however, ineffective in that it does not ensure that essential information is taken into account in the decision-making process. Federal and provincial levels of government did not make official presentations at the Niagara OMB hearings (Jackson, 1982), even though these levels of government have expertise or responsibilities relevant to the matter that was being considered. In the Niagara and Peel cases, important agroclimatic information was introduced at the OMB hearing stage only as a result of citizens' groups serving subpoenas on an expert witness to testify at a hearing; apparently no attempt had been made to make use of this information at an earlier stage of planning, such as during the preparation of the draft official plans. Decision making that affects rural land use also seems to be becoming less effective in obtaining public input. The practice of holding OMB hearings with respect to the annexation of rural land by a city, for example, appears to have been discontinued.

Much of the information needed in supporting farmland preservation is of a general nature and would be almost identical for every municipality in Southern Ontario, but because the decisions are made separately for each municipality, the process makes very inefficient use of expert witnesses' time, or it fails to obtain necessary information. For example, data was provided by the same expert at four different hearings, where one presentation could have sufficed. Similarly, farmland preservation groups are put at a great disadvantage in having to deal with each case separately.

IMPLICATIONS AND CONCLUSIONS

In any jurisdiction that has agricultural land it should be borne in mind that food shortages could occur in the future and that building houses on good farmland now will reduce future capacity to cope with such shortages. Future generations may be confronted with shortages of food to eat but with a good supply of (inedible) houses!

Already in many areas, farmland conversion to urban uses is significantly increasing the distances between where food is produced and where it is needed. The increased distances are affecting both the cost and the quality of food. At the same time, the reduction of high quality farmland due to this conversion process means that the land remaining for food production is of poorer quality, which raises the costs of production. Everyone, from the inner city population to the farmers, suffers in this situation.

In many cases there is a plentiful supply of land that is unsuitable for agriculture and that could readily be used for urban development, if needed. Conversion of good farmland to urban use in any territory reduces the ability of that territory to provide food for domestic needs and also in response to future shortages elsewhere in the world.

In the Ontario case, urban development so far has reduced the number of people that can ultimately be fed by three-quarters of a million. The process is continuing. In Peel Region alone, requests considered since 1980 for diverting good foodland to urban use would further reduce the number that could be fed by over 25,000.

A concerted effort is needed to redirect thinking so that in planning decisions people will consider themselves as stewards of the land. People must recognize a responsibility to pass the land on in as good a condition as that in which it was received, instead of viewing the land as a commodity to be bought or sold for short-term gain. It may appear that considerable research is being undertaken in the interests of farmland preservation, but much of this concentrates on fine-tuning the land evaluation process for local applications. This emphasis is natural in view of the present practice of basing land-use decisions on local considerations, but it fails completely to address the main research needs with respect to conservation of the resource in the broader context. Preservationists may contend that official farmland preservation programs are not working; politicians may say they are, but no one really knows. As Furuseth and Pierce (1982) point out, not enough has been done to monitor the impact and effectiveness of such programs. Also, urban and industrial growth seems to be considered synonymous with progress, and very little attention is given to the "diseconomics" of growth (Hodson, 1972).

Several research questions of immediate importance emerge.

1. Is more urban expansion really needed in a given region, province, state or country?
2. If so, where in the territory can it best be directed to minimize the adverse impact on the agricultural land base?
3. How can urban planning and building construction methods best be adapted for development on more difficult sites, in order that high capability agricultural land can be avoided for urban development?

4. How well are policy pronouncements (e.g., Ontario's Food Land Guidelines) working in practice?

5. To what extent is the jurisdiction espousing farmland preservation on the one hand, while on the other actively encouraging municipalities to pursue urban and industrial growth as a means of improving their fiscal situation?

6. At anticipated rates of farmland loss, is all the prime agricultural land likely to be converted to urban use in a few decades, as some analysts suggest, or would this take thousands of years, as implied by other results?

7. Even if the estimated "half-life" of farmland were many centuries, would it be acceptable or reasonable to continue converting good agricultural land to urban use?

It should be clear, from the writings of Brown (1981) and others, that a technological fix to overcome future needs for increased food production cannot be expected, and that it will not always be possible to import food from somewhere else. Each state, province or country that has agricultural land must learn to solve its own food supply problems. Halting the loss of foodland now would be an important step toward that solution.

NOTES

1. The CLI agricultural land capability system rates soils on a scale of 1 to 7, according to their capability to support agricultural practices on a sustained basis. Soils in classes 1-3 have no significant limitations for agriculture. Class 7 land is unsuitable for agricultural activities.

2. For Alberta, Saskatchewan and Manitoba farmland, the ACRI averages 1.5.

3. The OMB is a provincial body established to adjudicate planning disputes. Only the provincial cabinet can overturn OMB rulings.

ACKNOWLEDGMENTS

We wish to pay tribute to our friends in the Ontario Coalition to Preserve Foodland, and its member organizations PALS and APPEAL, for their past and continuing efforts, and to thank them for their help and encouragement. Interested readers may contact the Coalition at 25-295 Water Street, Guelph, Ontario, N1G 2X5; PALS at Box 1090, St. Catharines, Ontario, L2R 7A3; and APPEAL at P.O. Box 532, Streetsville, Ontario, L5M 2C1.

96

REFERENCES

Brown, L.R., 1981, "World Population Growth, Soil Erosion, and Food Security", Science, 214, pp. 995-1002.

Furuseth, O.J. and J.T. Pierce, 1982, "A Comparative Analysis of Farmland Preservation Programmes in North America", Canadian Geographer, 26 (3), pp. 191-206.

Gayler, H.J., 1982, "The Problems of Adjusting to Slow Growth in the Niagara Region of Ontario", Canadian Geographer, 26 (2), pp. 165-172.

Gertler, L.O., 1976, Urban Issues. Toronto: Van Nostrand Reinhold Ltd.

Government of Ontario, 1978, Food Land Guidelines. Toronto: Government of Ontario.

Hodson, H.V., 1972, The Diseconomics of Growth. New York: Ballantine Books Ltd.

Jackson, J.J., 1982, "The Niagara Fruit Belt: The Ontario Municipal Board Decision of 1981", Canadian Geographer, 26 (2) , pp. 172-176.

Krueger, R.R., 1977, "The Destruction of a Unique Renewable Resource: The Case of the Niagara Fruit Belt". In R.R. Krueger and B. Mitchell (eds.), Managing Canada's Renewable Resources. Toronto: Methuen Ltd., pp. 132-148.

Krueger, R.R., 1984, "Where Have all the Canadian Fruitlands Gone?", University of Waterloo Courier, September, pp. 3-8.

Krueger, R.R. and N.G. Maguire, 1984, "Changing Urban and Fruit Growing Patterns in the Okanagan Valley, B.C.", Environments, 16 (1), pp. 1-8.

Porenius, P., 1972, "Multiple Land Use in the Mälar Valley", International Geography, pp. 748-750.

Simpson-Lewis, W., J.E. Moore, N.J. Pocock, M.C. Taylor and H. Swan, 1979, Canada's Special Resource Lands. Ottawa: Map Folio No. 4, Lands Directorate, Environment Canada.

Troughton, M.J., 1981, "The Policy and Legislative Response to Loss of Agricultural Land in Canada", Ontario Geography, 18, pp. 79-109.

Warren, C.L. and P.C. Rump, 1981, The Urbanization of Rural Land in Canada: 1966-1971 and 1971-1976. Ottawa: Land Use in Canada Series No. 20, Lands Directorate, Environment Canada.

Williams, G.D.V., 1983, "Agroclimatic Resource Analysis, An Example Using An Index Derived and Applied for Canada", Agricultural Meteorology, 28, pp. 31-47.

Williams, G.D.V., N.J. Pocock and L.H. Russwurm, 1978, "The Spatial Association of Agroclimatic Resources and Urban Population in Canada". In R.M. Irving (ed.) Readings in Canadian Geography, 3rd Edition. Toronto: Holt, Rinehart and Winston, Ltd., pp. 165-179.

8
PROTECTING FARMLAND FROM WHOM AND FOR WHAT PURPOSE?
Geoffrey McDonald and Roy Rickson

INTRODUCTION

Markets are notoriously unreliable determinants of efficient, environmentally sound and equitable uses of rural land. They must be because governments the world over intrude a great deal into input and output markets in order to correct market distortions in the public interest. A case in point is that many countries have formulated policy to protect farmland from encroachment by non-farm uses. The purpose of this paper is to review farmland protection policies in the Australian context. Undoubtedly the situation in Australia is different from other counties, but one hopes that the analysis of the issues in Australia might bring into sharper focus the debate elsewhere.

A reasonable starting point for any argument about state intervention into the land allocation process is to define why and how free markets fail to maximize social welfare in allocating land to competing uses. The reasons are diverse and they are summarized in Table 8.1. This paper concentrates on the agricultural land protection issues; that too much land will be converted to non-agricultural uses and that this is undesirable for the long-term production of food and fibre.

THE SUPPLY AND DEMAND FOR LAND IN AUSTRALIA

The most notable feature of Australia's agriculture is its dependence on export markets. In 1985 the gross value of rural production was $15.6 billion of which 58 per cent ($9.1 billion) was exported (Table 8.2). Consequently, the demand for much of Australia's rural land can be assessed only in terms of world markets for Australia's major export commodities, namely cereals, wool, meat,

97

**TABLE 8.1: CAUSES OF FAILURE IN THE MARKET
FOR FARMLAND IN URBAN FRINGE AREAS**

CAUSE	EFFECT
Imperfect information for producers and consumers about future prices	Producers undervalue land. Consumers unwilling to pay for protecting farmland
Markets fail to compensate farmers for physical externalities of non-farm uses	Non-farm land overvalued; farmland undervalued
There are economic externalities due to natural monopoly, scale and agglomeration economies	Individual farmers rationally undervalue land where these externalities exist
The loss of farmland is irreversible	Social discount rate exceeds private discount rate; land is undervalued
There are unpriced public goods and externalities	Farmers are not compensated for their contribution to landscape values, views, etc.; farmland is undervalued

sugar and dairy products, in that order of importance. Export opportunities and export prices set the economic conditions under which most farmers operate and only few are protected by locational monopoly or government price support (e.g., fluid milk, horticulture). Despite attempts to establish higher prices for its farmers by trade negotiations, Australian rural exporters are price-takers in competition with highly protected farmers in importing countries and in recent years with subsidized exports from the European Economic Community.

Australian farmland prices are low in response to real and perceived future profitability. Australian farmers are notable for their high land: labour, output: man, capital: labour ratios and low outputs per unit of land. High transport costs and high costs of manufactured inputs magnify the tendency towards extensive production methods on Australia's farmlands.

TABLE 8.2: PRODUCTION AND EXPORT OF MAJOR RURAL COMMODITIES, AUSTRALIA 1984-1985

| COMMODITY | PRODUCTION | | EXPORTS | | |
	Volume 000s T	Value Mills $	Volume 000s T	Value Mills $	Volume %
Wheat and Flour	18666	3330	15775	2881	85
Barley and Malt	5554	807	4500	681	81
Sorghum	1885	217	1568	242	83
Rice	864	122	327	117	38
Dried Vinefruit	78	105	56	35	72
Sugar	3547	512	2524	574	71
Raw Cotton	249	425	140	260	56
Wool	815	2412	772	2538	95
Beef and Veal	1312	2148	416	1086	32
Mutton and Lamb[1]	516	602	312	364	60
Dairy Products[2]	569	1097	271	421	47
Other Commodities	-	3823	-	-	-
Total	-	15600	-	9199	-

[1] Includes live sheep
[2] Excludes fresh milk

Source: Bureau of Agricultural Economics (1986)

    For most of Australia's rural industries the major problem is finding a market and for rural landowners in general it is finding an enterprise that is viable. Irrespective of the pursuit, profit margins per unit of rural land are very low, especially relative to urban land-use activities.

    Such a setting is not one that is conducive to farmland protection at either the intensive or extensive margins of production.

And with respect to urban land development, it means that the opportunity costs will be low, at least in the foreseeable future.

This is not to say that Australia is particularly well-endowed with agricultural resources; quite the contrary. Only 10 per cent of Australia's land area is suited to agriculture, primarily due to climate but also due to topographic and soil factors. Various estimates have been made of the area of land available in Australia for rainfed agriculture (crops and sown pastures) but the consensus of expert opinion (Gifford, 1975; Hallsworth, 1976) is that 52 million ha are currently in use, leaving 28 million ha for further development. Such estimates are subject to wide margins of error and it is part of the national ethos in fact that there are unknown potentials, especially in Northern Australia.

Most of the land which exists for the expansion of agriculture is climatically marginal, or has production problems which would have to be overcome. It is an untestable but persuasive hypothesis put by some agricultural economists (notably Davidson, 1966), that it is more economical to increase agricultural output by intensification of use in existing farming areas than by developing new land. Suffice it to say that there is considerable scope to increase the production of food and fibre by at least a factor of two.

How much land has been lost temporarily or permanently to agriculture by urban expansion in Australia is not known, although it is small. Warren (1974) estimates that 10,000 ha are lost each year due to urban and related uses. This land is almost all in the climatically favourable east coastal belt between Bundaberg and Adelaide and in the southwest corner of the continent. Land is also lost to forestry and conservation, but these could not be regarded as losses in the long term.

Undoubtedly the biggest threat to Australia's ability to sustain agriculture in the long term is land degradation (i.e., agriculture itself). It is a serious problem in a nation practising extensive commercial agriculture, and without greater efforts in soil conservation long-term agricultural production in some regions is threatened. Woods (1984) estimates that over two-thirds of Australia's cropland requires significant conservation treatment (Table 8.3).

ATTITUDES TO FARMLAND PROTECTION

The National View

Agricultural land protection has received considerable attention in each of a series of inquiries that accompany the process of government in Australia. Problems that have been identified and

TABLE 8.3: EXTENT OF LAND DEGRADATION ON AUSTRALIA'S NON-ARID AGRICULTURAL AND GRAZING LAND

	NON-ARID GRAZING LAND		EXTENSIVE CROPLAND		INTENSIVE CROPLAND		TOTAL	
	000s Km²	%	000s Km²	%	000s Km²	%	000s Km²	%
Total Area in Use	1337	100	443	100	24	100	1804	100
Not Requiring Treatment	837	63	142	32	8	33	987	55
Requiring Treatment	497	37	302	68	16	67	815	45
Water Erosion	364	27	206	47	7	28	577	32
Wind Erosion	6	0	52	12	-	-	57	3
Water and Wind Erosion	13	0	42	10	0	0	55	3
Grassland Rehabilitation	92	7	-	-	-	-	92	5
Salinity	9	1	1	0	9	38	19	1
Other	13	0	1	0	-	-	14	1

Note: Totals may not agree due to rounding

Source: Woods (1984)

addressed, although not resolved, include water and wind erosion, salinity and salinization, grassland degradation and irreversible losses to other uses. A sample of statements taken from inquiry reports and submissions to inquiries are presented in Table 8.4. It is clear from the review that there exists little unanimity of opinion with respect to urban encroachment and farmland conversion in terms of either the seriousness of the problem or what policies are needed. This situation represents a significant impediment to the formulation and implementation of public action.

TABLE 8.4: ATTITUDES TO FARMLAND PROTECTION
EXPRESSED BY ADVISORY BODIES

SOURCE	STATEMENT
Committee of Inquiry into the National Estate (Hope, 1974, p. 336)	We recommend control by zoning to ensure that good agricultural land is not diverted from its productive use, either by uncontrolled urban sprawl or unwise rural subdivision into too small lots.
National Conservation Strategy (Australia Department of Home Affairs and Environment, 1981, p. 39)	... identify highly productive land and preserve its potential availability for agricultural use. Limit the encroachment of non-agricultural uses on prime agricultural land;
Australia Senate Standing Committee on Science, Technology and the Environment (1983, p. 970)	..., of all the possible justifications put forward, only the preservation of existing agriculture service facilities and the protection of agriculture from the adverse spillovers of other land uses hold up under close scrutiny. The assumptions required to justify controls as a form of insurance against high food prices in the future are simply not reasonable.
Australia Senate Standing Committee on Science, Technology and the Environment (1984, p. 2313)	The loss of strategic cane lands could significantly affect the regional viability of a sugar mill and its growers ... the loss of even relatively small amounts of certain strategic cane lands could lead to the premature closure of a mill.
Commonwealth Scientific and Industrial Research Organization (Hallsworth, 1976, p. 29)	... although Australia still has plenty of land capable of food production, the area suitable for agriculture and horticulture in the neighbourhood of the metropolitan areas is strictly limited. Encroachment on this land by urban development will inevitably increase the cost of foods in the city as a result of increased transportation and refrigeration.

Continued

TABLE 8.4 (Cont.)

SOURCE	STATEMENT
Institute of Agricultural Science (Leslie and Johnston, 1982, p. 1)	The Institute views with particular concern, the trends towards displacement of rainfed agriculture from high rainfall coastal areas and towards increasing dependency on dryland agriculture in lower rainfall areas and on irrigation schemes.
Queensland Agricultural Council (Eather, 1983, p. 11)	... the fruit and vegetable industry is heavily affected by urban expansion but appears to have scope for relocation elsewhere. Transport to central markets from the more distant areas would not appear to be overly difficult.
Working Group on Rural Policy (Harris, 1974, p. 255)	We would only wish to comment that the physical quality of land for agriculture does not itself justify reserving its use for agriculture if it has a higher value in urban use ... While the availability of land in Australia is not unlimited, capacity exists for intensification of existing uses of much of our agricultural land if economic circumstances warrant. In the absence of proper controls, the loss of land from soil erosion or salinization is likely to be much more than the loss from increasing urbanization.
Working Group on Agricultural Policy (Balderstone, 1982, p. 142)	It has often been suggested that agricultural land should be restricted in its use and more particularly that it should be effectively zoned agriculture only. However, the Group believes market forces should be the major influence in determining the use of land ... The Group recognizes that in some situations intervention may be necessary. Industry or recreation activities through their effect on water supplies, land productivity or

Continued

TABLE 8.4 (Cont.)

SOURCE   STATEMENT

cleanliness of air, may affect other activities within the same region including farming ...
Other than to note that problems can arise for other farmers the Group does not see major policy issues arising from increasing numbers of hobby farmers, provided they comply with the responsibilities required of all landowners with regard to pest, disease and weed control.

Farmers' Attitudes

Systematic efforts to measure farmers' views about protecting farmland from urban encroachment in Australia are unknown to the authors. Farmer organizations, responding to the major national inquiries discussed earlier, have not identified this to be an issue of great significance. And, indeed, they do not mention it in a recent submission on Australia's rural policy (National Farmers' Federation, [NFF] 1981). This is not to say that farmers are disinterested in the problem but that there are many issues of greater significance to most Australian farmers in terms of their use of land resources, and farmland protection is only important for some regions and farming systems. Examples where the issue is important include the sugar producing and irrigation regions.

Australian farmers share the agrarian values of their counterparts in most areas of the world and many believe that agriculture is, or should be, the basis of the economy and society. Maintenance of farming as a way of life is important to farmers despite the signs that this view is waning, and most believe in general terms that farmland should be protected from other uses. A serious internal inconsistency is inherent in this view with respect to individual rights, so central to farmers' ethos and yet so difficult to reconcile with farmland protection.

A recent survey of farmers in two shires on the fringe of metropolitan Brisbane sought to investigate farmers' attitudes to land-use problems and land-use planning (Rickson and Neumann, 1984). Farmland conversion to residential and other urban uses ranked third amongst the range of land-use problems identified by farmers in the area, after shortage of water and soil erosion.

While it is significant that 45 per cent of the 310 farmers saw it as a moderate or serious problem, there was a greater divergence of opinion on this issue than on any other (Table 8.5). The reasons for farmers identifying this as a problem are similar to those commonly cited in the literature on this topic. Perhaps they are best summarized in the words of one respondent:

> We would like to buy more good agricultural land but owing to stiff competition from doctors, lawyers, big businesses and just plain wealthy developers, it has become impossible for many genuine farmers to afford the prices they are paying. So the farmer of tomorrow who supplies the daily needs; milk, potatoes and vegetables hasn't a chance of acquiring anything he will ever own. Do we want a feed or don't we?

Divergence of opinion could result from different perceptions of the extent of farmland loss or from different values on the importance of retaining land in farming, although responses were similar among districts where the impact of urban land development differed widely. Farmers were also equally divided in their responses to the statement that land which is best suited to agriculture should not be used for other purposes (Table 8.6). Farmers further revealed their ambivalence on this issue when questioned on the balance between public and private rights over land-use decisions (Table 8.7). One farmer supplied a cryptic comment on the survey:

> Land-use planning is vital to ensure that productive land is preserved for the future of all Australians. I believe a farmer should have the right to sell his farm to the highest bidder.

Many farmers believed that non-farm uses could be accommodated without the loss of good farmland. In the words of one respondent:

> For non-farm use, use only areas of poor soil which is not useful for grazing or agriculture. The siting of Tarong Power Station is a good example. The top soil is so thin and poor that a bandicoot would need a cut lunch to cross the area.

THE CASE FOR FARMLAND PROTECTION IN AUSTRALIA

Given that Australia has not in fact placed a high priority on the protection of farmland from urban encroachment, has it been misguided? In other terms, is there evidence of significant market failure that would suggest reordering land-use policies?

TABLE 8.5: FARMERS' OPINIONS ON LAND-USE PROBLEMS, MORETON - BOONAH SHIRES (PER CENT)

	NOT A PROB.	MINOR PROB.	MODERATE PROB.	SERIOUS PROB.
Inadequate water supplies	11	11	29	49
Soil erosion on farms	10	35	37	19
Farmland conversion	25	29	22	22
Stream pollution by farmers	47	33	12	6
Loss of natural vegetation	31	29	23	16

Note: Number of respondents is 310

The Effect of Urban Encroachment on Food Prices

In the short term the displacement of farms may lead to higher food prices, depending on the level of production from substitute uses (such as hobby farms) and on the additional cost of supplying food from alternative lands. As far as supplying the Australian market is concerned, there is no product whose price would increase significantly as a result of the withdrawal of land near cities. The scope for land-use changes, especially for the production of horticultural and dairy products under supplementary irrigation is vast. The prices of export commodities will not be affected.

With respect to products with high transport costs (e.g., fruit, vegetables, milk) that are often found near urban markets, high haulage costs may be offset by agglomeration economies. Many of these products are sold on a seasonal basis on national markets and often their near-city location is unrelated to haulage costs. On this basis there is very little evidence to support the case that farmers, or consumers, are undervaluing the agricultural worth of land in the short term.

In the long term, changes in the supply and demand for agricultural products may lead to price increases. Farmers' willingness-to-pay reflects their expectations of future returns and the rate at which they discount these returns. There is no evidence to suggest

TABLE 8.6: RESPONSES BY FARMERS TO A SELECTION OF LAND-USE ISSUES, MORETON - BOONAH SHIRES (PER CENT)

ISSUE	DISAGREE	AGREE
Public goals should be given a higher priority in deciding the uses of land than the wishes of individual landowners.	74	27
Persons who own land should have the right to sell it to whoever they please, regardless of its future use.	71	29
Land which is best suited to agriculture should not be used for any other purpose.	49	51
There should be regulations prohibiting the conversion of high quality agricultural land to other purposes.	12	88

Note: Number of respondents is 310
         Totals may not agree due to rounding

TABLE 8.7: WHO SHOULD DECIDE ON FARMLAND CONVERSION (PER CENT)

The individual farmer	43
Farmers as a group	2
Voluntary government programs	38
Government regulations	17

Note: Number of respondents is 310

that farmers make unduly pessimistic market forecasts, although it is likely that the private discount rate will exceed the social discount rate when it comes to a finite resource like farmland. Farmers' valuation of their land will be less than the social value.

The extent of land undervaluation by farmers will depend on the strength of consumers' aversion to possible future price increases. If farmland protection results in lower food prices in the future all consumers will benefit, although it would be difficult to persuade Australian consumers of the need to pay now for that privilege. For export industries, most of these benefits would accrue to consumers in importing countries. Many Australians believe there is an ethical responsibility in this regard.

From the long-term point of view it is likely that Australian farmland is undervalued although this conclusion rests upon unpredictable changes in technology, population and trade policy at the global level.

Externalities

Many observers have noted that farmland is subject to physical externalities resulting from urban growth. These include:

1. pollution of surface and underground water supplies,
2. air pollution from industrial sources affecting the production of sensitive crops (e.g., grapes),
3. interference by people and domestic animals with livestock and crops in near-urban areas,
4. pest plants, especially woody weeds that flourish on poorly managed non-farm allotments, and
5. increased fire hazards.

Farmers are not compensated for these losses, suffer higher production costs and lower returns and agricultural land values are suppressed. Most of these problems could and should be solved by local planning schemes and land management regulations.

Economic externalities are more widespread and probably of greater significance in Australia. These arise in the form of scale and technical economies to agricultural supply, processing and marketing firms. In some cases the most economic number of firms is one and the unit costs of these firms will be affected by the expansion or contraction of agriculture in their localized service regions. Real resource savings may be gained by encouraging optimum levels of turnover for these firms and provide a justification for protecting farms from premature conversion to urban uses.

The Sugar Industry Example

The Australian sugar industry provides an excellent example of the operation of economic externalities. Under Australian conditions, mechanization, climate and terrain constrain the area of land suitable for cane production to subtropical and tropical floodplains which are also the location of many urban centres. Cane farms must be near mills due to the high bulk of cane and the requirement that it be processed within 36 hours of cutting. Agglomeration economies exist in the scale of mill operations, in the utilization of specialized light rail systems and in the concentration of support industries.

The distribution of existing mills in cane producing regions and the limited supply of land in some districts have made urban encroachment a significant problem. Four mills are threatened at present, namely, Rocky Point, Moreton, Racecourse (Mackay) and Hambledon (Cairns). Ryland (1969) estimated long-run cost functions for sugar mills and showed the classic J shape of average mill production costs. Critical levels of unit cost increase are reached when mill cane throughout declines below 350,000 tonnes.

The farmer is in a strange position in that while generally he owns his own farm in freehold title, he may only grow cane to the extent and location approved by the industry, and he may only sell his farm to another farmer as approved by the Central Cane Prices Board. If he chooses to vacate the industry and dispose of his property to urban development, all industry control ceases and the only constraints which confront him are those forces of the market place or town planning requirements.

The transferable cane assignment has a capitalized value that, at least in past years, was a significant buffer against urban encroachment. But with sugar prices extremely low, that value is declining and the tendency for farmers to sell increasing. In general terms, the existence of agglomeration economies in this industry leads to a significant difference between the private and social value of farmland and is an economically valid basis for protecting farmland against urban encroachment.

CONCLUSION

The protection of farmland from urban encroachment in Australia is not, in general, a major policy issue and the particular local circumstances under which it is an issue have been identified. Australian agriculture is export-dominated and land resources are not producing at maximum capacity. Farmers are silent or, at best, ambivalent about the restrictions on individual land rights necessary to protect land from urban encroachment.

There is a need to distinguish between protecting farms and protecting land in this debate. Protecting land cannot be simply equated with protecting farms. Cultivation of fragile farmland or using scarce water resources may well be a greater threat to Australia's long-term ability to produce food and fibre than many non-farm uses. It is a yet untested hypothesis that hobby farms and large-lot rural residential uses are more appropriate means of achieving farmland protection than is farming.

Agriculture and grazing have made a substantial impact on the Australian environment and its ability to sustain production in the long term. Some of these impacts include massive destruction of forests and other floral resources, and damage to the quality, quantity and reliability of water supplies over very large areas. These impacts have affected the productivity of forestry and fishing industries, among others. A very good case can be made that in Australia fewer, rather than more, land (and water) resources should be used in agriculture.

This is not to say that land-use planning should ignore farmland protection, although the justification may need to be on grounds other than protecting existing farms. Leaving land in farming may well be desirable from an aesthetic point of view and be efficient in terms of the timing and location of urban development.

REFERENCES

Australia Department of Home Affairs and Environment, 1981, National Conservation Strategy for Australia: Living Resource Conservation for Sustainable Development, Proceedings of a National Seminar, November 1981, Canberra.

Australia Senate Standing Committee on Science, Technology and Environment, 1983, Land Use Policy. Canberra: Official Hansard Report, Australian Government Publishing Service.

Australia Senate Standing Committee on Science, Technology and Environment, 1984, Land Use Policy in Australia. Canberra: Australian Government Publishing Service.

Balderstone, J.S., 1982, Agricultural Policy Issues and Options for the 1980s, Working Group Report to the Minister for Primary Industries. Canberra: Australian Government Publishing Service.

Bureau of Agricultural Economics, 1986, Quarterly Review of the Rural Economy, 8 (2). Canberra: Australian Government Publishing Service.

Davidson, R.B., 1966, The Northern Myth. Melbourne: Melbourne University Press.

Eather, D., 1983, An Agricultural Policy for Queensland. Brisbane: Queensland Graingrowers.

Gifford, R., 1975, "Biophysical Constraints in Australian Food Production: Implications for Population Policy", Search, 6, pp. 212-223.

Hallsworth, J., 1976, Principles of a Balanced Land Use Policy for Australia. Melbourne: Commonwealth Scientific and Industrial Research Organization.

Harris, S., 1974, Rural Policy in Australia. Canberra: Report to the Prime Minister by a Working Group, Australian Government Publishing Service.

Hope, R.M., 1974, Report of the National Estate. Canberra: Report of the Committee of Inquiry into the National Estate, Australian Government Publishing Service.

Leslie, J.K. and P.J.M. Johnston, 1982, Residential Encroachment on Rural Lands. Brisbane: Occasional Paper No. 3, Australian Institute of Agricultural Science.

NFF, 1981, Farm Focus: The 80s. Canberra: National Farmers' Federation.

Rickson, R.E. and R. Neumann, 1984, Farmers' Responses to Land Use Planning in Moreton and Boonah Shires. Brisbane: Institute of Applied Social Research, Griffith University.

Ryland, G.J., 1969, "Economies of Scale in Sugar Milling", Proceedings of the Queensland Society of Sugar Cane Technologists. Maryborough, Australia.

Warren, V.R.C., 1974, "The Planning Process and Land Use Options", In Proceedings of a Conference Agriculture on the Urban Fringe. Melbourne: Australian Institute of Agricultural Science.

Woods, L.E., 1984, Land Degradation in Australia. Canberra: Australian Government Publishing Service.

9
RISK-AVERSION VERSUS OPTIMAL STRATEGIES FOR PLANNING RURAL RESOURCES
John T. Pierce

INTRODUCTION

North American society is today faced with a variety of difficult choices in the use of its agricultural land resources. These land resources are valued for more than their productive capabilities, particularly in the vicinity of urban areas. And the growth in the productive capacity of the food system is not without its costs as soil resources are often traded-off for higher levels of output. The significance of the impact of urban land conversion and soil erosion upon the productive potential of the food system is the subject of considerable controversy. The sources of the controversy are similar to those in the debate over the adequacy of the natural resource base generally. Future levels of food demand, the relative importance of land in meeting that demand, tolerable levels of soil nutrient loss, the sustainability of certain practices and the growth in productivity are but a few unknowns which contribute to uncertainty about the operating environment and hence the adequacy of the food system.

It is within this context that the paper critically examines some of the major planning responses, actual and proposed, for the conservation of rural land resources. The major question to be answered is how effective are these strategies for dealing with different types and degrees of uncertainty in the use of agricultural land resources. These concerns are rooted in a more general concern of how public decision making deals with the questions of uncertainty and irreversibility.

ESTABLISHING A FRAMEWORK

Although soil erosion and loss of agricultural land are different sides of the same coin, their salient features and resource management implications have rarely, if ever, been examined in a collective framework. There are four points worth considering.

First, agricultural land is both a renewable and stock resource. Whereas the latter refers to the finite quantities of land suitable for production, the former refers to the flow characteristics of soil resources which with proper management can sustain a given level of production indefinitely. One of the notable features of North American agriculture during the past 40 years is that food production has consistently increased while both the stock and flow characteristics of the resource base have been diminished. Technological growth (land saving and yield augmenting) has effectively offset the loss in productive capacity (Figure 9.1: T_1 to T_3).

Second, the derivation of services from the stock and flow characteristics of the resource display threshold values as the quantity and quality of the resource decrease. In the case of the flow resource, numerous studies (see for example, Larson et al., 1983) have revealed that output drops sharply beyond a certain decrease in topsoil depth. And in the case of the stock resource, losses in the arable land base and its associated climatic resources can have a disproportionate effect upon production potential. Figure 9.1 illustrates these threshold effects (X_1 to X_3) for three different levels of technology. From a more general perspective, Ciriacy-Wantrup (1968) has identified a number of flow resources, including plant and animal species, as possessing a critical zone or threshold which defines the level of depletion which is irreversible.

Third, the distribution and extent of each process differs. Soil erosion, although varying between regions, is a non-point source phenomenon. Loss of agricultural land, on the other hand, is much more point specific, tending to be localized in regions of population and industrial concentrations.

Fourth, the rate of change in soil erosion and loss of agricultural land is heavily influenced by market conditions. Given the fact that both Canada and the United States are in a food surplus situation, the stress on the land resource base comes primarily from demands in export markets. Of equal importance and closely related to the economic climate for farming is the ratio of prices to costs, which has encouraged farm expansion and intensification and, in the opinion of some, poor land management practices. Along with this competition within the farm sector is the competition for agricultural land resources from other uses. In both cases the market price of agricultural land may understate its true long-term social value (Crosson and Stout, 1983). If this is so then both rates of soil erosion and land conversion may be excessive, leading to an externalizing of increased production costs to future generations and an overall decline in consumer and producer surplus.

**FIGURE 9.1: AGRICULTURAL OUTPUT GIVEN
CHANGES IN THE SOIL RESOURCE
AND TECHNOLOGY**

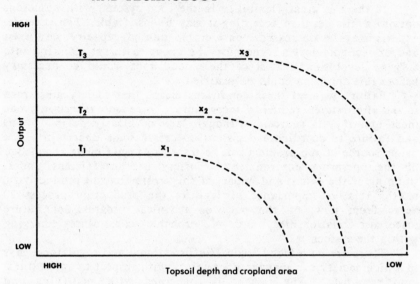

DEALING WITH UNCERTAINTY

Decisions within the public sector as to what and how to respond to real or perceived problems of soil erosion and farmland loss have been difficult to make. Hickling (1975) argues that the difficulty in making decisions in planning is due to three types of uncertainty:

1. about the operating environment in which there is insufficient knowledge about present relationships and future conditions,
2. about policy values (i.e., the lack of clearly defined objectives), and
3. about choices in related areas (i.e., the need for coordination between different sectors and jurisdictions).

Recognizing the existence of uncertainty is a necessary but not sufficient condition for its management. There are many instances in both Canada and the United States where the problem has been largely ignored. Assuming that side stepping the problem is an unacceptable approach, society is faced essentially with two alternatives: accept it or reduce it.

If there is great flexibility in the food system, with numerous options available, then accepting it may be justifiable. For example, exports may be decreased, considerable unused capacity may exist and/or technological advance may be about to thrust mankind into a "gene revolution". Most of these conditions would be necessary before this approach could be justified.

Failure to meet these conditions means that society must turn to the alternative: reducing uncertainty. To reduce uncertainty one must identify its source. Although lack of clearly defined goals and failure to coordinate decisions do create some uncertainty, the prime source of the problem can be traced to insufficient knowledge of the operating environment. Society has insufficient understanding of the extent and impact of soil erosion on soil productivity, of the relative importance of land in the production process 20 years from now, of the pace of technical progress, of future price/cost relationships, and of probable constraints emerging within the system.

There are both technological/informational and regulatory ways in which society can manage uncertainty with respect to agricultural land resources. The former is concerned with modifying and improving the mix of inputs in the production process to ensure a high and sustained rate of substitution of non-land for land inputs. This involves movements along and shifts in the production function (Figure 9.1). The success of this approach is heavily dependent upon a favourable relationship between prices and costs and a sustained investment by both public and private sectors into agricultural research.

The latter, which may substitute or supplement for the former, involves a variety of direct and indirect regulatory devices which affect the allocation and use of agricultural land and resources. These approaches generally fall into one of two categories: optimal strategies which strive to increase efficiency and maximize the benefits to society in resource use, and risk-averse which attempt in the face of uncertainty to minimize potentially large social losses through the depletion of a natural resource. Ciriacy-Wantrup (1968) has proposed the adoption of a safe minimum standard of conservation with respect to flow resources. Whereas this is equivalent in game theory to a minimax strategy, where the object is to minimize the largest possible losses (Bishop, 1978), the optimal strategy is much more akin to a maximax strategy in which the largest possible rewards or gains are pursued.

Loss of Agricultural Land

The most notable and representative planning responses to the urbanization and alienation of agricultural land can be categorized as follows:

1. indirect-financial (differential tax assessment [DTA]), evident in almost all North American states and provinces,
2. police power (DTA and centralized land-use controls), employed in the State of California and the majority of Canadian provinces,
3. integrated voluntary (DTA, agricultural districts, transfer of development rights), utilized in Prince Edward Island, Canada and such states as Maryland, Connecticut, New York and Wisconsin,
4. comprehensive-mandatory (DTA, exclusive agricultural zoning, land banking), employed in the provinces of British Columbia, Quebec and Newfoundland, and the states of Oregon, and Hawaii (Furuseth and Pierce, 1982).

How effective are these strategies in dealing with uncertainty? The first group of programs affects the allocation of agricultural land but it is not aimed specifically at farmland preservation. As such it does not answer the question of what is an acceptable rate of loss of land and it allows considerable cropland allocation to be influenced by market forces. Moreover, the relative uniformity of response occurs despite considerable variation in the importance of and pressures for conversion of farmland among jurisdictions.

The second group of programs, like the first, is not specifically designed for protection of agricultural land use. Instead, agricultural land belongs to a package of other land uses whose designation and protection are part and parcel of an official plan mandated by a planning act and enforced by a combination of zoning, subdivision controls and tax relief. The centralized planning strategies have tried to clarify goals and have attempted to coordinate growth and minimize land-use conflicts. Although these features reduce uncertainty, it is unclear if the specific designation of agricultural land is an optimal amount. Regardless of this, the centralized land-use strategies represent a first attempt at optimal land-use planning in the sense that efforts are made to maximize the net benefits from the use of land resources over time. Unfortunately, while these programs show great strength in statements of goals and policies, the reality of market differentials and urban political pressures are often contrary to the interests of the agricultural community.

The last two groups of programs rely much less on the market and much more on society's perceived needs for the allocation of agricultural lands. Not only are they specifically aimed at the agricultural sector, by giving agriculture exclusive right to the use of the land, there is an attempt to coordinate agricultural needs with other land-use needs. Through the establishment of a single goal, the preservation of agricultural land, these programs have attempted to reduce uncertainty regarding the environment for agriculture and future supply of arable land. To what extent this supply (particularly in the last group) matches future needs is not known. Hence if a surplus condition exists, land will remain unavailable for alternative uses and possibly result in high opportunity costs for society as a whole. The last group of programs is clearly concerned more with minimizing the loss of agricultural land and less with deriving the maximum net benefit from the use of land resources over time. Consequently these attempts at farmland preservation are risk-averse as opposed to optimal.

Current research into the development of a land evaluation model at the University of Guelph, Canada could contribute to a closer approximation of the optimal allocation of agricultural land over time (Smit et al., 1985). Within the context of the Province of Ontario, an attempt has been made to measure the degree of flexibility and criticality in the use of land. Both are determined by assessing the available land resource, in relation to expected requirements for products and services from the land. If the outcomes from this exercise are relatively insensitive to changes in constraints a more reliable picture and more certain view of future land-use needs may be developed and plans made accordingly. If the opposite is the case, reliability problems remain as will any attempt to allocate land optimally through the public sector. Proposals have been made for measuring sensitivity of the flexibility and criticality measures. By calculating differential sensitivity coefficients it may be possible to "provide relative indications as to where research effort should be expanded to increase parameter precision" (Chapman et al., 1984, p. 62).

Soil Erosion

Soil erosion has been a source of concern in North America ever since the 1930s. Problems in documentation, poor understanding of productivity losses, the diffuse (non-point) character of the process, rights of fee simple ownership to the land and economic constraints have combined to make it difficult to protect society's long-term interests in soil resources. The establishment in 1935 of the United States Soil Conservation Service and the Canadian Prairie Farm Rehabilitation Administration set the stage for the development of soil conservation programs in North America.

For more than 40 years in the United States, soil loss tolerance (T) values have been used as the basis for setting acceptable levels of soil erosion (commonly set at 11 tonnes/ha/yr). T-values have acted as convenient standards for both policy makers and farmers to judge the sustainability of farming practices and for targeting funding for soil conservation as in the Agricultural Conservation Program and the Conservation Operations Program. As a social goal or objective, T-values provide for equal treatment between present and future generations (Heal, 1981), and consequently the use of T-values is risk-averse or planning for the worst situation.

Since the adoption of T-values by farmers is entirely voluntary, the market has tended to be the prime determinant of rates of soil erosion. Results from the National Resource Inventory (United States Department of Agriculture [USDA], 1980) indicate that over one-third of the nation's cropland experiences rates of soil erosion in excess of the recommended 11 tonnes/ha/yr. In the Canadian Prairie Provinces average soil erosion is between 7 to 10 tonnes/ha/yr, with approximately one-quarter of the area above this figure (Prairie Farm Rehabilitation Administration [PFRA], 1983).

Despite these losses, the potential decline in yields has been more than offset by a further increase in technological and non-land inputs. Farmers have avoided yield decreases through a substitution process. One of the reasons farmers have ignored certain erosion control practices such as terracing, contour plowing and conservation tillage is that it has not been profitable to do so. T-values do not address this important issue and, unless society is willing to compensate farmers for lost production or higher production costs, there is often no incentive to conserve soil resources. An improvement in the use of T-values would be to make them more attuned to specific conditions. Pierce et al. (1983) have proposed the use of T-values associated with a certain tolerance loss in soil productivity. Specifically, the amount of soil loss (associated with a certain soil productivity loss) is divided by the number of years chosen as a planning horizon. Therefore, as the planning horizon expands, the T-value decreases.

Unlike in the United States, soil specialists in Canada have been somewhat ambivalent in their use of T-values. Only recently was it proposed that Canada adopt a flexible T-value approach as set by the United States Soil Conservation Service; and that "these values be employed in conservation planning until sufficient data are available to adjust them to Prairie conditions" (PFRA, 1983, p. 120).

An alternative to the previously used approaches is that "intergenerational equity is best expressed as avoidance of long-term increases in costs of production" (Crosson and Stout, 1983, p. 82). Technological enhancement of factors of production can prevent costs from rising as can a variety of conservation measures. The timing of intervention is very much dependent upon the nature of the productivity decline (i.e., linear or non-linear), the value of the discount rate and the planning horizon. In order to justify conservation programs, the present value of the cost of conservation must be less than the present value of lost income from lower yields. Still, this present value approach may underestimate the cost to society of erosion because of institutional failure.

Crosson and Stout (1983) argue that in order to ensure that society's interests are being protected, it would be necessary to give more weight than the market to the social value of the land. This would be done by imagining a future in which demand and input prices are high, whereas the growth in land saving technologies is low. By necessity there would have to be greater public involvement in terms of the technical information needs of farmers and even subsidies for erosion control. This proposal attempts to optimize where possible the benefits from erosion control and productivity growth. The main role and value of public intervention is to adopt a somewhat conservative view of the future through the use of a lower discount rate than the prevailing one, and to ensure that funds are available for research and development into erosion control measures and productivity growth.

CONCLUSIONS

In managing agricultural land resources, society has responded with a variety of programs and policies to affect the stock and flow characteristics of the cropland base. This paper has provided a broad-brush assessment of the effectiveness of some of these strategies in dealing with uncertainty. Programs and policies were categorized as optimal or risk-averse. Although highly generalized, these categories served to highlight some of the significant differences in the way in which society reconciles present and future interests under conditions of uncertainty.

Efficient allocation of resources over time, so that society derives the maximum benefit from their use, is an important and worthwhile goal. The attainment of this utilitarian goal of resource allocation has in many instances been elusive since decisions must be made about discount rates, the future cost of inputs and the price of outputs, future levels of demand, the rate of growth in technical progress and the prospective uses of resources. Arguments in favour of relying on the market to make these decisions lose much of their credibility when exposed to inefficiencies in the market because of externalities, the existence of public goods and information shortages.

A common approach for anticipating resource needs in the future is through some kind of prospective analysis. Assumptions are made about future supply and demand conditions, and a variety of modelling strategies are employed to test the impact of various scenarios upon the adequacy of the resource base. A number of optimal strategies contain elements of this approach. The reliability of this approach must be judged in relation to the sensitivity of the results to changes in the basic inputs of technological change or future levels of demand. If the results or outcomes are judged to be fairly robust or relatively insensitive to change, the range of uncertainty will have been reduced and a firm base for optimal planning strategies will have been provided. Conversely, if the outcomes are very sensitive to changes in the input parameters and there is no way of discriminating between these inputs then the reliability of the estimates must be questioned. In this case society is faced with considerable uncertainty. Of particular concern are those situations subject to threshold effects. A case in point is the inflection point in Figure 9.1 (X_1 to X_3) which reveals threshold relationships between food output and food constraints (topsoil depth and quantity of agricultural land). A region's or country's location on those curves could affect significantly food production potential.

Risk-aversion approaches are commonly associated with conservation of land resources and with the ethical concern that succeeding generations will be no worse off than present generations. While these approaches provide relatively clear objectives and establish minimum standards for rates of use, they are relatively inflexible and ignore important efficiency issues such as social opportunity costs of alternative uses. The decision to proceed with a safe minimum standard is extremely complex and traditionally has been based on the principle that unless the social costs are unacceptably large then one should proceed. Ciriacy-Wantrup (1965, p. 581) has justified its use when "the costs of maintaining it are small in relation to the possible losses which irreversibility of depletion might entail". The obvious question here is how to define unacceptably large or excessive costs. Bishop (1978) argues that since this is a distributional issue economics is not well-equipped to deal with it.

Nonetheless, given situations of uncertainty where the reliability of estimates can be questioned, risk-aversion strategies may be more successful in protecting society's needs than optimal approaches. They may be particularly useful as stop-gap measures while society with the aid of more research efforts explores ways and means of approximating a social optimum.

The general principles that emerge here are that: how well policy makers identify uncertainty (and its sources) will determine

122

the effectiveness of the policy response; and the range of uncertainty will dictate, all other things equal, the level and type of action required.

REFERENCES

Bishop, R.C., 1978, "Endangered Species and Uncertainty: The Economics of a Safe Minimum Standard", American Journal of Agricultural Economics, 60, pp. 10-18.
Chapman, G.R., B. Smit and W.R. Smith, 1984, "Flexibility and Criticality in Resource Use Assessment", Geographical Analysis, 16 (1), pp. 52-64.
Ciriacy-Wantrup, S.V., 1965, "A Safe Minimum Standard as an Objective of Conservation Policy". In I. Burton and R.W. Kates (eds.), Readings in Resource Management and Conservation. Chicago: University of Chicago Press, pp. 575-584.
Ciriacy-Wantrup, S.V., 1968, Resource Conservation: Economics and Policies. Berkley: University of California Division of Agricultural Science.
Crosson, P.R. and A.T. Stout, 1983, Productivity Effects of Cropland Erosion in the United States. Baltimore: John Hopkins Press.
Furuseth, O.J. and J.T. Pierce, 1982, "A Comparative Analysis of Farmland Preservation Programmes in North America", Canadian Geographer, 26 (3), pp. 191-206.
Heal, G.M., 1981, "Economics and Resources". In J.A. Butlin (ed.), The Economics of Environmental and Natural Resources Policy. Boulder: Westview Press, pp. 62-73.
Hickling, A., 1975, Managing Decisions: The Strategic Choice Approach. Rugby: Mantec Publications.
Larson, W.E., J.B. Swan and F.J. Pierce, 1983, "The Threat of Soil Erosion to Long-Term Crop Production", Science, 219 (4584), pp. 458-465.
PFRA, 1983, Land Degradation and Soil Conservation Issues on the Canadian Prairies. Regina: Agriculture Canada.
Pierce, F.J., W.E. Larson, R.H. Dowdy and W.A.P. Graham, 1983, "Productivity of Soils: Assessing Long-Term Changes Due to Erosion", Journal of Soil and Water Conservation, 38 (1), pp. 39-44.
Smit, B., M. Brklacich, J. Schildroth and T. Phillips, 1985, "The Capacity of Ontario's Land Base to Accommodate Growth in the Agri-Food Sector", Resource Management and Optimization, 3 (1), pp. 185-207.
USDA, 1980, Basic Statistics, 1977 National Resources Inventory. Washington, D.C.: Soil Conservation Service.

PART 3
RESOURCE INFORMATION SYSTEMS

Planning for the use of land resources in rural areas demands appropriate information. In the absence of adequate data relating to biophysical and socio-economic factors that influence resource use it cannot be expected that land-use planning will necessarily promote societal goals. Recognition of the need for appropriate data for use in rural land planning was an important incentive to the development of land inventory and classification systems, which many developed countries have adopted as a basis for rating the capability of land for specific uses. However, these systems do not in themselves provide sufficient information to constitute a base for land-use decisions. There is also a need for data systems that account for socio-economic variables in addition to biophysical elements. At the same time, it is widely acknowledged that there is a need to improve data collection processes, to organize the data more systematically and to increase accessibility to information.

Technological advances in areas such as remote sensing have greatly facilitated the collection of information that may be useful in planning the utilization of rural land resources. In particular, remotely sensed images provide relatively consistent coverage over large areas. As Ryerson et al. report, it is possible to discern from these images land-use patterns at various spatial scales, ranging from small areas through to patterns of use at regional and national levels. Moreover, since coverage is provided on a recurring basis, remote sensing provides a useful source of information on land use and other environmental changes through time. Previously there has been a paucity of consistent information on changes in resource use, and this relatively new capability should greatly enhance knowledge of temporal trends.

Further needs lie in the development of computer-based resource information systems. Systems such as that described by Jones and Davidson are designed to provide a comprehensive source of information on biophysical and chemical aspects of the land resource as well as perhaps economic, social and cultural aspects of regions. An important advantage of these computer-based resource information systems, demonstrated by van Kleef, is that the information can be rapidly retrieved, on a selective basis. Flexibility exists as to the form in which information can be retrieved, the options including tabular and map output. As these types of systems are built-up and refined, analysts and decision makers will be afforded ready access to extensive information bases which could then constitute the foundation for resource-use evaluation and planning.

Combining such systems, which might be described as general purpose information systems, with selected analytical procedures, allows for the evaluation of policy alternatives and assessments of the effects of environmental change. In land evaluation systems, biophysical data may be combined with information on land-use requirements, management techniques, demands for the products of the land, productivity and economic variables. In turn, the information may be input directly to appropriate analytical frameworks for the purpose of policy assessment. Not only is an extensive information base provided, but also this information can be processed in order to investigate options in resource use relative to policy initiatives and environmental change. With reference to the evaluation of land resource policy and the implications of land drainage schemes for regional agricultural production, respectively, Birch and Brklacich et al. demonstrate the powerful capabilities of land evaluation systems in assisting resource management decisions.

The level of technological sophistication that has been achieved with resource information systems is also well represented in the development of expert systems. An expert system is comprised of an information base and a set of decision rules that apply the information to specific resource problems, with the aim of identifying management alternatives. As Davis et al. note, expert systems may have much to offer in assisting decision makers in identifying appropriate resource management plans.

The considerable emphasis placed by governments, independent research organizations and members of the academic community on the development of reliable and comprehensive information systems is a clear testimony to their importance in planning for the use of rural land resources. The essays presented in this part describe and evaluate information systems of the various types that have been alluded to above. Collectively, they illustrate the diversity of research that falls within the general field of resource information systems. While each refers to experiences in the development of a particular information system, the general applicability of the concepts and techniques is clearly evident. These essays provide a useful overview of some important recent developments in the use of information systems to assist the effective management of rural resources, and a prospectus for further research.

10

MONITORING RURAL LAND-USE CHANGE: A PILOT PROJECT

Robert Ryerson, Marie-France Germain, Udo Neilson and Rosemary Villani

INTRODUCTION

Information on rural land-use change is required in Canada for planning at various spatial scales. Such information, when tied to both the Census of Canada and to specific land parcels, allows a wide range of socio-economic variables, as well as spatially variable physical factors such as soil types and land forms to be related to changes in land use. Currently, resource analysts and policy makers are interested in changes at the rural-urban fringe, the agriculture-forest interface, and changes in farm systems which may be related to current or future land degradation. Identification of trends and relationships between land-use change and other factors permits resource analysts to estimate the impact of various policy options and to suggest remedial measures to decision makers.

To be useful to both planners and decision makers, information on land-use change must be comparable to the broadest possible variety of factors. In Canada, this implies compatibility with the Census of Canada, as well as the various data bases on soils, land capability, land cover and land use maintained by the Federal Government.

The purpose of this chapter is to describe a pilot study aimed at developing an operational method for cost-effective and rapid monitoring of rural land-use change, and which is consistent with Canada's requirements. The primary objective of the project is to develop methods for obtaining data on rural land-use change that will allow comparisons to be made over space and time. It is widely recognized that remote sensing is well-suited to this particular application (Ryerson, 1980; Warren and Rump, 1981).

The following section provides a background to the pilot study, while subsequent sections detail a methodology based on the interpretation of aerial photography. The final section of the chapter discusses some implications of the findings for a broad-scale monitoring program.

BACKGROUND

In 1978 the Government of Canada established the Canada Land Use Monitoring Program (CLUMP). Comprising four distinct components, the Urban Centred Region Project, the Prime Resource Land Project, the Rural Areas Project and the Wildlands Project, the purpose of the CLUMP is to provide an information base relating to a range of land-use activities at various scales (Environment Canada, 1983). Two CLUMP projects, the Urban Centred Region Project and the Prime Resource Lands Project, are operational.

In order to devise and implement a cost-effective procedure to generate relevant and reliable information on rural land-use change, two pilot projects were undertaken. One project set out to assess a satellite-based data collection method, the other to evaluate a system of information procurement based on aerial photography. The later of these two pilot projects is the subject of this chapter. Southern Manitoba was the area chosen for the pilot study.

THE PROCEDURE

The air photo based system for information collection comprises four distinct steps:

1. sample design,
2. photograph acquisition,
3. photograph registration and interpretation, and
4. data compilation.

Sample Design

Given the large land area to be covered in a nation-wide application (2 million km^2), it was clear that constraints of time and money ruled out a method based upon total coverage. A sampling-based system was obviously suggested. Such methods are reviewed by Bryant and Russwurm (1979), and Bircham (1979) argues that cluster samples in the order of 2 km X 2 km are most efficient when compared to point samples or larger cluster samples (up to

16 km X 16 km).

The sampling design was based on the National Farm Survey (NFS) and the 1981 census, oriented primarily to agriculture. Since the purpose of the Manitoba test project was to evaluate land-use change, and owing to budgetary considerations, parts of the study area where major change was unlikely were omitted. Also omitted were those areas with relatively homogeneous land uses and covers. However, in order to capture the total range of land uses and covers, as mandated by the terms of reference for the test project, areas in which agriculture was not the predominant activity were added to the sample. A total of 349 segments (spatial units) were chosen. Of these, 253 were in agricultural enumeration areas (EAs) and 96 in non-agricultural EAs, such as forested land and military reserves.

The sampling procedure comprised three separate steps. First, EAs were categorized into agricultural EAs and non-agricultural EAs. They were further stratified by census division before selecting the sample. A stratum was defined as the intersection of a census division and type of EA. Second, a subset of the EAs was selected, chosen by systematic sampling to ensure a good geographic spread of units. Third, segments of land within each of the EAs, which would comprise the sample itself, were randomly selected.

Photograph Acquisition

General guidelines are well-established with respect to the most cost-effective aerial image types for interpretation (Ryerson, 1981). However, because of the narrow width of the sample plots proposed by Bircham (1979) and those currently used by Statistics Canada, standard survey photography in a 9 X 9 format was seen to be wasteful and too expensive when compared to smaller formats. Recent work at Statistics Canada (Ryerson, 1985) and the Ontario Centre for Remote Sensing (Mussakowski, 1984) has evaluated various small-format airborne imagery types for one component of land use of interest here - crop identification.

Imagery were obtained by the Manitoba Remote Sensing Centre from flights made during the summer and early fall of 1984. In concert with suggestions made by Meisner and Lindstrom (1984) and Best (1984) the film used was 70 mm colour infrared and flying height was 5,550 feet above the ground. The contact scale was 1:42,000. Normal problems such as cloud cover were encountered.

For the purpose of characterizing land-use change in the CLUMP, photographs used to establish benchmark data against which change is measured should be about 10 years old. Black and white photographs made in 1970 at a scale of 1:70,000 were obtained for this purpose.

Photograph Registration and Interpretation

Photographs for 1970 and 1984 were registered to one another in order to compare the sampled segments. A base map, at a scale of 1:50,000, was developed to record information on land-use activity and ground cover change. The classification system recognized 10 activity classes and 15 ground cover categories (Table 10.1).

Data Compilation

Sampled segments were then categorized according to the degree and nature of change with respect to land-use activity and ground cover. Segments were grouped as follows:

1. segments in which no change was observed,
2. segments in which partial change was observed (i.e., change recorded for part of the spatial unit only), and
3. segments in which complete change was observed.

Problems in Interpretation

Some problems were initially encountered with the interpretation and mapping of the 1984 data, the most serious being the quality of the map produced. A common problem was to digitize one or more segments twice. While differences in area were negligible, maps with some of the polygon boundaries drafted more than once did not appear to be of acceptable quality. The methodology, therefore, was changed in the manner described below.

All interpreted polygons were transferred onto drafting material on which the segment boundaries, water bodies, transmission and transportation corridors had been traced from 1:50,000 National Topographical Series (NTS) map sheets. Polygons were then numbered, coding sheets were completed and the data entered into the computer.

The segment map was digitized and the areas of each polygon stored in the computer as before, but no drafting was done by the plotter. The segment map was then placed on the plotter and labelling of each sheet was completed with computer and plotter.

Several other alternatives were tested but none were as efficient as the approach followed. For example, polygon numbering as well as drafting was done faster with the plotter than with

TABLE 10.1:LAND-USE AND GROUND COVER CODING SYSTEM

CODE	LAND-USE ACTIVITY CLASS
a	Annual tillage crops and forage
b	Grazing
c	Other agricultural activities
d	Summer fallow
e	Former agricultural activities
f	Productive land-forest
g	Productive land-wildlife
h	Productive land-recreation
i	Other activities
j	No activities perceived

CODE	GROUND COVER CLASS
1	Tall trees
2	Small trees and shrubs
3	Cereal grains
4	Oilseeds
5	Improved grains or legumes
6	Other close grown crops
7	Corn
8	Beans
9	Vegetables
10	Other row crops
11	Unimproved grasslands
12	Denuded surfaces
13	Construction cover
14	Water
15	Summer fallow

Leroy and pen, and photo-to-map transfer completed with the Kargl projector was slightly faster than transfer with digitizer and plotter.

To ensure that all polygons were digitized and no errors were committed, the area of the complete segment was compared to the sum of the areas of the polygons. If required, measurements were repeated.

It should be noted that some overlays do not perfectly match the corresponding 1:50,000 NTS sheets. This happens mainly where there is river and lake shoreline. These discrepancies are due to differences between photo and NTS maps.

Other problems encountered were not due to the methodology used, but organization. That is to say, some materials were not supplied, such as map sheets, wrong areas were photographed and segments could not be found on the 1970 images. As well, materials were not all delivered at the same time. This meant that a production flow could not be established and some delays resulted.

STATISTICAL ANALYSES AND RESULTS

Since all data were stored in computer files, the statistical analyses were completed without great difficulty. Old and new files were compared and the change was qualified and quantified. Listings were supplied in matrix form. Because of space considerations these cannot be presented here but are reported in Germain, (1985 and 1986). The first analysis was based on a stratification derived from the existing National Farm Survey Sampling Frame. Three estimates were made:

1. base level information (i.e., the total area in each land-use category at the first date),
2. estimates of absolute change (i.e., the absolute amount of change from one class to another), and
3. estimates of relative change (i.e., the relative per cent of any given class which has changed to another).

Virtually all of the coefficients of variation (CVs) for the changes exceeded 25 per cent. The only area with consistently good results was that of relative change. A second stratification was then done based on general land cover as interpreted from LANDSAT Multispectral Scanner data. A new set of results were then available. The new stratification, which was expected to lead to a general improvement, did so. A stratification based on broad land cover classes seems better than one based on administrative divisions. There are, however, some reservations.

The post-stratification has improved the estimates of absolute change and of relative levels of change, mostly for the more common changes or classes, but not in a substantial manner. The estimates remain of the same magnitude but the coefficients of variation are slightly better (lower CVs), especially for estimates of relative levels of change.

After looking at the estimates of gain in precision, it seems that the second stratification alone would produce estimates of better precision than the first one for common classes. Areas for "rare" changes or under "rare" classes seem difficult to estimate accurately from both stratifications.

The second stratification does not seem to be efficient for the activity class "no perceived activity" and the cover classes "denuded surfaces" and "water", this last class being the most difficult to estimate.

Finally, the overall quality of the post-stratified estimates and the estimates of gain in precision are difficult to assess due to the bias of the estimates (from a ratio estimation) and to non-sampling errors such as measurement errors, collapsing of strata and non-randomness of the sample. Therefore, the estimates should be used with caution.

The following comments summarize the observations made on the new estimates.

1. Most of the post-stratified estimates of absolute change are of the same magnitude as the old estimates (within a ±10 per cent difference. There is an approximately equal number of losses (higher post-stratified CVs) and gains (lower post-stratified CVs) in precision. Finally, the larger differences in the estimates and large losses or gains in precision appear for rare changes (few segments with non-zero value).

2. For the estimates of levels in 1984, the post-stratified estimates are of the same magnitude as the old ones but most CVs are better. Again, the larger differences in magnitude and of losses or gains in precision are for rare classes.

As mentioned previously, the overall "quality" of the post-stratified estimates is difficult to assess, but a few remarks should be made and taken into account when using these estimates.

1. The post-stratified estimates are very likely to be biased because of the high CVs observed for the estimates of area in new strata.

2. Because of the small number of non-zero segments used in the calculation of change area or level for some characteristics, the ratio estimates should be used with caution as point estimates.

3. The exactness of the correction factor is questionable due to the errors in measuring the true areas of the new strata and the high variability of the estimated areas of the new strata.

4. The amount of collapsing of new and old strata necessary to ensure sufficient sample sizes to calculate the estimates reduces to some extent the benefits of the new

stratification; that is, the homogeneity within the new strata.

5. Because the final sample is not a random subsample of the initial one, it may not be adequately representative of the population. Also, it does not respect the optimum allocation and therefore does not minimize the variance of the estimators.

CONCLUSION

This chapter has described a pilot project in which a methodology based on the interpretation of aerial photography has been examined as a possible means of generating reliable information on rural land-use change. The study demonstrated that for common land-use classes the sampling approach with airborne imagery was adequate for identifying relative levels of change. However, for rare classes, to obtain absolute values other methods must be considered. The second component of this study will focus on evaluating satellite data to identify the rare classes noted in the previous section, as well as to obtain absolute values on change.

For most jurisdictions with more dense population and/or smaller land areas, it is expected that much of the baseline information would be better obtained from total coverage or an efficient point sample. For tropical areas with almost continuous cloud cover, the imagery source one should consider would be airborne Synthetic Aperture Radar (SAR), or high resolution Systéme Probatoire d'Observation de la Terre (SPOT), rather than the normal colour or colour infrared imagery considered here. Subsequent change information would, from the preliminary work reported here and that of others, be available from either airborne SAR, LANDSAT Thematic Mapper (TM), or SPOT data.

ACKNOWLEDGMENTS

This work was funded by the Canada Land Use Monitoring Program, the Canada Centre for Remote Sensing, Agriculture Canada, and Statistics Canada (Agriculture Division).

REFERENCES

Best, W., 1984, Personal communication. Manitoba Centre for Remote Sensing, Winnipeg, Manitoba.

Bircham, P., 1979, Sampling Methodology Study for Land Use Monitoring in Canada: A Detailed Methodology and Data

Report. Ottawa: Land Use Monitoring Division, Lands Directorate, Environment Canada.

Bryant, C.R. and L.H. Russwurm, 1979, Area Sampling Strategies in Relation to Land Use Monitoring-Needs and Objectives. Ottawa: Working Paper No. 24, Lands Directorate, Environment Canada.

Environment Canada, 1983, Canada Land Use Monitoring Program-An Evaluation of a Methodology for Determining Presettlement and Existing Wetlands in Canada. Ottawa: Lands Directorate, Environment Canada.

Germain, M.F., 1985, Rural Land Use in Manitoba: Results of a Statistical Analysis. Ottawa: Unpublished Contract Report, Methodology Division, Statistics Canada.

Germain, M.F., 1986, New Stratification Analysis of Rural Land Use Results in Manitoba. Ottawa: Unpublished Contract Report, Methodology Division, Statistics Canada.

Meisner, D.E. and O.M. Lindstrom, 1984, "Design and Operation of a Colour Infrared Aerial Video System". In 50th Annual Meeting of the American Society of Photogrammetry, Washington, D.C., pp. 518-525.

Mussakowski, R.S., 1984, "The Application of Video Remote Sensing to Resource Surveys and Environmental Monitoring". In 8th Canadian Symposium on Remote Sensing, Montreal, pp. 91-99.

Ryerson, R.A., 1980, Land Use Information from Remotely Sensed Data. Ottawa: Users' Manual 80-1, Canada Centre for Remote Sensing, Canada Department of Energy, Mines and Resources.

Ryerson, R.A., 1981, Results of a Benefit-Cost Analysis of the CCRS Airborne Program. Ottawa: Research Report 81-1, Canada Centre for Remote Sensing, Canada Department of Energy, Mines and Resources.

Ryerson, R.A., 1985, "Crop Identification on Airborne Video and 70 mm Colour Photography". Ottawa: Unpublished Research Note, Agriculture Statistics Division, Statistics Canada.

Warren, L. and P. Rump, 1981, Urbanization in Canada, 1966-1976. Ottawa: Land Use in Canada Series No. 20, Lands Directorate, Environment Canada.

11

APPLICATION OF A LAND RESOURCE INFORMATION SYSTEM TO A SMALL AREA IN SCOTLAND
Gareth Jones and Donald Davidson

INTRODUCTION

The most cursory consideration of land evaluation will show that the specialists who are involved in the construction of a land-use policy demand the most detailed and contemporary data at their disposal, require direction from their political and economic masters, and require a particular sensitivity for understanding the feelings of the population who will be affected by any changes in land use. Land-use policies can rarely be judged to be totally successful. At best, the planning process works on the principles of compromise in which the well-being of the region, or the nation, takes priority over the individual. In such a situation, dissent by groups of individuals can sometimes sway the decision making processes. Planners have thus been anxious to use as much information as possible in order to evaluate the potential usefulness of the land resource, including its constituent parts. Mapped data is a well-established source of information, and includes, for example, geology, soils, vegetation and climatic statistics, all of which represent important information in an evaluation program. Traditional data sources, while still of great value, have considerable defects which are summarized in the following.

1. Maps based on traditional methods of data collection and production have become very expensive to produce both in terms of manpower and production cost.
2. Some maps, for example those showing soil attributes, are of a technical nature and require specialist knowledge in order to extract information.
3. Occasionally, there can be a plethora of maps, published at differing scales and with differing accuracy. Owing to problems of interpretation and comparability, the potential usefulness of some of these maps can be very difficult to

assess.

4. Traditionally produced maps become rapidly outdated; often before a map is published the data on which it is based is obsolete but because of the expense involved in updating it, it is retained in use.

Computerization of data sources appears to hold much promise in overcoming many of these deficiencies, including improvements in the quality of data available to the planner and in permitting greater flexibility both in the use of the data and in the way in which the results are presented. This paper describes the development of a relatively low cost computer-based land resource information system (LRIS). A brief historical sketch of LRISs in Britain sets the stage for the more specific discussion which follows.

COMPUTER-BASED INFORMATION SYSTEMS

The advent of the electronic computer has made possible a re-evaluation of the ways in which data can be collected, stored, interpreted and made available for the user. The large, impersonal mainframe systems of the 1960s and early 1970s were poorly suited for use by the non-specialist user. However, the development of user-friendly systems along with specialist software has enabled the semi-skilled computer user to make use of computer facilities (Wehde et al., 1980). In Britain, one of the earliest practical applications of computer storage and analysis of data for planning purposes was the Tourism and Recreation Information Package (TRIP) Computer Assessment for Tourism and Recreation Potential in Scotland (Tourism and Recreation Research Unit [TRRU], 1974). Quality of output was limited due to use of lineprinter symbols but the efforts were highly commendable and sufficiently encouraging to allow further development. The TRIP system was a grid-cell data base with each cell representing an area of 10 km^2. Since 1980, the TRIP has been succeeded by the highly sophisticated GIMMS mapping program (Waugh, 1983). At the same time, Lyall (1980) reported on the Rural Land Information System in which 54 sets of variables covering physical, biotic, economic and population data were assembled for the Fife Region of Scotland. This system showed considerable promise but made little progress due, apparently, to lack of funding.

The most expensive British study to date has been that conducted by the Institute of Terrestrial Ecology, which has produced a comprehensive survey of Britain at a 1 km^2 grid square interval. This system collected data on 186 characteristics and then by means of dendrogram sorting via 15 divisions and 15 thresholds produced 16 classes of land (Institute of Terrestrial Ecology, 1982).

Despite its relatively crude scale, the data has been used by a number of planning bodies to aid the construction of a regional planning strategy. The mapping scale of 1 symbol per 1 km^2 is acceptable at a national level, but for detailed area studies a much finer grid mesh is desirable.

DEVELOPMENT OF THE LRIS

One of the objectives of the LRIS study developed by the present authors was to examine the practicalities of working with an intensive grid sampling system over an area of ground which showed extreme physical and biotic variation. A number of sampling intervals were considered before finally selecting a 100 m^2 interval. The system was also intended to test the feasibility of producing high quality symbol maps which would be acceptable to land users. Initially, it was considered that the GIMMS mapping program would be used to process the data bank but after some trials the alternative symbol mapping program GINO-F was used (CAD Centre Ltd., 1983). This is a graphics package which takes the form of a library of drawings and administrative subroutines. Control of line type, pen size and type and area fill with default or user defined hatch styles is possible.

The test area selected is located approximately 12 km west of Stirling in Central Scotland (Figure 11.1). This site is 14 km x 5 km and was chosen deliberately as it includes considerable variation in topography. At the northern end of the transect terrain is flat, comprising low-lying carse lands of the River Forth. South of this area, the land rises abruptly over a basaltic scarp slope which continues as a dissected plateau. Consequent upon the topographical variations are equally wide ranging differences in soil type, land use, climate and land value. It is an area of contrasting land uses, ranging from intensive farming in the north of the transect to extensive sheep farming, forestry and water catchment in the central and southern portions of the transect.

A sampling grid of 100 m^2 was superimposed over the entire transect area and data were collected from grid intersection points. The only exceptions were presence/absence data, such as information relating to the presence/absence of roads, tracks and streams. These data referred to the grid square as a whole. In order that the LRIS could be developed as quickly as possible, it was decided that all data would be collected from existing map, air photograph or statistical report sources. Some field verification was undertaken. Twenty-one different variables were judged to be both relevant to the LRIS study and available in published form (Table 11.1). A total of 7,800 observations for each variable were collected. Data were collected, tabulated and entered into a computer data bank

FIGURE 11.1: LOCATION MAP OF THE LRIS
STUDY AREA

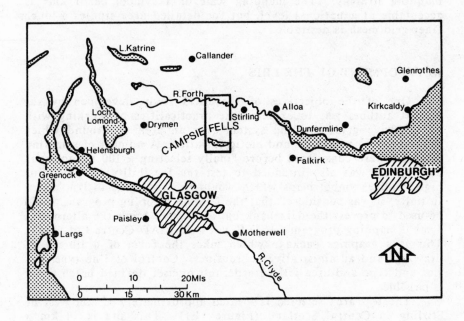

within the space of 23 worker-weeks. Short programs were written
to check that variable data values were within the specified range,
though it was impossible at the initial stage to authenticate every
data value. Visual checks were made much later in the exercise
when mapped data were checked for rogue values.

The collection of data at a 100 m^2 interval had certain advantages as well as disadvantages. A major benefit associated with
the use of this scale was the ability to record small-scale variations
in site conditions; this was judged to be essential for projects
requiring detailed information. As a result, it was possible to
produce small-scale computer-drawn maps which possessed a high
degree of visual acceptance. The disadvantages were essentially
those of high financial cost and the length of time necessary for the
assembly of the data. The data collection was slow, tedious and
expensive while the development of the mapping programs was
consumptive of computer time. A further disadvantage was that
not all the variables could be assessed at equivalent levels of
sophistication, creating obvious difficulties with respect to

TABLE 11.1: VARIABLES USED IN THE LRIS
DATA BANK

1. Grid Reference; 6 figure number
2. Land/Reservoir/Land Beyond Study Area
3. Elevation in Metres
4. Slope; 7 categories
5. Aspect; 9 categories
6. Streams, Rivers, or Drainage Ditches; present/absent
7. Rock Outcrops, Crags, Rock Facies or Quarries; present/absent
8. Marsh, Peat or Bog; present/absent
9. Roads; Metalled; present/absent
10. Tracks; Unclassified; present/absent
11. Buildings; Any Form; present/absent
12. Solid Geology
13. Drift Geology; categories 12 and 13 were not assessed because of variability in data sources
14. Soils; Soil Series or Mapping Unit; 27 categories
15. Land-Use Capability Class; 7 categories
16. Land-Use Capability Subclass; 7 categories
17. Vegetation; 13 categories
18. Land Type; 6 categories
19. Tree Type; afforestation; 7 categories
20. Yield Class of Afforested Area; 5 categories
21. Exposure as Assessed by TOPEX; 2 categories

comparability between certain variables.

A fundamental component of any LRIS must be the ability to display information in a form that makes sense to potential users. Since maps have long been used by resource managers, it is clear that the capability to display data in map form is essential. Using the GINO-F graphics software package, four different types of map can be produced.

1. At the simplest level, direct plotting of symbols to correspond with data as collected from published sources. Figure 11.2 illustrates a general pH map in which five pH classes have been defined.
2. A development of Map Type 1, in which evaluators were included such as IF ... THEN ... statements. Figure 11.3 shows the distribution of prime agricultural land in which the base data was searched for land below 150 m, a slope of $<7^0$, free or imperfect soil drainage and moderate stoniness, and a rooting depth of >40 cm. All grid cells

FIGURE 11.2: LRIS DISTRIBUTION MAP - pH VALUES

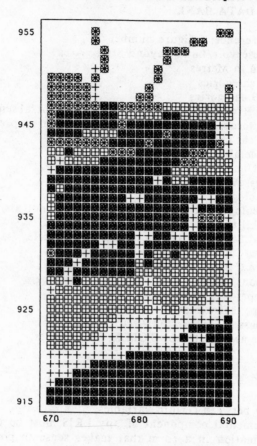

	pH USUALLY >6
▦	pH USUALLY 5-6
■	pH USUALLY <5
▨	pH VERY VARIED
‡‡	NO INFORMATION
—	RESERVOIRS
•	LAND BEYOND STUDY AREA

**FIGURE 11.3: LRIS INTERPRETATIVE MAP -
PRIME AGRICULTURAL LAND**

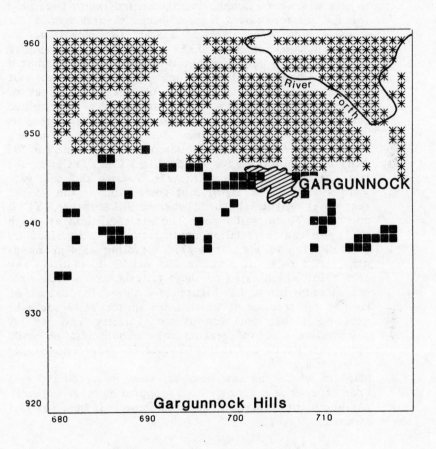

■ Prime Agricultural Land
(Definition 1)

▨ Unique Agricultural Land
(Carseland)

1 km

which met these specifications were plotted as prime agricultural land.

3. Data can be statistically or mathematically manipulated to produce derived data values; these could be plotted as in Map Type 1. Rainfall and temperature maps were produced in this way. For example, average annual rainfall readings for ten meteorological sites adjacent to and within the transect area were regressed against site elevation. A regression equation, $Y = 113.81 + (1.65 * X)$, was applied to all elevation points within the transect, and predicted rainfall amounts plotted to one of six categories. Of greater relevance, it is possible to make predictions of vegetation productivity using statistically determined correlations. The Forestry Commission made available its Timber Yield Class values for the area (Forestry Commission, 1971). A Chi-squared test was made on 507 pairs of observations for which Yield Class (YC) for the tree species Sitka spruce (*Picea sitchensis*) and soil type were available. A significant correlation at the 95 per cent level was established between Sitka spruce, YC12, and six different soil types. The site conditions at which the significant correlation applied could be described by the following values: slope $<25^{\circ}$, elevation <394 m, Landuse Class 5 or 6. A program was written to identify any grid point which satisfied these criteria, and which were not already forested. Figure 11.4 shows the extent of land in the transect at which Sitka spruce YC12 could be expected if that land was given to forestry land use. A comparative study of grazing values could also be made using the Relative Grazing Values for vegetation types (Bibby et al., 1982).

4. Maps in which the raw data has been interpreted (based upon experience and/or methods proposed by other workers). Air photo interpretation forms an important base for this assessment.

An Example: Soil Data

One of the most important considerations in a land evaluation study is that which concerns soil information. The physical and chemical conditions of a soil will, to a large extent, determine the uses to which that soil can be put. Many regions of Britain now have available a soil survey memoir comprising a handbook of detailed information on the soils of an area. Accompanying the memoir is a soil survey map at a scale of 1:50,000. It was unfortunate that no such information existed for the transect area. Field

**FIGURE 11.4:   LRIS PREDICTIVE MAP - LAND SUITABLE,
SITKA SPRUCE TREES, YIELD CLASS 12**

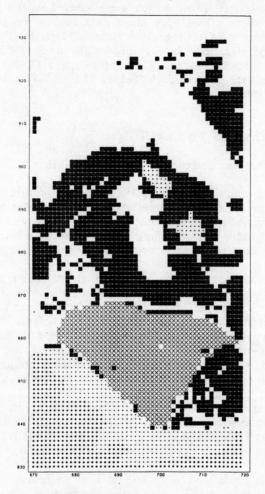

■ LAND CAPABLE OF SUPPORTING
   SITKA SPRUCE YC 12
   SLOPE LESS THAN CLASS 6
   LAND USE CAPABILITY CLASS 5 OR 6
   SOIL TYPE NUMBERS 6/7/10/11/12 OR 26
   ELEVATION LESS THAN 394m
   95% CONFIDENCE LEVEL ON RESULTS
⊠ EXISTING FOREST PLANTATION
∷ RESERVOIRS
∷ **LAND BEYOND STUDY AREA**

and laboratory data did exist, however, and the Departments of Soil Survey and Mineral Soils of the Macaulay Institute made available the data for 92 sites, 18 of which were located in the transect, the remainder close by. This very large data source was assembled on a microcomputer data management system. Details of this part of the project are described in Davidson and Jones (1985). The soil data yielded information for 13 separate maps (Table 11.2). Full details of the data described in Tables 11.1 and 11.2 are contained in Davidson (1984).

AN ASSESSMENT OF THE LRIS

The system was designed to test the feasibility of:

1. the production of a detailed land information system,
2. the creation of a system with maximum flexibility, useful to specialist and non-specialist users alike, and
3. the production of computer drawn maps with emphasis on high quality, visually acceptable output.

The system met these criteria though demands on time and finance were considerable. To illustrate, the transect area was small, 70 km^2, yet the data took 23 worker-weeks to prepare. Several adjustments might be considered to redress this problem. First, the data collection grid could be enlarged, although this would lead to an inevitable loss in definition at the map output stage. Second, the number of variables collected could be reduced. Experience shows, for instance, that the presence/absence data were of little use in this project (Variables 6 - 11, Table 11.1). Neither of these adjustments could be undertaken without considerable consultation with potential clients, a consideration which is often overlooked when LRISs are being developed. Third, automating data collection could be justified, especially if a large area was to be studied.

The LRIS described here has met all expectations regarding flexibility and ease of use. Elementary knowledge of FORTRAN is advisable, however. A free format data base allows maximum ease of transfer between program operating systems. Threshold values and critical variable combinations can be easily set into the control program. Screen editing facilities on computer terminals allows rapid modification of the programs.

Considerable surprise has been expressed at the quality of the map output. There existed considerable reservation as to the acceptability of the computer drawn maps, especially to non-specialist users. Despite GINO-F having only eight basic symbols available for plotting, it was possible to combine symbols in a way that a

TABLE 11.2:   SOIL VARIABLE MAPS PRODUCED
BY THE LRIS

1. Major Soil Groups; 10 categories
2. Parent Material Types; 9 categories
3. Soil Drainage; 8 categories
4. General pH Values; 5 categories
5. Depth of Organic Horizons; 6 categories
6. Exchangeable Bases; 5 categories
7. Per Cent Base Saturation; 5 categories
8. Organic Matter; A Horizon; 6 categories
9. Phosphate (soluble); A Horizon; 6 categories
10. Silt Content; 5 categories
11. Sand Content; 5 categories
12. Stoniness; 5 categories
13. Maximum Rooting Depth; 5 categories

graded shading system could be produced. To date there have been
no negative comments regarding the quality of the maps. The maps
can withstand substantial photographic reduction and still remain
legible (40 per cent reduction is the norm). Individual symbol size
can be changed and, depending on the plotter, multicolour maps can
be produced. The use of a symbol plot method imparts great
accuracy, unlike an isopleth, contour mapping system which may
have a plus or minus 10 per cent line position error. Because the
symbol plotting method is linked to the grid coordinates of an area,
it is possible to identify a mapped symbol position with considerable
accuracy in the field.

CONCLUSION

The LRIS described can provide the planner and the land user
with a highly accurate, flexible assessment of land attributes. It
can be used to predict areas where specific land uses can be best
located in respect to physical and chemical site conditions. The
LRIS can also be used to make predictions of productivity. The
addition of agricultural statistics would allow a wider comparison to
be made between alternative uses of land.

A flexible methodology has been devised which, with further
development, could provide the land user and the land-use planner
a technique with which to optimize land utilization. It is now the
responsibility of the planner to indicate, precisely, the combinations
of variables which are of greatest use in the task of producing

planning strategies. When applied to specific field data, the LRIS can help improve the productivity of forestry and agricultural land use. It can locate areas which are of minimal economic use, as well as those areas of ecologic uniqueness and of amenity value. In its present form, the LRIS is suitable for small area land evaluation ($<100m^2$). Automation of data collection, or direct data input from Landsat satellite imagery would make available a very sophisticated planning technique for large areas. With ever greater pressures being placed upon resources, it becomes imperative that the management of resources is conducted according to the soundest of scientific principles.

REFERENCES

Bibby, J.S., et al., 1982, Land Capability for Agriculture. Aberdeen: The Macaulay Institute for Soil Research.

CAD Centre Ltd., 1983, GINO-F Users Guide. CAD Centre Ltd.

Davidson, D.A., 1984, LRIS Working Report. Glasgow: Department of Geography, University of Strathclyde.

Davidson, D.A. and G.E. Jones, 1985, "The Use of a Low Level Data Base Management System for the Analysis of Soil Survey Records", Soil Survey and Land Evaluation, 5 (3), pp. 88-92.

Forestry Commission, 1971, Forest Management Tables (Metric). London: Forestry Commission Booklet No. 34, Her Majesty's Stationery Office.

Institute of Terrestrial Ecology, 1982, The Use of Land Classification in Resource Assessment Rural Planning. Natural Environment Research Council.

Lyall, G.A., 1980, "Planning and Land Assessment in Scotland: - Role of the Rural Land Information Systems Working Party". In M.F. Thomas and J.J. Coppock (eds.), Land Assessment in Scotland. Aberdeen: Aberdeen University Press, pp. 107-118.

TRRU, 1974, Systems Description. Edinburgh: TRIP Series No. 1, Research Report No. 11, Edinburgh University.

Waugh, T.C., 1983, GIMMS Users Handbook. Edinburgh: Edition 4.5, GIMMS Ltd.

Wehde, M.E., K. Dalstead and E.K. Worcester, 1980, "Resource Applications of Computerized Data Processing: The AREAS Example", Journal of Soil and Water Conservation, 35 (1), pp. 36-40.

12

AUTOMATION AND THE SUPPLY OF INFORMATION FOR LAND-USE MANAGEMENT
H.A. van Kleef

INTRODUCTION

The supply of information for land-use management in rural areas presents a problem, due to the requirements in terms of time and money. Of particular concern are the collection and processing of data which are not available in a general graphics data system. The choice in that situation between using the limited information that is available and the collection of data with a minimum of effort can have the following results:

1. plans are unbalanced in that components with better data become more clearly articulated,
2. plans are vague,
3. there is no interaction between plans at different scales, such as the local and regional level,
4. there is no interaction between planning and implementation,
5. the same data are collected more than once,
6. the collected data do not satisfy the conditions of an information system, such as uniformity of concepts and classification, and
7. the collected data are not managed adequately.

Generally, information is scattered and is difficult to obtain. It is not surprising, therefore, that more attention is being paid to the management of information systems in order to optimize the observation, registration, processing, presentation and maintenance of information. It will be demonstrated in this paper that automation can make an important contribution to solving this problem.

Two developments in the Netherlands in relation to the supply of information for land-use management will be discussed here. The first concerns the use of data bases in which graphics data are linked to nongraphics data. A simple example is an information system called the Land Division Survey for General Land-Use Management (CIAB). This is a farm-level data base in which the coordinates of farm buildings are combined with farm data. The second development concerns the linking of several data bases which contain graphics data. This is done by means of digitizing basic information from topographic map sheets.

LAND DIVISION SURVEY FOR GENERAL LAND-USE MANAGEMENT

The term land-use management, while used in connection with a great many activities, normally implies the control and guidance of development within a framework of policy that has the support of most, though not necessarily all, of the interested parties. Examples of issues for which policy initiatives are presently being prepared or revised in the Netherlands are, respectively, the excavation of sand for construction projects and that of surplus manure in areas with intensive animal husbandry. A reliable source of information, which can be regularly updated, can be extremely valuable in policy formulation.

The information source most commonly used in the Netherlands for the development of agriculturally oriented policy is the annual inquiry of farm data. Each of the more than 160,000 farm operators in the Netherlands is required to participate in this census which is executed by the Central Bureau of Statistics (CBS). Data are collected for over 200 variables relating to farm operators and their businesses. Included is information on the age and occupation of farm operators, characteristics of farm labourers, holding size, the acreage and production of crops, and details relating to animal husbandry.

Despite some appealing features, such as the annual collection of data, researchers have complained that the system is incapable of providing flexible output. To illustrate, even though data are collected for individual agricultural holdings, the information is aggregated into geographic units with set boundaries. Data are available only at the national, provincial and municipal levels, as well as for selected large agricultural areas. It was for this reason that the province of Gelderland requested that the Institute for Land and Water Management (ICW) develop an agricultural geographic information system to provide data for use in land-use management. The system is called the Land Division Survey for General Land-Use Management (CIAB).

CIAB: An Outline

The basic structure of the system is outlined in Figure 12.1. After a farm visit, a land users map and a farm buildings map are composed at a scale of 1:10,000, and data relating to the holding are collected. These data refer to the size of a holding, the acreage of land around the farm buildings and the number of lots. On the land users map the lots of each holding are marked. The graphics data and that pertaining to the individual holdings are updated on an annual basis. On the farm buildings map, the locations of the farm buildings are marked together with the holding number and the other holding data (Figure 12.2). These data, taken together with the information from the CBS, constitute the CIAB data base.

Use of the CIAB Data Base

To date, the data base has been used in two ways. First, in the identification of holdings with specific characteristics, and second for the production of tables and maps. Identification of holdings with particular characteristics is possible with a list of holding numbers or through a list of attributes, such as the number of breeding pigs and fattening pigs, or the total number with specific characteristics, such as the number of breeding pigs weighing less than 50 kg or the number of fattening pigs heavier than 50 kg. Selection also can be made by digitizing the boundaries of one or more areas drawn on a map.

Once holdings have been identified, it is possible to produce primary and secondary tables and maps. The primary tables and maps provide information at the individual farm level. The tables may contain basic farm data or refer to specific characteristics, such as perhaps a list of holdings that are located within a specified radius of a particular farm (Table 12.1). Flexibility exists in relation to the layout of the tables and in terms of the information that is incorporated. A primary map is a map on which the calculated results or the primary table have been recorded (Figure 12.2).

The secondary tables are cross-tabulations of the data and also offer a high degree of flexibility in terms of the information that can be provided. Table 12.2, for example, presents a cross-tabulation of holding size and the number of lots per holding. Additional secondary tables can be generated by expressing the absolute values or percentages of row or column totals. Secondary maps can then be generated from the information contained within these tables as, for example, Figure 12.3.

FIGURE 12.1: THE CIAB SYSTEM

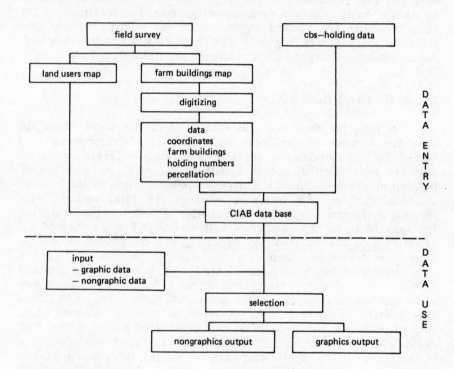

FIGURE 12.2: FARM BUILDINGS MAP

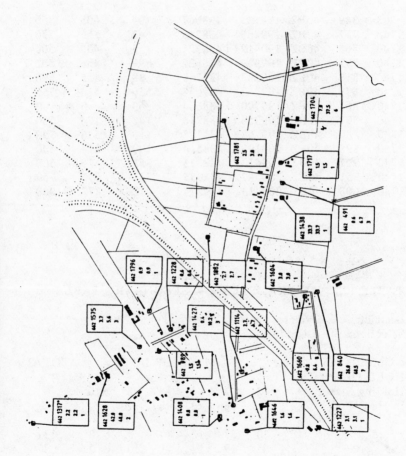

TABLE 12.1: AN EXAMPLE OF A PRIMARY TABLE

Area: Duiven-Westervoort
Selection: Holding with pigs within a particular distance to holding number 17400861

HOLDING NO.		MAP 991	X COORD 992	Y COORD 993	NO. OF PIGS 256	DIST IN M 1002	PART. DIST 1003
997	998						
1740	349	40BZ	199185	438667	104	605	750
1740	757	40BZ	199460	438216	42	556	750
1740	768	40BZ	199412	438525	5	403	500
1740	797	40BZ	199336	438622	199	456	500
1740	810	40EZ	200233	438768	39	455	500
1740	833	40BZ	199443	439038	530	510	750
1740	861	40BZ	199790	438664	363	0	0
1740	871	40BZ	199956	438716	148	174	250
1740	880	40BZ	199768	438128	110	536	750
1740	898	40EZ	200103	438614	100	317	500
1740	927	40BZ	199413	438375	358	475	500
1740	951	40EZ	200287	438985	557	592	750
1740	1003	40EZ	200413	439274	32	872	1000

TABLE 12.2: AN EXAMPLE OF A SECONDARY TABLE

District: Lymers
Selection: All holdings

NUMBER OF HOLDINGS Holding Size in Ha	NUMBER OF LOTS						TOTAL
	<2	≥2 <4	≥4 <6	≥6 <8	≥8 <10	≥10	
<5	70	57	10	0	0	0	137
≥5, <10	5	19	12	1	0	0	37
≥10, <20	2	15	22	5	2	0	46
≥20, <30	0	4	8	2	0	1	15
≥30, <40	1	1	1	4	1	1	9
≥40	0	1	5	2	1	2	11
TOTAL	78	97	58	14	4	4	255

FIGURE 12.3: AN EXAMPLE OF A SECONDARY MAP

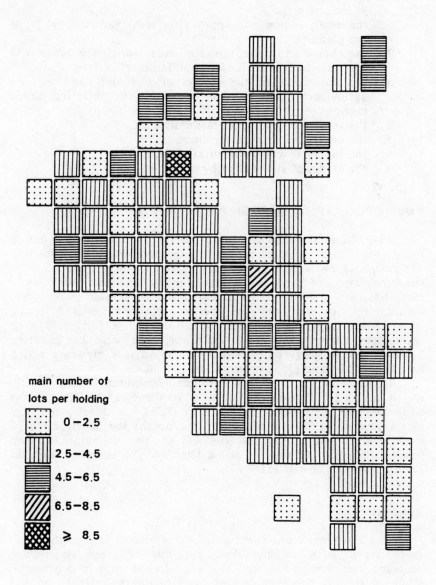

main number of
lots per holding

0 – 2.5

2.5 – 4.5

4.5 – 6.5

6.5 – 8.5

≥ 8.5

The system is used in connection with the management of land uses in the province of Gelderland. Further possible applications relate to the following:

1. the draft, review and approval of local and regional land-use plans,
2. the choice and delimitation of areas which are considered for reallotment and land consolidation,
3. the indication of the effects of changing land uses in agricultural areas (outdoor recreation, urbanization, sand-mining),
4. the control of plant and cattle diseases,
5. the control of manure surpluses,
6. the supply of energy in rural areas, and
7. the effect of inundation by rivers.

THE TOPOGRAPHIC BASE MAP

The second development to be discussed relates to the use of topographic maps as a base for linking information contained in various other geographic information systems. In connection with the preparation of land consolidation projects in the Netherlands, there has been a proliferation of automized geographic information systems relating to land use, relief, soil, traffic and roads, watercourses, landscape, outdoor recreation, and so forth. Most of these systems have a relation to the topographic map. The problem, however, is the geographic linking of the various elements which are all part of stand-alone information systems.

In cooperation with the technical computer centre RAET, which has an INTERGRAPH system at its disposal, the Institute for Land and Water Management Research (ICW) has developed a low cost system to solve this problem. It concerns the construction of a geographic data base derived from the topographic map (scale 1:10,000). The base is called Digitized Topographic Map for Land Consolidation (DIGTOP-LI).

The System

The most important function of the digitized topographic map is to serve as a common base for the different stand-alone geographic information systems that are relevant for a land consolidation project. In this way data entry, data linking, calculation and production of tables and graphics output can be automated. It means that the map has to satisfy the following conditions:

1. geographic orientation must be possible,
2. it must contain the elements which are necessary to link attributes, and
3. it must approximate the exactness of the photogrammetic map of the Netherlands which is at a scale of 1:10.000 (Figure 12.4).

When Figures 12.4 and 12.5 are compared it will be clear that all line elements in the rural area are included in the data base. Buildings and symbols for smaller features such as dams, bridges and churches are not part of the base, and larger villages and towns are also excluded. All existing roads in a land consolidation area are usually included in the data base, however.

The DIGGTOP-LI system offers several useful facilities. Among these are a data base with trigonometric coordinates which are consistent with the photogrammetic map sheets of the Topographic Service, or other coordinates if required. The system also provides for phased data entry, data editing, and the overlaying of sheets. The facility exists to extract coordinates for any area chosen, and to plot data at any scale chosen. The DIGTOP-LI system also provides a base from which to calculate lengths and sizes of lots or other polygons in the area. The data entry and the management of the data base is executed by the RAET.

There are several major advantages to this system. These include the fact that problems with linking stand-alone bases are avoided. Digitizing and other activities which are necessary to build up a data base, including control plotting, are minimized. Under the system described here, more maps can be produced which, in terms of scale, form and orientation, are adjusted to the particular requirements of the user. The base can be installed in any computer system and maps can be produced on a wide variety of hardware. Also, geographic information systems bases on DIGTOP-LI can be developed by RAET or by the user. Finally, nongraphic linking is possible by generating unique area and line numbers.

The DIGTOP-LI is used in conjunction with land consolidation projects. This means that each year 36,000 ha are added to the base. More important is that the base is used as a frame for geographic information systems such as the land division survey, the landscape survey, the nature survey, and so on, that are carried out as part of land consolidation projects. An example is given in Figure 12.6, which is a ditch capacity map that was produced through the linking of DIGTOP-LI and the water management survey. The system could, therefore, also be used by ministerial, provincial and municipal departments which otherwise rely on photogrammetic maps. In that way an important step to improve

156

FIGURE 12.4: PHOTOGRAMMETIC MAP (1:10,000)

220.570

219.570

FIGURE 12.5: DIGITIZED PHOTOGRAMMETIC MAP

FIGURE 12.6: DITCH CAPACITY MAP

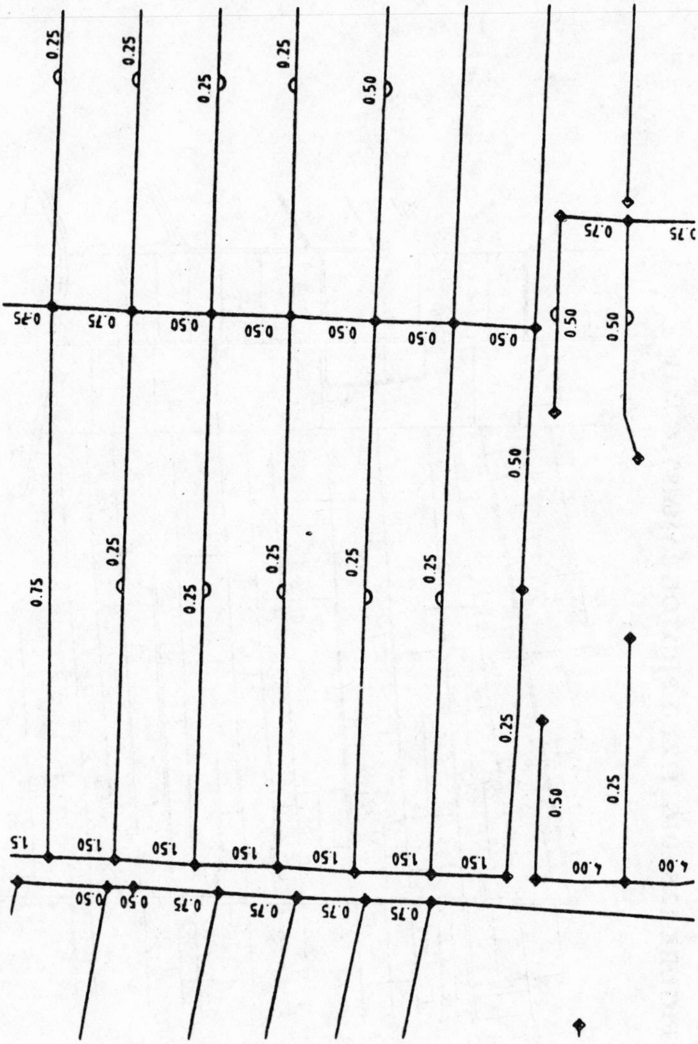

the supply of information for land-use management would be made.

CONCLUSION

In this paper a description is given of two operational systems for the supply of information for land-use management, both of which represent a significant improvement over sources of information commonly used in the formulation of agriculturally oriented policy in the Netherlands. It was the intention to call attention to developments in relation to automation. With the help of these techniques it will be possible to improve land-use management in rural areas significantly.

13

THE AGRICULTURAL LAND BASE STUDY: NATURAL RESOURCE POLICY RESEARCH IN ALBERTA
Alfred Birch

INTRODUCTION

The allocation and management of natural resources are matters of increasing concern. Governments are being forced to play a more conscious and prominent role in these processes and are requiring more information in order to plan resource allocation and management in accordance with basic societal objectives.

The Agricultural Land Base Study, being conducted in the Canadian province of Alberta, is designed to answer a wide range of questions on selected agricultural resource development alternatives (Government of Alberta, 1983). The objective of this paper is to describe this research project, in the context of the policy formation process, as an example of inter-agency response to resource planning issues.

POLICY FRAMEWORK

The management and allocation of land, water and other natural resources is closely related to the characteristics and distribution of property rights. The ownership of these resources, whether public or private, carries with it a certain set of rights which define allowable uses, the distribution of rents or benefits from use, and the rules for exchange of ownership. However, property rights inevitably involve limitations or recognition of the rights and interests of others to use, benefit from, or to be free of certain negative effects that result from the use of a resource. Indeed, the failure of the market to adequately protect the interests of innocent parties is recognized as a basis for state intervention in the first place.

The use of privately owned land, for example, is at the discretion of the owner within the limits of such things as zoning regulations and legal restrictions regarding nuisance or negligence. These rules express the interests of non-owners in the use of private land. In a similar manner, property taxes are the public or non-owner share of the profits or rent from private land use. In general, government regulations, incentives or penalties, and the direct management of publicly owned resources are indications of the recognition of certain property rights of non-owners. The balancing of property rights is inevitable, though the way in which it is done is guided by political philosophy.

Property rights are only meaningful where some degree of scarcity of resources exists. The transition from abundance to scarcity of natural resources is both ubiquitous and inevitable and is characterized by the transition from the "frontier" to the "spaceship" mentality. Because of the complexity of the physical and biological relationships which are involved, however, the true extent of the scarcity which exists in natural resource systems and of the trade-offs which are involved is seldom fully recognized. As these relationships are revealed, the interests of non-owners become apparent and the competition for property rights through legal, political or other means takes place.

With resource scarcity, the role of public policy in explicitly or implicitly allocating property rights has increased considerably. One result of this change is that decisions are increasingly centralized and conscious, rather than being the aggregate effect of dispersed private choice. A subsequent result is the rising demand for information by public decision makers on the physical effects of resource management alternatives and the public valuation of those effects.

While the evaluation of resource management and allocation alternatives is not new, the range of effects which are being considered and the complexity of the relationships and trade-offs has increased. This has raised the need for both quantifiable information and some logical decision criteria related to broad public objectives. Quantitative indicators for natural resource management may include such measures as agricultural or forestry output, recreational user-days, wildlife numbers, or measures of water or energy resource quality or availability. While these may be informative for decision makers, it is often desirable to bring such indicators into common units by converting them into, for example, economic terms.

Some effects may lend themselves well to this economic assessment because they are directly or closely related to markets. In many cases, however, markets are not available on which to base estimates of value. In such cases, values may be attributed through some market simulation technique. While there is valid scepticism in this regard, considerable progress is being made in the development of techniques for economic valuation of resource management effects. The level of reliability of the estimated values should be kept in mind. Despite the recognized lack of precision of the available techniques, there is pressure on natural resource agencies to bring their subject material into the main ʳtream of political consideration by estimating economic values.

The criteria available for evaluating resource management alternatives are based on broad public objectives. Foremost among economic criteria is the concept of efficiency, the maximization of benefits over costs. Although the concept may appear straightforward, problems of aggregating individual preferences, of measuring true social values, and of the effect of wealth and income distribution make this simplicity deceptive. Another common economic criterion is that of equity. This implies some political or social definition and, in practice, is difficult to define or balance with the efficiency criterion in a consistent manner. Other economic criteria include stability and diversification, full employment, public investment limitations and various macroeconomic and international trade related criteria. Among non-economic criteria employed in natural resource decision making are such factors as environmental quality and the availability of amenities and other quality of life indicators.

Politicians, government agency staff, and interest groups all play a role in the process of choice and the resolution of competition for resources and property rights. These participants act both as decision makers within certain contexts, and as representatives of client groups or broader objectives within other contexts. The process of competition for property rights places a high value on information, and considerable resources are devoted to research on both physical and social questions.

The quantity and quality of information which can be assembled by an agency will have a strong effect on resource management and allocation decisions. Decision makers at higher levels require information presented in a comprehensive and multicriteria manner. This requires or places a higher value on inter-agency and interdisciplinary research. While such research undertakings have potentially greater validity for problem solving, they are both costly and involve a greater degree of commitment by the participating agencies to endorse the results. Agencies may therefore attempt to keep the visibility of such research or their commitment to it limited until its results and consequences can be foreseen.

THE AGRICULTURAL LAND BASE STUDY

History

In 1982, an Alberta government task force was assembled to develop an approach to determining the potential for expanding the provincial agricultural land base and increasing the intensity of production on existing agricultural land. This action was in response to growing pressure to increase the availability of public land for agricultural production. The demand for new land corresponded with the provincial goals of increasing the contribution of the renewable resource sector to the provincial economy, increasing the rate of rural development, and decentralizing economic development activity to all regions of the province.

Over 4 million ha of public land with potential for cultivation were known to exist in the province. Most of this land was not being used for any type of agriculture, although a small portion was used for livestock grazing. It was also recognized that considerable agricultural land in Alberta was being converted to urban, rural residential, industrial and other nonagricultural uses. During the period of 1976 to 1980, an average of almost 21,000 ha per year were permanently removed from the agricultural land base.

There was also strong local pressure for more agricultural land development from individual farmers, farm organizations and communities in close proximity to public land with undeveloped agricultural capability, particularly in northern Alberta. That pressure was reinforced by statements from some prominent Albertans, including one former provincial minister of agriculture who suggested that there should be 4 million ha of public land in Alberta converted to an agricultural use in the next ten years.

The response to this pressure among provincial government natural resource management agencies was mixed. Much of the land in question was being managed for other uses such as recreation, wildlife habitat, timber production and watershed protection. Those agencies, and the public interests which they represent, were concerned about the possibility of a large-scale shift in public land-management policy. They correctly pointed out that there were many other agricultural resource development opportunities involving private land in Alberta. They maintained that agricultural development policy should be formulated only in the context of a comparative examination of the potential for both expansion of the agricultural land base and intensification of production on existing agricultural land. They also maintained that any decision to undertake expansion or intensification of agricultural production should explicitly recognize the trade-offs involved with other sectors relying on the same land base.

The Alberta Department of Agriculture, the provincial government agency concerned primarily with the promotion of agricultural development, saw in this situation the opportunity to assess the relative development potential of a number of natural resource management alternatives. The opportunity was also seen by the Department of Agriculture to rationalize its own policy in this regard and to promote development through its leadership in a coordinated response to public pressure.

The 1982 task force recommended that a joint research project be undertaken to assess a number of development alternatives for both public and private land, as well as certain water resource alternatives having a direct bearing on agriculture. Public land allocation and management in Alberta was already being affected at this time under a system of integrated resource planning. That system, under the leadership of the Alberta Department of Energy and Natural Resources, established a tradition among provincial agencies of comprehensive and cooperative planning based on land and other resource capabilities and on public demand. Despite strong agency interests, this integrated resource management tradition or model, as well as other joint resource planning activities, contributed to the decision to adopt the task force recommendation and initiate the Alberta Agricultural Land Base Study in October 1982.

The provincial departments in Alberta which agreed to participate in the study are Energy and Natural Resources, incorporating the provincial mandates for public lands, forestry, fish and wildlife, and integrated resource evaluation and planning, Agriculture, Environment, with the primary provincial water management mandate, Transportation, and Municipal Affairs. This range of representation illustrates the early recognition of the scope and interrelatedness of the issues involved in agricultural resource management.

Objectives

The four major objectives expressed in the terms of reference for the Agricultural Land Base Study are as follow.

1. To enhance understanding of how Alberta's land and water resources could be more effectively allocated and managed to increase agricultural production.
2. To gain an understanding of how other land and water resource users may be affected by any such management

and allocation changes.

3. To gain an appreciation for the relative economic benefits of any such management and allocation changes.

4. To identify information gaps and provincial government program deficiencies and make recommendations on actions to enhance the information base and improve programs.

The agricultural orientation of the study is illustrated in these objectives. The objectives also spell out the various criteria which will be used to evaluate agricultural development options: the potential for increasing agricultural production, the impacts on other land and water resource users, and the economic efficiency effects of each of the alternatives. The fourth objective is primarily administrative and will ensure that the results are presented in terms relevant for policy formation. These objectives correspond to the major component tasks which are being undertaken in the Agricultural Land Base Study.

Another important aspect of the study, although not explicitly mentioned in the objectives, is the presentation of results on a regional or subprovincial basis. The distribution of benefits and costs is an essential aspect of policy related research. A number of broad soil zones in Alberta were selected as the basis for displaying regional results since these have agricultural development significance and provide a manageable number and distribution of subprovincial units (Figure 13.1).

In 1948, a broad zoning system for lands in Alberta was adopted, dividing the province into three major areas for the administration of public lands. The Green Area, which covers over half of the province, corresponds to the forested non-settled lands managed primarily for timber production, watershed protection and multiple use, including some grazing. The remainder of the province, the White and Yellow Areas, are primarily settled lands available for agricultural use and development (Figure 13.2). The Agricultural Land Base Study is restricted to the White and Yellow Areas and that portion of the Green Area that is believed to have potential for cultivated crop production. A number of other minor restrictions in coverage, such as the exclusion of urban areas, parks and Indian Reserves, were also made.

It is understood that the study will not lead to specific land and water allocation decisions and that more detailed planning will be required as will careful assessment of demand and socio-economic objectives. The study is therefore being conducted at a very broad scale without attention to many of the local details which implementation studies will need to take into account. Final area estimates will be reported to the nearest 100,000 acres (40,500 ha) and economic results to the nearest 100 dollars per acre (247 dollars per ha).

FIGURE 13.1: SOIL ZONES OF ALBERTA

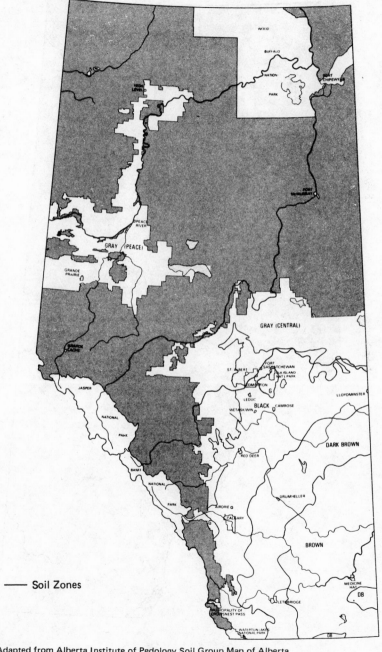

— Soil Zones

Adapted from Alberta Institute of Pedology Soil Group Map of Alberta

168

FIGURE 13.2: ALBERTA PUBLIC LANDS
ADMINISTRATIVE AREAS

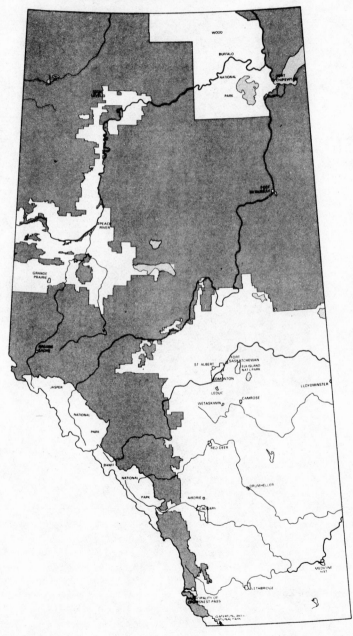

The study is examining eleven agricultural development options. These options are restricted to land and water allocation opportunities and management practices which directly affect the resource base.

1. The expansion of cultivated agriculture onto lands not currently allocated to an agricultural use. Lands suitable for cultivation within the Green Area a⁻e examined in this alternative.

2. The expansion of the irrigated land base by bringing new land under irrigation, both with and without new water supply development. In 1981, Alberta accounted for two-thirds of the irrigation in Canada, with close to 500,000 irrigated hectares. The potential exists for expanding this irrigated area through such means as additional water storage and further development of the water distribution system.

3. The deep plowing of solonetzic soils. These soils are characterized by an impermeable hard pan layer which may severely restrict root and water penetration. Deep plowing physically breaks up the hard pan layer, improves soil structure and can improve crop yields.

4. Liming of acid soils. Soils with a pH level of 6.0 or less are considered acidic. Acids affect the physical, chemical and biological properties of soils which, in turn, affect nutrient availability and reduce crop yields. Lime can be applied to neutralize the soil and increase the range of crops which can be grown.

5. The reduction of summerfallow area, defined as cultivated land allowed to lie idle during the growing season. Benefits from summerfallowing include increased soil moisture and weed control. The increased use of fertilizers and herbicides make it possible to reduce summerfallow while maintaining average yields. In addition to increasing cropped hectares, summerfallow reduction will reduce soil degradation through such processes as erosion, salinization and the loss of organic material.

6. The provision of flood control on agricultural land. Agricultural production occurs on many of the floodplains of Alberta's streams, rivers and lakes. Dykes, reservoirs and channel alignments can be used to reduce crop damage.

7. The drainage of wet and waterlogged land. Agricultural production may be limited by excess water causing delayed seeding, crop damage or permanently inaccessible land. Drainage can correct these problems in many cases and improve the efficiency of farming operations on entire

fields.

8. Prairie and woodland range improvement. This includes the breaking and reseeding of prairie rangeland and the clearing, breaking and seeding of woodland range, including the increased use of fertilizer and fencing. Rangeland improvement allows an increase in the capacity of such land to support livestock grazing.

9. The conversion of rangeland to cropland. A portion of the land currently used as pasture has the capability of producing cultivated crops. This alternative involves rangeland in the native grass areas of southern Alberta.

10. The clearing of brush from land with cultivation potential within the current agricultural area (woodland conversion). As with the preceding alternative, this involves the conversion of land previously used for grazing to cultivation.

11. The reclamation of salinized land. Saline soils occur throughout the province but are most common in southern and eastern Alberta. Salinization occurs as a result of excess groundwater depositing dissolved salts at or near the surface, causing crop yield reduction. The problem may be associated with summerfallowing, excess irrigation or water seepage from irrigation canals.

These development alternatives cover a broad range of opportunities for developing land and water resources for agricultural purposes and for altering the management of these resources currently in agricultural production. Where adjustments in the management of privately owned resources are considered, approaches such as education, financial incentives or disincentives, or regulations are available for implementing public policy.

The alternatives listed above do not include a number of means for increasing agricultural output such as increased agricultural research and improvements in farm management other than the specified alternatives. The terms of reference of the study also exclude an explicit investigation of the price and marketing situation, although it is acknowledged that these will have a critical effect in determining the rate at which agricultural development will take place.

Methodology

The four objectives of the Agricultural Land Base Study correspond to the four major tasks being undertaken in the study. The first task is a determination of the potential for increasing agricultural production through each of the identified development alternatives. This requires an estimation of the area of land available for each alternative and of the potential yield increase per unit of land. In most cases, the land area is identified by using Canada Land Inventory (CLI) maps of soil capability for agriculture. The CLI classification system for agriculture evaluates land according to its potential to grow a broad range of crops and its sensitivity to soil degradation. The first three classes are capable of sustained production of common cultivated crops, the fourth class is considered marginal for cultivated crop production, the fifth is capable of use for only permanent pasture and hay, the sixth is capable of use for native grazing and the seventh has no capability for agricultural use. In the Agricultural Land Base Study, CLI Classes 1 to 4 are grouped together as being capable of cultivated crop production, Class 5 is considered for grazing, and Classes 6 and 7 as well as organic soils are excluded from the study. Normal yields are determined from published data and are established for each major soil zone or region in the province. A more detailed description is found in Environment Canada (1972).

The economic analysis in the study includes both a financial analysis conducted from the farmer's perspective to determine private profitability, and an economic analysis including farm effects and broader social costs and benefits. The farm financial analysis is conducted by using representative farm models for each region of the province, including such things as representative farm size and crop information for reporting effects on farms, but broadens the analysis by reporting many of the economic effects of the development alternatives on the rest of society. The public investment requirements associated with alternatives such as the opening of agricultural lands in the Green Area and irrigation and drainage development are estimated. Secondly, a number of the economic values associated with the impacts of agricultural development on other resource-using sectors are estimated and reported. These include foregone opportunities for timber production and the loss of wildlife and associated recreational and subsistence values. The sectors which are identified for investigation are forestry, fish and wildlife, human settlement and services, industrial and commercial development, and recreation and tourism. In addition to the social costs associated with agricultural development, social benefits such as secondary or spin-off economic benefits are reported, although it is recognized that the inclusion of these assumes unemployed and mobile economic resources.

Not all of the effects of agricultural development on other resource sectors can be quantified and economically valued. The third major task of the study is, therefore, to report, in qualitative terms, as many of the environmental effects as possible. This task also includes the identification of the physical impacts on other resource-using sectors which are evaluated in the economic analysis.

The final aspect of the Agricultural Land Base Study is the documentation of current government programs serving to promote the development of agricultural resources. The conclusions of the study will be reported in terms of the adequacy of these programs or recommendations for new steps to guide resource development and management.

PRELIMINARY RESULTS

Table 13.1 shows the estimated maximum increases in agricultural production from the various resource management options, which are ranked according to the estimated value of the increase in production. The drainage option is omitted since results are not yet available. The reclamation of saline soils is shown separately for irrigated and dryland areas because the management techniques and the study results differ considerably between these. Table 13.1 does not account for the possibility of double counting or interactive effects between these development possibilities. For example, land with potential for irrigation expansion may also be suitable for conversion from range to dryland cultivated crop production.

In terms of the total potential for increased production, the expansion of cultivated crop production onto suitable lands in the Green Area and onto woodland in the White and Yellow Areas show a significantly larger potential than the remaining options, largely due to the considerable land area available. Study results do not yet show what proportion of this land in the White and Yellow Areas is under public ownership and could be made available for transfer to private ownership and development. Figure 13.3 shows the public lands in the White and Yellow Areas of Alberta.

The potential for irrigation expansion shown in Table 13.1 is the estimated maximum with current and developable water supplies in southern Alberta where the climatic potential is greatest. The relatively high potential for increased production associated with this strategy is related more to the potential crop yield increase than to the total land and water available. Irrigated crop yields range from 60 to 200 per cent above dryland yields in that part of the province.

Another output from the analysis of development potential is the mapping of lands for each of the alternatives. Figure 13.4 illustrates the lands in the Green Area with potential for cultivated crop production. It is estimated that 15 per cent of these lands would not be suitable for actual agricultural development because of unmapped local physical limitations.

Table 13.2 shows the economic consequences for farmers of each of the development options. These results do not include the costs associated with required public investments for such things as

**TABLE 13.1: POTENTIAL INCREASES IN
AGRICULTURAL PRODUCTION**

DEVELOPMENT ALTERNATIVE	VALUE OF PRODUCTION INCREASE Mills $	LAND AREA AFFECTED 000s Ha
Agricultural Expansion in Green Area	763	3.70
Woodland Conversion	612	2.90
Irrigation Expansion	350	0.50
Rangeland Conversion	212	1.50
Summerfallow Reduction	137	0.60
Deep Plowing Solonetzic Soils	104	0.90
Saline Soil Reclamation (Dryland)	59	0.90
Liming Acid Soil	54	1.10
Saline Soil Reclamation (Irrigated)	53	0.10
Range Improvement	18	0.60
Flood Control	1	0.04
Drainage	na	na

irrigation development or the expansion of cultivated crop production in the Green Area, nor the economic effects on other resource sectors, nor the indirect benefits to non-farmers from agricultural development. Those effects will be incorporated later. The range of values in Table 13.2 for each strategy is due to differing results in the various soil zones or regions of the province.

The ranking of the development options in Table 13.2 differs considerably from that in Table 13.1. Irrigation expansion, for example, has higher average annual net returns for the farmer than does the expansion of cultivated crop production in the Green Area. While this would suggest that irrigation is more attractive to farmers, these possibilities are not available to the same farmers and, therefore, have different implications in terms of regional development and the distribution of benefits.

FIGURE 13.3: PUBLIC LANDS IN THE WHITE AND YELLOW AREAS

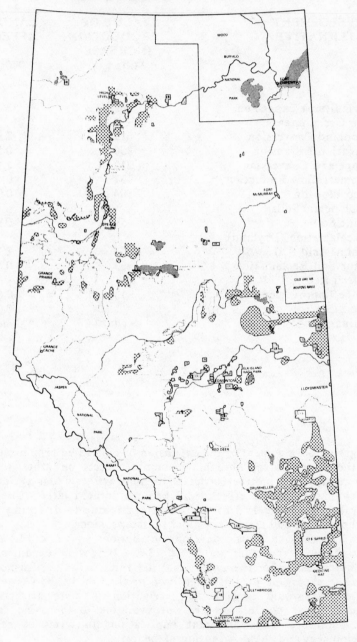

PRODUCED BY THE RESOURCE EVALUATION AND PLANNING DIVISION, ALBERTA FORESTRY, LANDS AND WILDLIFE.

FIGURE 13.4: GREEN AREA LANDS WITH CULTIVATION POTENTIAL (CLI CLASS 1-4)

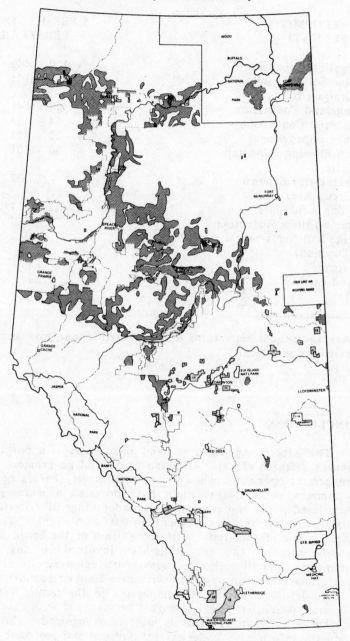

PRODUCED BY THE RESOURCE EVALUATION AND PLANNING DIVISION, ALBERTA FORESTRY, LANDS AND WILDLIFE.

176

TABLE 13.2: ON-FARM NET ECONOMIC RETURNS FROM DEVELOPMENT ALTERNATIVES[1]

DEVELOPMENT ALTERNATIVE	$ PER HECTARE PER YEAR
Irrigation Expansion	100 - 440
Saline Soil Reclamation (Irrigated)	141
Rangeland Conversion	94 - 148
Woodland Conversion	54 - 124
Range Improvement	22 - 111
Deep Plowing Solonetzic Soils	30 - 101
Agricultural Expansion in Green Area	37
Liming Acid Soils	12 - 17
Summerfallow Reduction	5 - 27
Saline Soil Reclamation (Dryland)	2
Drainage	na
Flood Control	na

[1] Average annual net returns to land, hired labour, management and existing investment

CONCLUSIONS

The Alberta Agricultural Land Base Study is a novel natural resource research effort. Although provincial government resource management agencies have worked cooperatively before on matters of common concern, this study has addressed a wider range of interrelated issues and employed a broader range of criteria than is usual, a significant development in its own right. The major characteristic of the study is its recognition of the broad nature of resource scarcity and the trade-offs involved in any resource management and allocation decisions. Although agricultural development in Alberta is an objective with broad public support, the costs of that development are also important in the public view. Not only must provincial fiscal resources be managed with care, but the distribution of rents or benefits must be recognized. The study is producing information under several physical and economic headings which will allow decision makers and the public to be aware of the trade-offs which are involved in resource management policy choices.

The commitment of government agencies to this type of natural resource investigation is still somewhat untested in Alberta. Although there is a process of integrated resource planning for public lands in the province, as well as other joint resource management processes, the required commitment of staff and funds and the range of issues being addressed is new. Also, the study has gained some prominence at senior management levels in the provincial government and therefore has committed agencies to some extent to respond to its results. There appears to be, however, a general consensus that resource policy based on comprehensive research will be more widely acceptable than more narrowly focussed, single agency initiatives.

It would be possible to attribute the existence and design of the Agricultural Land Base Study to the particular set of events which preceded it and to the particular natural resource management environment in Alberta. Nevertheless, it is possible to draw certain recommendations from this experience for similar resource management needs in other locations. First, interagency, interdisciplinary investigations should be promoted if significant progress is to be made in working out realistic resource management policies which have the commitment of those who will be in charge of implementing them. This may be a difficult step to take if agency interests and objectives are entrenched and a climate of cooperative activity has not been developed. Achievements in this area will be incremental and may be slow.

Second, resource management issues must be viewed in sufficiently broad terms to incorporate the major effects of the alternatives to be considered. The diversity of these effects has become increasingly apparent to the public and should not be ignored by government. There is an inevitable choice which must be made by government concerning whose interests or property rights are to be supported. It is much better for government to recognize the decision and make it on the basis of good information, including information on public perceptions and desires.

This comprehensive information will need to be organized under the headings of many different criteria. The Agricultural Land Base Study has used the potential for increased agricultural output, the farm financial effects, and the physical and economic consequences for other resource sectors as criteria to evaluate the development alternatives being examined here. Other studies of this nature would have to specify both the criteria and the alternatives to be examined at an early stage.

Finally, the inclusion of economic analysis in such a study must be based on sound information on physical resource management effects. Because the economic analysis is conducted, in general, by attributing values to effects which are not dealt with by normal market operations, research on these physical effects must precede the economic research.

REFERENCES

Environment Canada, 1982, Soil Capability Classification for Agriculture. Ottawa: Canada Land Inventory Report No. 2, Lands Directorate, Environment Canada.

Government of Alberta, 1983, "Agricultural Land Base Study, Potential for Expansion and Intensification: Terms of Reference". Edmonton: Government of Alberta.

14

LAND EVALUATION AND ENVIRONMENTAL CHANGE: THE CASE OF LAND DRAINAGE AND FOOD PRODUCTION

Michael Brklacich, Barry Smit
and Ray McBride

INTRODUCTION

Possible changes in environmental conditions and the implications of these changes in terms of the long-term potential for food and fibre production have stimulated considerable debate among resource analysts (Pierce and Furuseth, 1983). It would appear that much of this controversy can be attributed to two sources. In many instances, the debate can be traced to alternative assumptions relating to the direction and the extent to which particular environmental conditions might change. For example, there is general acceptance that man's activities are increasing atmospheric concentrations of CO_2 and that the resulting greenhouse effect will cause a gradual warming of the earth. There is no consensus, however, with respect to either the extent to which temperatures might increase or the degree to which precipitation patterns might shift (Hengeveld and Street, 1985; Phillips, 1985). Other environmental issues for which there is no apparent consensus include the severity of land degradation and its potential impacts on production opportunities (Coote, 1983; Crosson, 1985; Larson et al., 1985; Sparrow, 1985; Weetman, 1983), the potential implications of acid precipitation on aquatic and terrestrial production systems (Altshuller and McBean, 1979; Evans, 1982; Irving, 1983), and the aggregate effects of land improvements such as artificial land drainage, on production prospects (van Vuuren and Jorjani, 1983).

The absence of consensus can also be attributed to the fact that analytical procedures for assessing the long-term opportunities for food and fibre production and for gauging the sensitivity of these opportunities to environmental change are not well developed (Clapham et al., 1979; Environment Canada, 1980). Until recently, comprehensive assessments of production prospects for large geographic regions and of the implications of environmental change have relied heavily on subjective evaluations. Advances in computing technology now allow for the efficient management and systematic processing of relatively large data sets. These technological developments, along with the compilation of land-related data sets that are spatially compatible, have facilitated the implementation of various types of land evaluation systems (Schultink, 1983). These systems have the potential to identify the implications of environmental change on the long-term prospects for food and fibre production.

The purpose of this paper is to demonstrate that it is feasible to develop a land evaluation system which can be used to assess the implications of specified changes in environmental conditions on food production prospects, and to illustrate the utility of the system as a policy assessment tool. A land evaluation system for the agri-food sector of the province of Ontario is outlined, and applied to the selected issue of the expansion of artificial land drainage and its implications for food production potential.

THE ONTARIO LAND EVALUATION SYSTEM

The Ontario land evaluation system is comprised of a land-related information base and a variety of analytical tools for integrating selected components or the entire data base (Figure 14.1). All components of the data base are compiled on a consistent basis for the entire province. This means, for example, that data on yields pertain to the same spatial units as those used to compile estimates of land availability. This consistency facilitates the assessment of the long-term prospects for agricultural production.

The Data Base

The main components and structure of the data base are illustrated in Figure 14.1 and are outlined below.

1. Land Availability: Ontario's land resources for agricultural production are described as land units and are defined on the basis of seven climatic zones, six administrative regions and seven land types (Figure 14.2 and Table 14.1). The data base stores estimates of the current availability of each land unit for crop production, and these are adjusted to reflect possible changes in future conditions such as further drainage of agricultural land and urban expansion.

FIGURE 14.1: THE ONTARIO LAND EVALUATION SYSTEM

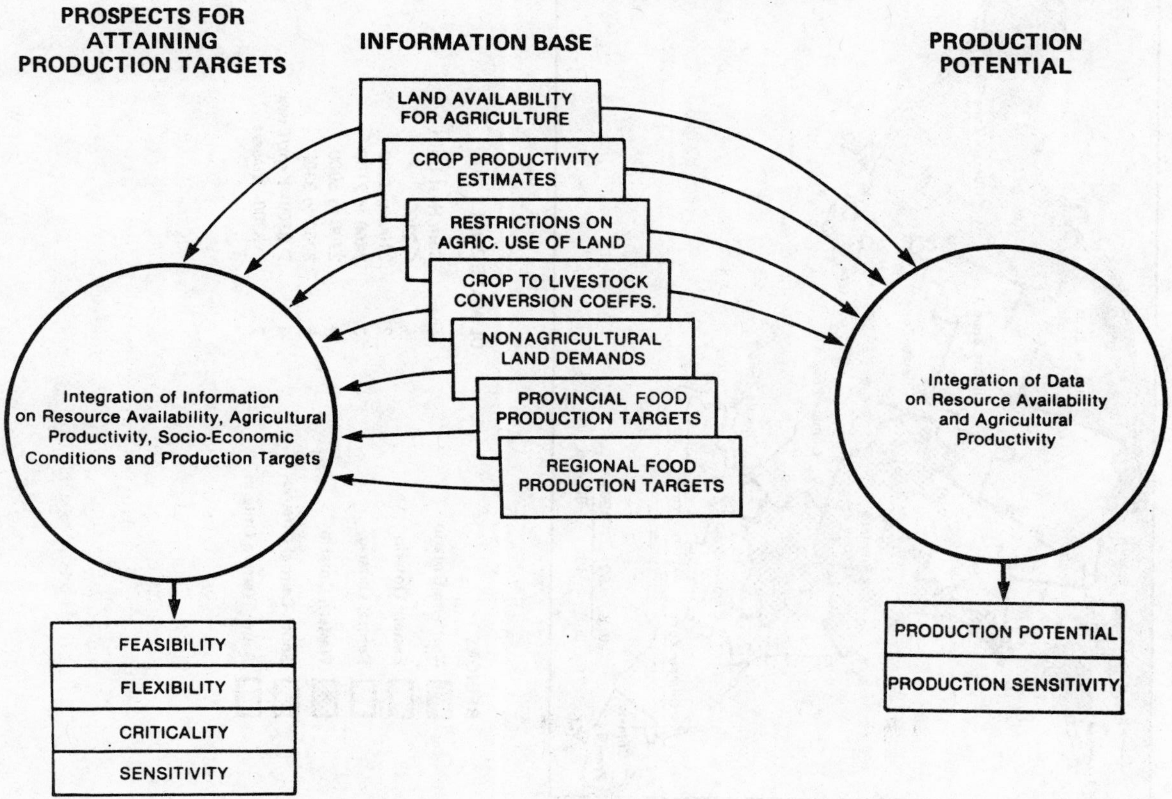

PROSPECTS FOR
ATTAINING
PRODUCTION TARGETS

INFORMATION BASE

PRODUCTION
POTENTIAL

LAND AVAILABILITY
FOR AGRICULTURE

CROP PRODUCTIVITY
ESTIMATES

RESTRICTIONS ON
AGRIC. USE OF LAND

CROP TO LIVESTOCK
CONVERSION COEFFS.

NONAGRICULTURAL
LAND DEMANDS

PROVINCIAL FOOD
PRODUCTION TARGETS

REGIONAL FOOD
PRODUCTION TARGETS

Integration of Data
on Resource Availability
and Agricultural
Productivity

PRODUCTION POTENTIAL

PRODUCTION SENSITIVITY

Integration of Information
on Resource Availability, Agricultural
Productivity, Socio-Economic
Conditions and Production Targets

FEASIBILITY

FLEXIBILITY

CRITICALITY

SENSITIVITY

FIGURE 14.2: REGIONS IN ONTARIO

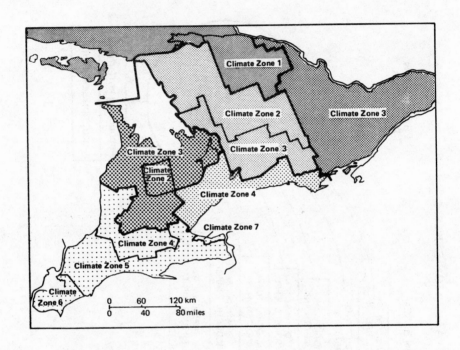

REGIONS

▨	Northern Ontario
▨	Eastern Ontario
▨	Central Ontario
▨	Western Ontario
▨	South Central Ontario
▨	South Western Ontario

CLIMATE ZONES

Zone	Corn Heat Units
1	< 2100
2	2100 to 2400
3	2400 to 2700
4	2700 to 3000
5	3000 to 3300
6	> 3300 – Kent/Essex
7	> 3300 – Niagara

TABLE 14.1: AN OVERVIEW OF THE LAND CLASSIFICATION SYSTEM

LAND TYPE	BIOPHYSICAL CHARACTERISTICS
A	- well-drained loamy soils - relatively level topography
B	- fine-textured clays - moderately well to well-drained
C	- coarser-textured sands and gravel, or shallow soils (less than one metre to bedrock) - well to excessively well-drained
D	- imperfectly to poorly drained soils which have been tile drained
E	- imperfectly to poorly drained soils which have not been tile drained, and all poorly to very poorly drained soils
F	- extremely stony or shallow soils
G	- well-drained loamy soils - rolling to hilly topograpy

Note: Ontario's land resources are classified according to biophysical characteristics that are relevant to the production of crops

2. Crop Productivities: Eighteen crops representing the major agricultural land uses in Ontario are considered (Table 14.2). The productivity of each crop on each land unit is estimated given current conditions for climate, technology and management, and given adjustments to these parameters.

3. Restrictions on Agricultural Land Use: Land conservation, and hence sustainable productivity levels, are incorporated by specifying land-use practices which would control soil erosion and prevent the build-up of pests and disease organisms. These include the rotation of row crops with forages and cereals, and remedial measures such as grassed

TABLE 14.2: GROWTH PROJECTION FOR ONTARIO'S AGRI-FOOD SECTOR TO 2001

COMMODITY	1976-1981 PRODUCTION	PROJECTION TO 2001	
	000s T[1]	Prov. Prod. Requirement 000s T[1]	Change from 1976-1981 %
Grain Corn[2]	4693	7382	57
Oats[2]	664	528	−21
Barley[2]	1059	1418	33
Winter Wheat[2]	639	1152	80
Soybeans[2]	707	1200	70
Canola		220	
Hay Crops[3]	5165	6708	30
Fodder Corn[3]	7022	9861	40
Grazing and Rough Grass[3,4]	2866	4543	58
Apples	137	291	113
Peaches	28	37	30
Grapes	64	113	75
Peas	29	44	48
Sweet Corn	142	277	95
Tomatoes	439	700	60
Potatoes	369	385	4
Tobacco	88	76	−14
White Beans	62	65	5
Chicken	141	180	28
Turkey	43	40	−7
Pork	208	413	98
Beef	266	363	37
Mutton and Lamb	1	4	400
Milk Products	2520	2580	2
Eggs	127	125	−2
Horses[5]	250	250	0

---

[1] Compiled by Agriculture Canada (1983)

[2] Livestock feed requirement based upon feed crop-to-livestock product conversion rates developed by the Land Evaluation Group ([LEG], 1984)

[3] Based upon feed requirements to support specified levels of production of livestock products. Conversion coefficients developed by the LEG (1984)

[4] Grazing and rough grass are converted into a hay-crop equivalent

[5] 000s of units

waterways and windbreaks.

4. Livestock Production: Eight types of livestock are considered, accounting for the majority of Ontario's livestock sector (Table 14.2), and the production of livestock is linked to the land base via feeding requirements for livestock. The data base houses feed-to-livestock product conversion coefficients, based upon present feeding practices and possible changes in feeding practices and technology.

5. Nonagricultural Uses: Future requirements for nonagricultural uses (e.g., land for housing, forestry, recreation and so on) are estimated exogenously, and incorporated into the data set by making appropriate adjustments to the land availability estimates.

6. Agricultural Production Levels: Regional and provincial levels for agricultural production are estimated as a function of provincial population and per capita consumption patterns, regional development schemes, and trading patterns for agricultural commodities. Stored in the data base are estimates of regional and provincial production levels given current conditions and possible changes from these norms.

One of the major applications of the Ontario system is to provide data to resource and policy analysts. The data are compiled on a consistent basis for Ontario, and hence it is possible to conduct interregional assessments of resource suitability for crop production. The data base, therefore, can be readily used to address such issues as:

1. in which regions are there the greatest opportunities for expanding or upgrading the agricultural land base?

2. what is the current productivity of different types of land for particular crops?

3. how sensitive are these productivity levels to specified changes in environmental conditions such as climatic change, land degradation, acid precipitation and artificial land drainage?

Production Potential

Production potential refers to the possible levels of production given specified conditions for land availability, crop productivities, restrictions on agricultural land use and livestock production (Figure 14.1). In other words, it estimates the extent to which biophysical conditions constrain production opportunities. These assessments can be conducted for individual agricultural activities or for groups of activities. For the latter case, it is also necessary to specify spatial patterns of production.

The production potential approach to resource assessment can be used to indicate in which regions of Ontario there are the greatest opportunities for agricultural production. It can also indicate the sensitivity of these production opportunities to changes in environmental conditions such as artificial land drainage, climatic change and land degradation.

Prospects for Attaining Production Targets

This approach to resource assessment is designed to estimate the feasibility of meeting specified levels for agricultural production. The procedure utilizes mathematical programming techniques to integrate information on resource availability and productivity with information on production levels and other socio-economic conditions for land use (Figure 14.1).

If it is feasible to meet the specified levels of production given the available land base, estimated productivity levels and so on, the Ontario system also estimates the ease with which these production levels could be met. Two measures are of specific relevance. The measures of flexibility relate to the difference between production potential and production levels for the agricultural system as a whole. Measures of criticality refer to the strategic importance of particular land units for specific crops given specified conditions. These concepts and their measurement are discussed in Brklacich et al. (1984) and Chapman et al. (1984).

The Ontario land evaluation system can also measure the sensitivity of these evaluations (i.e., feasibility, flexibility and criticality) to changes in biophysical and/or socio-economic conditions by making appropriate adjustments to the input parameters (Figure 14.1).

ONTARIO'S AGRICULTURAL LAND RESOURCES AND LAND DRAINAGE

The Current Land Base

The biophysical resource base in the South Western Ontario region poses fewer limitations to agricultural production than available resources elsewhere in Ontario. Currently, there is more

cleared land available for agriculture in South Western Ontario than
in any other region of Ontario, and about three-quarters of this
available land base is physically well-suited for the production of a
wide range of field and horticultural crops (Land Types A, D and G)
(Table 14.3).

Similar to the South Western Ontario region, the majority of
the available land base in the South Central and Western Ontario
regions consists of Land Types A, D and G. There is, however,
considerably less land available for the production of crops in
either of these two regions (Table 14.3).

While there is a larger area of cleared land available for agriculture in Eastern Ontario, much of the land is currently of poor
quality for crop production (Table 14.3). Land currently available for
agriculture in each of the Central and Northern Ontario regions is
constrained to a relatively small proportion of each region's total
land base, and adverse soil and climatic conditions severely limit
the quality of these lands for crop production (Table 14.3).

Agricultural Land Drainage

Artificial drainage of lands which are either imperfectly or
poorly drained has proven to be an effective means for ameliorating
limitations imposed by excessive moisture and hence improving crop
yields. Imperfectly to poorly drained lands total some 979,000 ha,
representing about 19 per cent of the available agricultural land
resources in Ontario. It is estimated that about half of these lands
have been improved by tile drainage (Table 14.3 - Land Type D).

Artificial land drainage has been installed more extensively in
South Western Ontario than in other regions (Table 14.3). Approximately 80 per cent of the 474,000 ha of imperfectly to poorly
drained land in the region has been tile drained. These farm-level
improvements have resulted in considerable increases in crop yields
and enhanced production opportunities throughout the region.

A comparison of each of the other regions to South Western
Ontario indicates that there is considerably less imperfectly to poorly
drained land in these regions (Table 14.3). Furthermore, the
proportion of these lands which have been improved via on-farm
drainage range from 17 per cent in Eastern Ontario to 40 per cent
in Central Ontario. The greatest opportunities for upgrading
existing agricultural lands via artificial drainage exist in Eastern
Ontario. On-farm land improvements would be sufficient to enhance
the productivity of an additional 225,000 ha in this region. In all
other regions, the potential for artificial land drainage ranges from
about 8,000 ha to 88,000 ha.

**TABLE 14.3: CURRENT EXTENT AND POTENTIAL
FOR AGRICULTURAL LAND DRAINAGE
IN ONTARIO**

	SWO[1]	SCO	WO	EO	CO	NO
Total Land Area (000s ha)	2521	1024	2126	2872	3000	15752[2]

CURRENT LAND BASE FOR AGRICULTURE

Land Available for Agriculture

	SWO	SCO	WO	EO	CO	NO
% Total Land	76	59	57	32	13	2
(000s ha)	1892	606	1201	922	382	342
Land Type A	877	378	679	177	127	130
Land Type B	171	37	65	81	22	41
Land Type C	161	41	99	173	55	36
Land Type D[3]	373	2	41	45	12	24
Land Type E	141	16	96	257	19	77
Land Type F	32	67	101	185	103	31
Land Type G	136	62	120	3	44	4

Potential for Drainage[4]

	SWO	SCO	WO	EO	CO	NO
(000s ha)	101	8	88	225	18	42

---

[1] SWO = South Western Ontario   EO = Eastern Ontario
SCO = South Central Ontario   CO = Central Ontario
WO = Western Ontario   NO = Northern Ontario

[2] Limited to the area covered by the Canada Land Inventory, which although small in comparison to the total land area of Northern Ontario does incorporate most of the land suited to agricultural uses

[3] Imperfectly to poorly drained land which has been improved by artificial drainage at the farm level. Represents current extent of artificial land drainage

[4] Imperfectly to poorly drained land which has not been drained

Source: LEG (1983)

EFFECTS OF AGRICULTURAL LAND DRAINAGE
ON FOOD PRODUCTION PROSPECTS

Overview

The Ontario land evaluation system is employed to assess the effect of agricultural land drainage on the long-term prospects for food production. The analyses are conducted for the five scenarios illustrated in Figure 14.3, and the sensitivity of overall opportunities for agricultural production (i.e., flexibility) is estimated given adjustments to selected environmental and socio-economic conditions.

Scenario 1 is the base scenario, in which the variables for the environmental and socio-economic conditions for agricultural production throughout Ontario are specified as the prevailing values for the 1976-1981 period.

Scenarios 2 through 5 represent alternative sets of conditions in the year 2001, and are specified by adjusting selected environmental and socio-economic conditions. Scenario 2 differs from the base scenario in that:

1. provincial requirements for crop production are increased to reflect a growth in provincial population, development of agricultural markets and a more efficient conversion of livestock feeds to livestock products (Table 14.2), and
2. lands available for crop production are reduced by 84,000 ha to reflect the possible expansion of Ontario's major urban centres.

Under Scenario 3, there is the additional assumption that advances in agricultural technology will increase yields in all areas for all crops by 1 per cent per annum during the 1981-2001 period.

Expansion of agricultural drainage is introduced under Scenarios 4 and 5. Scenario 4 differs from Scenario 3 in that it is assumed that the 267,000 ha of imperfectly to poorly drained land in Northern and Eastern Ontario which could benefit from artificial land drainage would be tiled by the year 2001. This is extended under Scenario 5 to include the entire 482,000 ha of imperfectly to poorly drained land throughout Ontario which could benefit from farm-level drainage schemes.

For all five scenarios, the following conditions are assumed to be constant:

190

FIGURE 14.3: SCENARIO SPECIFICATION: ADJUSTMENTS TO ENVIRONMENTAL AND SOCIO-ECONOMIC CONDITIONS

CONDITION	SCENARIO 1 (Base)	SCENARIO 2	SCENARIO 3	SCENARIO 4	SCENARIO 5
1. Land Availability	5.34 mil. ha.	Urban expansion reduces total to 5.26 mil. ha			
2. Provincial Levels for Food Production	Current	Growth Projection to 2001			
3. Conversion of Feed Crop to Livestock	Current Rates		More Efficient		
4. Crop Productivity	Current Levels		Increases of 1% per annum		
5. Agricultural Land Drainage		Current Extent		Increase of 267,000ha in N.&E. Ontario	Increase of 482,000ha throughout Ontario
6. Soil Conservation Practices		Sufficient to Maintain Land Quality			
7. Economic Conditions			Current		
8. Regional Levels for Crop Production		Current or greater, except when prov. prod. levels decline			

 CHANGE FROM CURRENT

1. the quality of the land resource is maintained by rotating row crops with forages and cereals, and using 5 per cent of the land base for non-crop soil conservation practices.
2. the production of grain corn, soybeans and winter wheat is limited to lands on which yields would be sufficient to generate a profit under present economic conditions, and
3. regional levels of crop production are maintained at or above current levels.

Findings

Food Production Prospects Under Current Environmental Conditions (Scenarios 1 and 2)

The 5.34 million ha of cleared land available for crop production in Ontario could support substantial increases in the production of all crops without jeopardizing either the long-term quality of land resources or current levels of crop production in each region. In fact, it would be physically feasible to expand provincial production levels for all crops by as much as 30 per cent (Figure 14.4). While the production of particular crops could be increased beyond this estimate, this would necessitate a smaller increase or perhaps a decrease in production levels for at least one other crop.

Scenario 2 assumes current environmental conditions, a modest expansion of Ontario's major urban centres, improvements in livestock feeding efficiencies, and projected increases in crop production requirements. Under these conditions, the productive capacity of Ontario's land resources would fall short of the projected increases in provincial crop production targets by 13 per cent (Figure 14.4). It would be feasible to meet and exceed the projected levels for the production of some crops, but this would widen the gap between productive capacity and production levels for other crops to more than 13 per cent.

Effects of Yield Increases on Production Prospects (Scenario 3)

Advances in agricultural technologies which would increase crop yields by an average of 1 per cent per annum through to 2001 would enhance production prospects to such an extent that it would be feasible to exceed all projected targets for crop production by as much as 8 per cent (Figure 14.4). This gap of 8 per cent between productive capacity and productive levels is considerably less than the current slack in Ontario's agri-food system, indicating that there would be substantially more pressure on Ontario's agricultural

FIGURE 14.4: EFFECTS OF AGRICULTURAL LAND DRAINAGE ON LONG-TERM PRODUCTION PROSPECTS

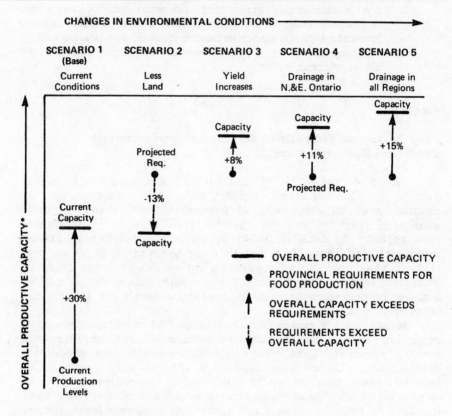

*Given cumulative effects of changes in environmental conditions

Source: Land Evaluation Group (1984)

land resources under Scenario 3 than under the base scenario.

Effects of Agricultural Land Drainage on Production Prospects (Scenarios 4 and 5)

Agricultural land drainage in Northern and Eastern Ontario (Scenario 4) would have a substantial impact on crop production possibilities for the entire province. Drainage of 267,000 ha of imperfectly to poorly drained land in these regions along with increases in crop yields throughout the province would enhance the productive capacity of the province's land base to such an extent that it would be feasible to exceed projected targets for crop production by 11 per cent (Figure 14.4).

The combined impacts of tiling the estimated 482,000 ha of imperfectly to poorly drained land throughout Ontario which have not been improved by on-farm drainage and of increases in crop yields (Scenario 5) would be that the productive capacity of the province's land resources would exceed the projected levels for crop production by 15 per cent (Figure 14.4). These enhancements in environmental conditions would obviously result in considerable increases in production potential, but these increases would not keep pace with the projected increases for provincial crop production targets. As a result, there would be far fewer options for agricultural land use under Scenario 5 than under the base scenario.

CONCLUSION

The implementation of the Ontario land evaluation system described in this paper and its application to the effects of agricultural land drainage on long-term prospects for food production indicate that it is feasible to develop systems which operate at the broad scale and which have the capacity to measure the aggregated impacts of environmental change on the long-term adequacy of the resource base.

This application of the Ontario land evaluation system demonstrates the potential for using land evaluation systems to provide:

1. ready access to land-related information,
2. aggregate measures of feasibility and flexibility, and
3. assessments of the sensitivity of feasibility and flexibility to discrete adjustments in environmental and socio-economic conditions.

It is also possible to extend the analyses and identify those specific conditions (i.e., resource availability, productivities, production targets, etc.) which effectively limit production opportunities.

The analyses have been directed at examining the effects of an adjustment in a selected environmental parameter, agricultural land drainage, on production opportunities. It should be apparent that other environmental issues, including climatic change and land degradation, could be assessed using the procedures outlined in this paper. Furthermore, this systematic approach to integrated resource evaluation is well-suited to gauging the sensitivity of production opportunities to predetermined adjustments in environmental and

194

socio-economic conditions.

In the policy arena, the approaches to resource assessment implemented via the Ontario land evaluation system have proven to be extremely effective in assessing the effects of alternative courses of action on agricultural production possibilities. By its very nature, policy formulation is a cyclical process exploring options under different sets of conditions. The procedures for land evaluation outlined in this paper recognize this process and have been designed to facilitate assessments of long-term resource adequacy under alternative sets of environmental and socio-economic conditions.

ACKNOWLEDGMENTS

The authors gratefully acknowledge contributions from all members of the Land Evaluation Group and the support of Agriculture Canada and the Ontario Ministry of Agriculture and Food.

REFERENCES

Agriculture Canada, 1983, Provincial Profile: Commodity Projections to the Year 2000. Toronto: Unpublished Report, Regional Development Branch.

Altshuller, A.P. and G.A. McBean, 1979, The LRTAP Problem in North America: A Preliminary Overview. United States - Canada Research Consultation Group on the Long-Range Transport of Air Pollutants.

Brklacich, M., B. Smit and T. Phillips, 1984, "Long-Term Prospects for Sustainable Agricultural Production in Ontario, Canada", Presented to the Eighth Annual Meeting of the Canadian Regional Science Association, May 1984, Guelph, Ontario.

Chapman, G.R., B. Smit and W.R. Smith, 1984, "Flexibility and Criticality in Resource Use Assessment", Geographical Analysis, 16 (1), pp. 52-64.

Clapham, W.B., R.F. Pestel and H. Arnaszus, 1979, "On the Scenario Approach to Simulation Modeling for Complex Policy Assessment and Design", Policy Sciences, 11, pp. 157-177.

Coote, D.R., 1983, "Stresses on Land Under Intensive Agricultural Use". In P. Loshak (ed.), Stress on Land. Ottawa: Environment Canada, pp. 228-257.

Crosson, P., 1985, "National Costs of Erosion Effects on Productivity". In Erosion and Soil Productivity - Proceedings of the National Symposium on Erosion and Soil Productivity. St. Joseph: American Society of Agricultural Engineers, pp. 254-265.

Environment Canada, 1980, Land Use in Canada: The Report of the Interdepartmental Task Force on Land-Use Policy. Ottawa.

Evans, L.S., 1982, "Biological Effects of Acidity in Precipitation on Vegetation: A Review", Environmental and Experimental Botany, 22 (2), pp. 155-169.

Hengeveld, H.C. and R.B. Street, 1985, Development of CO_2 Climate Change Scenarios for Canadian Regions. Toronto: Unpublished Report, Canadian Climate Centre, Environment Canada.

Irving, P., 1983, "Acidic Precipitation Effects on Crops: A Review and Analysis of Research", Journal of Environmental Quality, 12 (4), pp. 442-453.

Larson, G.A., F.J. Pierce and L.J. Winkelman, 1985, "Soil Productivity and Vulnerability Indices for Erosion Control Programs". In Erosion and Soil Productivity - Proceedings of the National Symposium on Erosion and Soil Productivity. St. Joseph: American Society of Agricultural Engineers, pp. 243-253.

LEG, 1983, Analysis of the Production Possibilities of Ontario Agriculture: Regional Assessments of the Prospects for Sustainable Agricultural Production. Guelph: Publication No. LEG-16, University School of Rural Planning and Development, University of Guelph.

LEG, 1984, Analysis of the Production Possibilities of Ontario Agriculture: Prospects for Growth in Ontario's Agri-Food Sector Under Alternative Conditions of Supply and Demand. Guelph: Publication No. LEG-18, University School of Rural Planning and Development, University of Guelph.

Phillips, D.W., 1985, "Canada's Climate Impacts Program", Land, 6 (1), p. 8.

Pierce, J. and O. Furuseth, 1983, "Assessing the Adequacy of North American Agricultural Land Resources", Geoforum, 14 (4), pp. 413-425.

Schultink, G., 1983, "Integrated Remote Sensing and Information Management Procedures for Agricultural Production Potential Assessment and Resource Policy Design in Developing Countries", Canadian Journal of Remote Sensing, 9 (1), pp. 4-18.

Sparrow, Hon. H.O. (Chairman), 1985, Proceedings of the Fifth Annual Meeting - Expert Committee on Soil Survey. Ottawa.

van Vuuren, W. and H. Jorjani, 1983, "Evaluation of Net Benefits from Sub-Surface Drainage", Presented at the 1983 Winter Meeting of the American Society of Engineers, Paper No. 83-2616.

Weetman, G.F., 1983, "Forestry Practices and Stress on Canadian Forest Land". In P. Loshak (ed.), Stress on Land. Ottawa: Environment Canada, pp. 260-301.

15

THE USEFULNESS OF COMPUTER AIDS THAT CAPTURE EXPERT KNOWLEDGE ABOUT LAND MANAGEMENT

Richard Davis, Paul Nanninga and Douglas Cocks

INTRODUCTION

Land management is the making of decisions about the application of non-land resources (money, personnel, equipment) so as to bring about or maintain the efficient, equitable utilization of land resources (minerals, water, productive land, etc.) (Cocks et al., 1986). Unlike land-use planning, which involves the long-term commitment of land resources, management is generally a short-term decision-making activity which must necessarily be based upon information currently available to the decision maker. Although the following discussion of land management is set in the Australian context, most of the features identified will be common to countries possessing pluralistic and democratic systems of federal government.

In Australia, management of public land is the responsibility of various special purpose state government departments and agencies (Forestry Commissions, National Parks and Wildlife Services, Crown Lands Departments, etc.), while local governments have responsibility for imposing occasional management conditions upon private landowners. Federal agencies have land management responsibilities over the small portion of the Australian land mass in federal ownership (less than 1 per cent) and only indirect power elsewhere. Of course, all private landowners are either themselves land managers or, when large tracts of land are in freehold ownership, employ specialised land managers.

In all states of Australia, the legislation which governs the activities of most special purpose government agencies sets out their broad management aims and requires them to draw up management plans for each of the tracts within their jurisdictions (Cocks et al., 1986). However, local government authorities, which possess largely indirect powers over land-use activities, can still mobilize their limited resources to achieve desirable patterns of land use. Their land management activities consist principally of approving or forbidding (according to predefined criteria) development applications and, less effectively but more directly, providing infrastructure and services in advance of development. There are several features common to the land management tasks of all these responsible organizations that have influenced the design of the knowledge-based management aid, GEOMYCIN, described later in this paper. These features, which have been identified empirically and are not based upon a coherent theory of information needs for land management follow.

1. The characteristics of the land base relevant to management vary significantly across the management region.

2. Because diverse issues have to be addressed by land managers, they must be able to access a corresponding diversity of expertise in order to manage effectively.

3. Many natural processes of importance to land management cannot yet be described by traditional scientific models to the point where managers can easily use them. Consequently, managers must rely upon common sense, the accumulated understanding of other experienced managers, and the specialized knowledge of external experts (such as consultants and scientists) when faced with problems outside their area of competence.

4. Many land managers are unfamiliar with computers. Although Australian local governments have made wide use of computers for over a decade now (Davis and Walker, 1980) this has occurred mostly in administrative and financial sections and not in land planning and management sections of the authorities. Although no comparable studies of the extent of computerization have been carried out among state resource agencies, it is the experience of the authors that most land management agencies possess computers in their central offices and a small number have placed computers in the headquarters of the larger tracts of land under their jurisdictions.

SOURCES AND REPRESENTATIONS OF KNOWLEDGE

Knowledge, as a concept, has been extensively studied by philosophers, cognitive psychologists, educators and, more recently, by computer scientists interested in artificial intelligence (AI). The work described here draws upon the research of the latter group. Waltz (1985) has classified artificial intelligence research into approximately 500 categories within a four level hierarchy, but a simple classification, suitable for the present purpose, is one based upon those activities of the mind that AI researchers seek to understand and emulate (Table 15.1). This paper is specifically concerned with attempts to apply human decision-making procedures to problems that normally require considerable expertise to solve. Computer programs of this type are called expert systems (Hayes-Roth et al., 1983). Although there is no widely accepted definition of an expert system (Barr and Feigenbaum, 1981; Hayes-Roth et al., 1983), a definition appropriate for this paper is a computer program that undertakes difficult decision-making tasks by using the accumulated knowledge of, and mimicking the solution methods of, a human expert.

Brachman et al., (1983) provide an extended definition through the enumeration of seven semi-independent characteristics which an ideal expert system should possess, characteristics which Buchanan (1982) summarizes as utility, performance and transparency.

Before further describing the characteristics and possible role of expert systems in land management, it is useful to introduce several of the representations that can be used to record expert knowledge in computer-compatible form.

Scientists commonly construct computer models to express procedural knowledge. These models are designed to carry out a predefined procedure known by the expert to produce conclusions in accordance with observations. As Reichelt et al. (1983) point out, the purposes of model building in science (and, concomitantly, the types of models built) are different to those of management. Natural scientists create procedural models for the purposes of explaining and predicting phenomena by linking up representations of already-understood natural processes. Such procedural models are termed process models. Other procedural models, used for prediction rather than explanation, are not based on an understanding of underlying processes (e.g., the Group Method of Data Handling [GMDH] of Ivakhnenko [1978]). Managers do not always use models for explanation or prediction but for control purposes, which only sometimes require explanation and prediction (Bradbury et al., 1983).

Scientifically developed procedural models (whether process-based or not) usually express the expert's knowledge in a set of equations (if the procedure is continuous), although conditional statements about relationships between classes of material entities may be included. Such models provide conclusions quickly and reliably, partly because the one model suffices for all occurrences of the phenomenon being modelled and partly because most common computer languages (FORTRAN, BASIC, COBOL, etc.) and computer architectures have been specifically designed for building and applying procedural models. When a procedure is based upon well-accepted descriptions of underlying processes, results will be reliable for a broad range of occurrences of the phenomenon being modelled

TABLE 15.1: CLASSIFICATION OF ARTIFICIAL INTELLIGENCE RESEARCH

HUMAN ACTIVITY	AREA OF RESEARCH
Decision making	Expert Systems
Learning	Learning Systems
Movement	Robotics
Seeing	Vision Systems
Speaking	Natural Language Systems

(i.e., the process model possesses a wide domain of applicability).

Although these are efficient representations of acquired knowledge for scientific purposes, procedural representations do possess a number of shortcomings for land managers. The formulation of reliable procedures can be a slow process, particularly if undertaken by scientists interested in developing process understanding. Also, when embedded in computer programs, their usefulness for explaining conclusions is low since the encapsulated knowledge is inextricably combined with the program's mechanisms for applying the knowledge (e.g., a FORTRAN program consists of a mixture of control statements [GOTO, PRINT, etc.] and knowledge representing statements [Y = aX + b, etc.]). Using the language of expert systems research, typical procedural computer programs combine the knowledge of a programming expert and a problem domain expert, and, consequently, when new understanding about the problem domain is to be incorporated into an existing model, the services of both a professional programmer and a land management expert are required.

Process understanding is the ultimate goal of scientists, but the understanding accumulated by land managers and other experts is generally of a different type. This understanding is commonly expressed as a set of individual, semi-independent assertions and so is termed declarative knowledge. A number of alternative ways of representing declarative knowledge have been developed for different applications (Barr and Feigenbaum, 1981; Michalski et al., 1983). Essentially these differ in the *a priori* connectiveness and the range of operators allowed in the representations. Nevertheless, these differences are only ones of degree and knowledge stated in one representation can always be transformed to another representation (Barr and Feigenbaum, 1981).

The extensive discussion that occurred during the formative period of AI research over the relative merits of procedural and declarative representations first raised many of the issues touched on here; this discussion is summarized in Winograd (1975). It focussed essentially on questions of modularity, efficiency, understandability, completeness and certainty.

Although there is no intrinsic reason why expert systems should not utilize either (or both) procedural and declarative representations, it is true that the latter type has dominated expert systems research and applications. Despite the fact that there has been considerable interest recently in frame-based (Minski, 1975) and first-order logic (Clocksin and Mellish, 1981) representations, the production rule representation remains the most common form used for declarative knowledge, because of its simplicity, modularity and ease of interpretation (Davis and King, 1977; Barr and Feigenbaum, 1981).

Each rule consists of a simple premise-conclusion pair:

Rule 1 If: it is the hot season and there is a strong wind
       Then: the fire danger is high,
Rule 2 If: the fire danger is high and the available biomass is dry
       Then: the height of flames will be high.

The premise is typically made up of one or more triplets: a parameter (e.g., season), an operator (e.g., equal to) and a value (e.g., hot). Individual triplets are themselves linked by the usual logical operators. In most production rule systems the Right-Hand-Side (RHS) contains only one conclusion with the operator constrained to "equal to", although it is relatively simple to incorporate multiple conclusions. Because of their ubiquity, subsequent discussion will be couched in terms of production rule systems. As an aside, it is worth noting that, although expert systems have generally been used for practical applications, they can also be applied to the purposes of science - namely, transforming declarative knowledge into procedural knowledge and eventually process understanding - either directly or by using learning systems (e.g., Michalski et al., 1983).

ANATOMY OF AN EXPERT SYSTEM

Two of the central components of production rule-based expert systems are clearly alluded to in the previous definition; a knowledge base that contains the expert's knowledge and an inference engine that applies the knowledge base to the problem domain in order to simulate an expert opinion. Additionally, information about the particular occurrence of the problem being investigated (case data) is recorded in a third component, usually called the working memory.

In production rule systems, the knowledge base simply consists of a set of production rules, usually ordered so as to aid later alteration and application of the knowledge. Pure production rule systems of the type proposed by Post (1943) are seldom used today; Davis and King (1977) describe modern production systems which typically extend Post's proposals through the incorporation of uncertain knowledge, conflict resolution, explanation, and flexibility in controlling the inferencing.

Although it is a fundamental design characteristic of expert systems to separate the domain knowledge from the application mechanism, the design of the inference engine is still dependent on the particular type of knowledge representation used. Inference engines designed for applying production rule knowledge bases operate in one of two basic modes - forward or backward chaining (Davis and King, 1977). In the former mode, the inference engine attempts to infer a range of conclusions from a particular occurrence of the phenomenon of interest to the manager (a data-driven approach), while in the latter, the inference engine tests the knowledge base against the characteristics of a particular occurrence recorded in the working memory in order to ascertain the validity of a specific hypothesis of interest to the manager (a goal-driven approach).

As its name implies, the inference engine attempts to infer values for parameters of interest to the manager from the knowledge contained in the rules. When backward chaining, the inference engine searches the knowledge base for a rule that can determine a value for the parameter of interest (the goal parameter), makes the parameters in the premise of that rule new goal parameters, and attempts to establish the validity of the premise of the rule by searching for further rules that can establish values for these new goal parameters, and so on. A rule is satisfied when the condition contained in the premise can be matched to the data contained in the working memory. When there is insufficient knowledge available to infer a value for a parameter through this chaining process, most inference engines ask the user to supply a value so that the working memory can be augmented and the inferencing can proceed. If this cannot be done, or if the value supplied does not satisfy the premise, then the inference engine will search the knowledge base to see if there is an alternative set of rules that can be used to determine a value for the goal parameter. Eventually the inference engine will have explored all possible paths and will have either established a value (or several possible values) for the goal parameter or will be unable to determine a value for that occurrence of the phenomenon given the current state of the knowledge base. There are many variations possible upon this basic description of inferencing (Davis and King, 1977; Hayes-Roth et al., 1983) but they will not be described here.

Whereas traditional procedural scientific models contain the one global model of the phenomenon, in rule-based systems each combination of rules that leads to a value for the goal parameter constitutes a separate, occurrence-specific model of the phenomenon. Thus the inference engine contains a model for building occurrence-specific models of the phenomenon. Normally, this model is represented as a procedure but, in an example of self-referencing, it is possible to build part or all of the inference engine using a rule-based representation of knowledge about human decision making. Davis (1980) has recognized this possibility in his proposal for meta-rules to control the application of the knowledge base.

The inference engine also contains a number of other components. A "tracer" keeps track of the rules used in the inferencing so that the system can provide the user with explanations of the understanding reached at any point in the inferencing. Thus, asking the system why it reached a certain decision will lead to an explanation such as:

> I have concluded that the height of flame is high because the fire danger rating is high and the available biomass is dry (Rule 2), and I know that the fire danger rating is high because it is the hot season and the wind strength is strong (Rule 1).

Not all of the knowledge in the rules need be held true with equal confidence. Another component of the inference engine keeps track of any measures of confidence attached by the expert to each rule, and it attempts to assign a level of confidence to the parameters of interest to the user. Conflicting conclusions can be reached by the inference engine if it discovers multiple sequences of rules that can each determine values for the same parameter (this occurs particularly often when knowledge has been obtained from different experts). To cope with this, the inference engine also needs to contain a module that can at least identify, and preferably resolve, such conflicts.

THE GEOMYCIN EXPERT SYSTEM SHELL

Although expert systems have been applied to a wide variety of problems (Bramer, 1982), neither a clear understanding of the types of problems to which they are well-suited nor simple methods for designing a system for a particular application have yet been achieved. In spite of this, a number of standard, general purpose inference engines (together with editors for building and modifying knowledge bases) have been constructed, under the belief that they will be suitable for many simple problems. These programs are termed shell programs.

The EMYCIN program (van Melle, 1979), perhaps the best known of these shells, is widely regarded as representing the most consistent and comprehensive design available (Cendrowska and Bramer, 1984). Two of the present authors (Davis and Nanninga, 1985) have added features to both the knowledge base representation and the inference engine of EMYCIN to make it better suited to problems of land management, and have named this augmented shell program GEOMYCIN. The four features of land management problems, outlined in the first section of the paper, have been used to guide these changes, as outlined below.

1. The GEOMYCIN program sequentially considers each distinguishable part of the management region, making a separate management decision for each. These parts are not treated independently since the values determined for a particular parameter in one part can be automatically transferred to another part. Thus the system can be initially set up to "know" that the value determined for the parameter season will be common throughout the management region. However, more complicated spatial interdependencies, such as the dependence of the value of one parameter on the value(s) of other parameters in other management units, have not yet been included. In addition, each rule in the knowledge base can be identified as being relevant to only certain parts of the management region. Thus, different subsets of the knowledge base are utilized when parameter values are being inferred for different locations.

2. A fact is a particular type of knowledge, an assertion accepted to be unconditionally true within a problem domain to a prescribed level of problem "graininess". When a fact is known to be true for a wide range of occurrences of a phenomenon, it can be recorded in either a data base (when it is spatially invariant) or a geographic data base (when it is spatially variant). For instance, the underlying geology of a part of the management region constitutes a fact that can be recorded in a geographic data base. In the GEOMYCIN system, allowance is made for the inference engine to gain access to relevant geographic data bases, so that the user is not asked to supply known parameter values during a consultation.

3. Where expert procedural knowledge is available, the GEOMYCIN shell can utilize such information together with the (rule-based) declarative knowledge for which

EMYCIN was designed. Thus GEOMYCIN can take advantage of the efficiencies afforded by the use of algorithms, although the shortcomings of these representations remain (Winograd, 1975).

4. GEOMYCIN possesses a number of features that make it particularly attractive to land managers who have had little experience with computers. For example, at any point, the manager can ask a number of additional questions, apart from the usual "why", in order to determine the progress of the decision making, and can override some features of the inferencing process (e.g., the automatic transference of the value of common parameters such as the season) during a consultation if wished.

Two other features that will improve the representation of geographic knowledge and the naturalness of interactions between the system and the user are currently being implemented in GEOMYCIN. First, given that spatial problems require knowledge to be expressed about relative locations and the dependencies of one location on another, it is important that not just logical and arithmetic, but spatial relationships between parameters should be able to be expressed simply in the knowledge representation. Second, GEOMYCIN presently displays output information in tabular and numerical form, a format which many land managers find difficult to interpret. Computer systems, comprising hardware and software components, which can display data graphically appear to hold much promise. Interactive computer graphics, the term often used to describe such systems, allows results to be displayed in a form that provides a spatial context, and is one with which land managers have far more familiarity.

APPLYING GEOMYCIN TO A LAND MANAGEMENT PROBLEM

The GEOMYCIN program has been applied to the problem of fire management in Kakadu National Park, Northern Territory, Australia (Davis et al., 1985). Fire has been used by the Aborigines of this area as a deliberate management tool for millennium. Over the last 150 years, however, the intensities and frequencies of the fires have increased, to the point where the park managers are uncertain of the long-term effects on the environment.

A knowledge base consisting of 120 production rules was obtained over a four month period from an acknowledged expert on fire behaviour in tropical environments. Many of the features of the GEOMYCIN system were specifically developed during this work in order to represent the expert's knowledge more efficiently and to ensure that the program behaved in a reasonably consistent fashion during its application to realistic problems. The expert system was demonstrated to a group of park managers, and its predictions were consistently found to be in close accordance with those of the managers.

CONCLUSIONS

This paper has discussed some of the possibilities for land managers offered by recent developments in artificial intelligence research, especially expert systems. Expert systems research attempts to develop computer programs that behave like experts in a problem domain; in the present case, to develop expert computer programs for land managers. It is worth emphasising that expert systems are not necessarily alternatives to procedural scientific models; it is possible (although uncommon) to design a scientific model as an expert system. In the course of developing such systems, AI researchers have realized that the procedural representations of knowledge sought by scientists constitute only one form of knowledge, and that the wealth of declarative knowledge available from experts also needs to be incorporated in these decision-making systems.

Additional features of an expert system shell program, called GEOMYCIN, which has been designed for land management purposes have also been described here. The system has been determined empirically, and work is still needed to establish the essential attributes of such a system from first principles. Although it has been demonstrated that GEOMYCIN is applicable to the problem of fire management in Kakadu National Park, it is clear that the hardware requirements and complexity will mean that it is unsuited to many practical applications. At present a simpler shell program, incorporating many of the same features, is being written in the PROLOG language for microcomputers and it is expected that this program, together with a knowledge base obtained from researchers and park managers, will form the basis of a practical fire management tool for Kakadu National Park.

The current enthusiasm for expert systems, like that surrounding many newly emergent technologies, is likely to be replaced by a more realistic understanding of theoretical and practical limitations in the next few years. However, expert systems will continue to have much to offer those land managers who are not themselves experts but who, from time to time, rely on expert advice.

REFERENCES

Barr, A. and E.A. Feigenbaum, 1981, The Handbook of Artificial Intelligence. Stanford: Heuristech Press.

Brachman, R.J., S. Amarel, C. Engelman, R.S. Engelmore, E.A. Feigenbaum and D.E. Wilkins, 1983, "What are Expert Systems?". In F. Hayes-Roth, D.A. Waterman and D.B. Lenat (eds.), Building Expert Systems. London: Addison-Wesley, pp. 31-58.

Bradbury, R.H., R.E. Reichelt, and D.G. Green, 1983, "Explanation, Prediction and Control in Coral Reef Ecosystems III: Models for Control". In J.T. Baker, R.M. Carter, P.W. Sammarco and K.P. Stark (eds.), Proceedings: Great Barrier Reef Conference. Townsville: James Cook University Press, pp. 165-169.

Bramer, M.A., 1982, "A Survey and Critical Review of Expert Systems Research". In D. Michie (ed.), Introductory Readings in Expert Systems. New York: Gordon and Breach, pp. 3-29.

Buchanan, B.G., 1982, "New Research on Expert Systems". In J.E. Hayes, D. Michie and Y.H. Pao (eds.), Machine Intelligence 10. New York: John Wiley and Sons, pp. 269-299.

Cendrowska, J. and M.A. Bramer, 1984, "A Rational Reconstruction of the MYCIN Consultation System", International Journal of Man-Machine Studies, 20 (3), pp. 229-317.

Clocksin, W.F. and C.S. Mellish, 1981, Programming in PROLOG. Berlin: Springer-Verlag.

Cocks, K.D., J.R. Ive and J.R. Davis, 1986, "Developing Policy Guidelines for the Management of Public Natural Lands", Land Use Policy, 3 (1), pp. 9-20.

Davis, J.R., 1980, "Meta-Rules: Reasoning About Control", Artificial Intelligence, 13, pp. 179-222.

Davis, J.R., J. Hoare and P.M. Nanninga, 1985, "The GEOKAK Fire Behaviour and Fire Effects Expert System". In J. Walker, J.R. Davis and A.M. Gill (eds.), Towards an Expert System for Fire Management at Kakadu National Park. Canberra: Technical Memorandum 85/2, Division of Water and Land Resources, Commonwealth Scientific and Industrial Research Organization.

Davis, J.R. and J. King, 1977, "An Overview of Production Systems". In E.W. Elcock and D. Michie (eds.), Machine Intelligence 8. New York: John Wiley and Sons, pp. 300-332.

Davis, J.R. and P.M. Nanninga, 1985, "GEOMYCIN: Towards a Geographic Expert System for Resource Management", Journal of Environmental Management, 20 (4), pp. 377-390.

Davis, J.R. and P.A. Walker, 1980, "The Use of Computers in Local Government", Urban Systems, 5, pp. 55-68.

Hayes-Roth, F., D.A. Waterman and D.B. Lenat (eds.), 1983, Building Expert Systems. London: Addison-Wesley.

Ivakhnenko, A.G., 1978, "The Group Method of Data Handling in Long-Range Forecasting", Technological Forecasting and Social Change, 12, pp. 213-227.

Michalski, R.S., J.G. Carbonell and T.M. Mitchell, 1983, Machine Learning: An Artificial Intelligence Approach. Palo Alto: Tioga.

Minski, M., 1975, "A Framework for Representing Knowledge". In P. Winston (ed.), The Psychology of Computer Vision. New York: McGraw-Hill, pp. 211-277.

Post, E., 1943, "Formal Reductions of the General Combinatorial Problem", American Journal of Mathematics, 65, pp. 197-268.

Reichelt, R.E., D.G. Green and R.H. Bradbury, 1983, "Explanation, Prediction and Control in Coral Reef Ecosystems I: Models for Explanation." In J.T. Baker, R.M. Carter, P.W. Sammarco and K.P. Stark (eds.), Proceedings: Great Barrier Reef Conference. Townsville: James Cook University Press, pp. 231-235.

van Melle, W., 1979, "A Domain-Independent Production-Rule System for Consultation Programs". In 6th International Joint Conference on Artificial Intelligence. Tokyo: International Joint Conference on Artificial Intelligence and Information Processing Society of Japan, pp. 923-925.

Waltz, D.L., 1985, "Scientific Datalinks Artificial Intelligence Classification Scheme", AI Magazine, 6 (1), pp. 58-63.

Winograd, T., 1975, "Frame Representations and the Declarative/Procedural Controversy". In D.G. Bobrow and A. Collins (eds.), Representation and Understanding: Studies in Cognitive Science. New York: Academic Press, pp. 185-210.

PART 4
ANALYSIS FOR RESOURCE-USE POLICY

Comprehension of land resource issues and the development of policy to address those issues, invariably requires not only data but also analysis. Resource problems are analyzed most generally to understand better the nature of the issues, but also to assess the magnitude of the problems, to determine the need and nature of policy responses, to locate priority areas for such responses, and to evaluate policy both before and after its implementation.

Most of the issues addressed in this volume stem from environmental and other constraints to meeting those demands on the uses of lands. One important avenue of analysis involves characterizing the relationships between the availability of resources and the human needs they are expected to meet. An example of this type of analysis is supplied by Wisner et al., who apply a resource accounting framework to the problem of meeting energy needs from limited wood supplies in a Third World context. Analyses of this type can assist in decisions about the use of resources, especially by highlighting the options which are possible and the trade-offs involved.

The contentious issue of farmland protection also derives from pressures on limited land resources. Advocates and policy makers need analytical tools to assess the urgency for public policy and to identify those lands which are most important for food production or for meeting other needs. Increasingly, attention has been directed to developing more comprehensive approaches to land rating. Some of these novel approaches are explored by Flaherty and Smit. These approaches offer distinct advantages over interpretive schemes which rate lands according to physical suitability, and which have conventionally been used as a basis for land-use planning.

Land resources are not fixed; environments are frequently modified, particularly by human activity, and changes in requirements from lands also shift interpretations of lands. An important field of analysis involves assessing the implications of environmental changes on rural lands and their uses. This research includes studies of the ecological response to changes and extends to assessments of implications for "productive" uses of lands and the socio-economic sectors they support. Investigation by Ludlow and Smit of acid rain and agriculture illustrates some of the prospects and difficulties involved in this type of research.

A vast array of policies, programs and management strategies has been developed to reduce environmental constraints on productive uses of lands, particularly for agriculture. These initiatives have met with an equally wide range of successes and failures, prompting evaluative analysis of programs, before, during and after their implementation. Van Vuuren and McCaw provide an evaluation of programs intended to stimulate rural development by enhancing land drainage.

Rural areas are essentially those which are not urban, and many of the most prominent planning issues relate to the "fringe" areas between urban and rural, and to the processes occurring therein. Unravelling the dynamics of population growth, residential development, demands on space and land-use change in these fringe areas represents a major challenge for resource analysts. Both Moffatt and Dawson provide examples of modelling approaches to the analysis of the dynamics of urban fringe areas. These papers are reflective of the increasingly popular use of modelling as a means of characterizing the dynamics of these fringe areas.

What has become clear in recent times is that effective planning for rural resource use does demand analysis for the various purposes listed above, and this may necessitate the development of new approaches and procedures. The papers contained within this part provide some interesting examples of how rural resource analysts have responded in rather novel ways to the need for structured inquiry with respect to specific issues. And while each type of analysis is presented in relation to particular resource concerns, the opportunities for application of the methods to other issues, either directly or in modified forms, is quite evident.

16

A MATRIX-FLOW APPROACH TO RURAL DOMESTIC ENERGY: A KENYAN CASE STUDY

Ben Wisner, Hans Gilgen, Nicolas Antille, Peter Sulzer and Dieter Steiner

INTRODUCTION

Since the massive petroleum price rises of 1974 and 1979, many Third World countries have been faced with the task of understanding complex interactions among sectors of their energy systems. If urban and industrial demand for petroleum products has caused a crisis of foreign exchange in the petroleum-importing countries, rural woodfuel shortage has emerged as the other crisis that will not go away (Eckholm, 1976; Eckholm et al., 1984).

In Kenya an attempt has been made by a combined Swedish Academy of Sciences/Ministry of Energy team to capture the inter-relations of the energy system (O'Keefe et al., 1984). Supported by more than a dozen person-years of field operations in the period 1981-1983, the team concluded that around 80 per cent of primary energy consumed in Kenya comes from wood rather than petroleum.

As a result of previous research by the team, an energy accounting model was developed to estimate wood consumption at the level of the seven administrative provinces. This model is known as the LDC Energy Alternatives Planning Model (LEAP). A major limitation of the LEAP is that it is really only useful for planning at a national scale. Increasingly, however, it has been recognized that effective planning for rural development necessitates a district-level approach, allowing for the involvement of local inhabitants. Recognition of this need led the authors to develop a woodfuel accounting system for use at the local level. The woodfuel matrix is capable of identifying the allocation of wood among specified social groups and possible fuel shortages, given information on resource availability and traditional access patterns determined by social status.

The format of this woodfuel matrix and its data requirements are described in this paper. The utility of the framework is then illustrated through the presentation of results from two scenarios;

211

one assuming that all woodfuel demands are satisfied and the other assuming conditions of sustained yield.

THE LEAP AND ENERGY PLANNING IN KENYA

To a large extent the development of the woodfuel matrix described herein was initiated in response to the perceived limitations of the energy accounting model known as the LEAP. The LEAP is consistent with a planning approach which defines the woodfuel cycle as the key to Kenya's immediate energy future. Three varieties of wood consumption are distinguished:

1. household and rural industrial woodfuel use in direct combustion, accounting for about two-thirds of total resource use,
2. urban household and a small amount of industrial charcoal consumption, accounting for about another third, and
3. a small amount of wood use in construction and other non-energy industrial uses.

Household and rural industrial woodfuel is generally collected locally, and in the situations in which it is marketed commercially, it is not transported more than about 80 km (Hosier, 1982). Charcoal, by contrast, is almost exclusively marketed commercially and is transported up to 150 km by road and 350 km by rail (Openshaw, n.d.).

The energy accounting model, LEAP, developed by the Beijer/Ministry of Energy team, estimates future wood consumption in these three categories for seven provincial Kenyan subregions with the help of models of demographic and economic growth. The LEAP is capable of assuming that each subregion must cover its own future wood demand from internal production (annual increment or stock). Importation of wood from other subregions is allowed, however. Within each subregion ecological zones are distinguished for the purpose of estimating wood production under different biomass productivity conditions. Furthermore, within each ecological zone, major land-use and tenure types are distinguished. Land use is a major factor in determining available biomass stock and annual yield through the effect it has on the spatial distribution of trees (isolated trees, shrubs, hedgerows versus closed forest).

The model is thus able to estimate present stock and yield of woody biomass by aggregation across land-use types, ecological zones, and provinces. In the base year, 1980, three provinces were already consuming wood stock, unable to meet demand from their annual increment plus interprovincial transfers. It was projected that the proportion of wood supplied from stock would increase, if this base case continued, until 1995. However, such a scenario is clearly not sustainable. Indeed, by the year 2000 an enormous gap of 32 million tonnes of wood would exist, representing the difference between demand (nearly 50 million tonnes per year) and supply (only 18 million tonnes). In 1980, Kenya actually consumed just over 20 million tonnes. This trend toward deforestation is measurable using remote-sensing technology (Epp et al., 1983; Geiser and Sommer, 1983), but description of a problem stops short of explanation and control.

These early results of the Beijer/Ministry of Energy work influenced strategic thinking about woodfuel and energy in general in Kenya, and since spring 1984, the LEAP has been successfully operationalized as a planning tool in the Ministry's planning section.

The Limits of the LEAP

Despite attempts to build in the variability of social and ecological conditions at the subprovincial scale, the LEAP remains functional for planning purposes only at the national policy level. It lacks effective spatial resolution below the provincial level, whereas the planning process in Kenya is increasingly focussed on the 41 administrative districts (Figure 16.1). The LEAP's provinces are too heterogeneous, and its ecological zones and land types cannot be built up into districts. In addition, the LEAP lacks sufficient social resolution for effective planning. The reality of social access to woodfuel is far more complex than the simple assumptions the LEAP makes. O'Keefe et al. (1984, p. 75) assume that "under conditions of scarcity, households would obtain access to whatever woodstocks were available, either directly or through commoditization". But what of the many ways in which kinship, temporary employment and other associations give households access to wood on the lands controlled by others outside of a commercial or market context? The Beijer/Ministry team realized further work on these questions would be necessary, noting that "future research needs to focus more closely on the determinants of accessibility and its impacts on fuel availability" (O'Keefe et al., 1984, p. 75). More recent statements from field projects underscore the extreme variability and complexity of the determinants of access in Kenya. For instance, Bradley (1985), working with the Kenya Woodfuel Development Programme, writes:

In Kakamega trees mean money, which means men. Kuni[1] is (or was) a free food like water ... It is for women to collect. The fact is that in South Maragoli, despite population densities approaching 1,000/sq. km, 20% plus of land is devoted to woody biomass. Very little of that 20% is accessible to the

214

FIGURE 16.1: DISTRICTS AND PROVINCES
OF KENYA

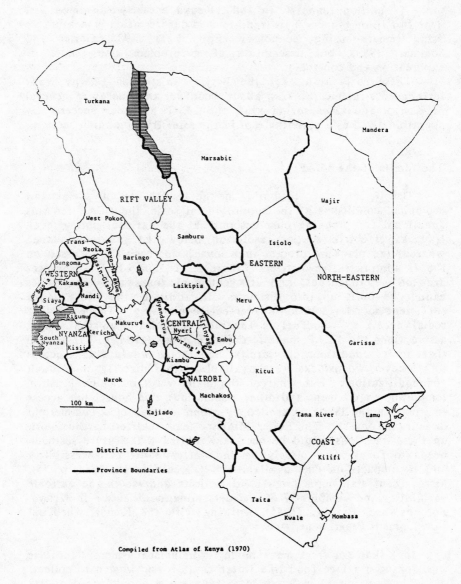

Compiled from Atlas of Kenya (1970)

women, and the men will not allow them to plant trees of any description ... [Wood on farms] fulfills the role of an emergency bank. When school fees are desperately needed a few trees are felled and sold. It is a vital monetary resource, and to consider it as wastable for kuni is a gross misperception.

There is a growing consensus that rural development of all kinds is more effective if local inhabitants are involved in as much of the planning, implementation, and evaluation cycle as possible (Chambers,1983). But popular participation or community participation stands little chance at the scale of projects embracing large administrative units such as the province (approximately two million people). The district planning process is where participatory innovations are more likely, although some have argued that even the district is too big (Miller, 1985; Rocheleau, 1985).

It was with such a district-level process of action-research (Brandão, 1984; Dubell et al., 1981; Kassam and Mustafa, 1982) in mind, that the authors tried to test, in a preliminary way, the feasibility of using a flow-matrix approach to woodfuel access. This exploratory work is obviously not meant as a substitute for the district-based process just described. The research was undertaken in order to design a local-level accounting system of sufficient simplicity and flexibility to serve as a tool in the district-level participatory process. Use of matrix formalism is not meant to disguise the fact that fundamental questions are being asked: who gets what? where? how? This exploratory work seems both a logical extension of the earlier success of the LEAP and a response to the growing interest in decentralized, participatory planning in Kenya.

Such an attempt was explicitly foreseen in work summarizing and reflecting upon the results of the earlier Kenyan studies (Wisner, 1983). Subsequently, it has been learned that such work might fill an international gap (Greeley, 1985; Howes, 1985a; Sachs, 1985).

Data from the process of developing the LEAP and other published Kenyan sources were available during summer semester 1984 and winter semester 1985. Details of the computer system supporting the woodfuel matrix and of the data used are available in two diploma theses (Antille, 1985; Sulzer, 1985).

THE WOODFUEL MATRIX

Woodfuel consumption for meeting domestic energy need in any district of Kenya (Figure 16.1) can be specified for a given year as follows:

$$C = aN, \tag{1}$$

$$= bY + cS \qquad a,b,c \in [0,1], \tag{2}$$

where C is woodfuel consumption,
N is domestic energy need,
Y is biomass yield,
S is biomass stock,
a is the proportion of energy need satisfied,
b is the proportion of yield required,
c is the proportion of stock required.

The calculations involve estimation of the proportions a, b and c. The expressions in (1) and (2) can be disaggregated into the following:

$$C = \sum_i C_i, \tag{3}$$

$$aN = \sum_i a_i N_i, \tag{4}$$

$$bY = \sum_j b_j Y_j, \tag{5}$$

$$cS = \sum_j c_j S_j, \tag{6}$$

where C_i is the woodfuel consumption of social class i,
N_i is the woodfuel need of social class i,
Y_j is biomass yield for land-use/tenure category j,
S_j is biomass stock for land-use/tenure category j.

The values for N_i, S_j and Y_j are stored in the cells at the extreme left edge and top of the woodfuel matrix, respectively (Table 16.1). These are labelled "need", "stock" and "yield".

One district, Machakos, in the eastern, drier foreland plateau is presented as an example (Table 16.1). Machakos District was chosen because of the wide range of social classes and land-use/tenure types represented in this district. In a number of other districts some of these categories of social class and/or land types are missing. Given that there are reliable values for N_i (i = 1,...,9), as well as for S_j (j = 1,...,5) and for Y_j (j = 1,...,5), the task is to calculate the values for F_{ij}, which are the flows of woodfuel from land types to user groups; that is, the cells in the central portion of the woodfuel matrix.[2]

TABLE 16.1: EXAMPLE WOODFUEL MATRIX, MACHAKOS

SUSTAINED YIELD MACHAKOS	HOUSEHOLDS	NEED (T)	LARGE FARMS >4HA	SMALL FARMS <4HA	COMMON LAND	FOREST	OCCUPIED RANGELAND	TOTAL	RESIDUAL NEED (T,%)
STOCK (T) / YIELD (T)			3 792 000 / 252 900	791 700 / 52 800	2 597 400 / 67 400	916 500 / 36 300	16 117 200 / 418 200	24 214 800 / 827 600	
LARGE FARMERS	9 570	47 850	47 850					0 / 47 850	0 / 0
LANDLESS WITH NO NO ACCESS	5 800	29 000	29 000					0 / 29 000	0 / 0
SMALL FARMERS WITH NO ACCESS	21 730	108 650	98 091	10 559				0 / 108 650	0 / 0
SMALL FAR. WITH COMM. LAND	32 600	163 000		15 841	25 193			0 / 41 034	121 966 / 74
SMALL FAR. WITH ACC. TO FOREST	54 330	271 650		26 400		18 315		0 / 44 715	226 935 / 83
LANDLESS WITH COMM. LAND	8 700	43 500			7 117			0 / 7 117	36 053 / 82
LANDLESS WITH ACC. TO FOREST	14 510	72 550				5 418		0 / 5 418	67 132 / 92
FARMERS ON OCCUPIED RANGELAND	21 780	108 900					108 900	0 / 108 900	0 / 0
URBAN	16 920	203 040			34 760	12 567		0 / 47 327	155 713 / 76
TOTAL	185 940	1 048 140	0 / 174 941	0 / 52 800	0 / 67 400	0 / 36 300	0 / 108 900	0 / 440 341	607 799 / 57
RESIDUAL STOCK (T) (%)			3 792 000 / 100	791 700 / 100	2 597 400 / 100	916 500 / 100	16 117 200 / 100	24 214 800 / 100	
RESIDUAL YIELD (T) (%)			77 959 / 30	0 / 0	0 / 0	0 / 0	309 300 / 73	387 259 / 46	

SATISFIED NEED MACHAKOS	HOUSEHOLDS	NEED (T)	LARGE FARMS >4HA	SMALL FARMS <4HA	COMMON LAND	FOREST	OCCUPIED RANGELAND	TOTAL	RESIDUAL NEED (T,%)
STOCK (T) / YIELD (T)			3 792 000 / 252 900	791 700 / 52 800	2 597 400 / 67 400	916 500 / 36 300	16 117 200 / 418 200	24 214 800 / 827 600	
LARGE FARMERS	9 570	47 850	47 850					0 / 47 850	0 / 0
LANDLESS WITH NO NO ACCESS	5 800	29 000	29 000					0 / 29 000	0 / 0
SMALL FARMERS WITH NO ACCESS	21 730	108 650	98 091	10 559				0 / 108 650	0 / 0
SMALL FAR. WITH COMM. LAND	32 600	163 000		15 841	79 759 / 67 400			79 759 / 83 241	0 / 0
SMALL FAR. WITH ACC. TO FOREST	54 330	271 650		26 400		208 950 / 36 300		208 950 / 62 700	0 / 0
LANDLESS WITH COMM. LAND	8 700	43 500			43 500			43 500 / 0	0 / 0
LANDLESS WITH ACC. TO FOREST	14 510	72 550				72 550		72 550 / 0	0 / 0
FARMERS ON OCCUPIED RANGELAND	21 780	108 900					108 900	108 900 / 0	0 / 0
URBAN	16 920	203 040			203 040			203 040 / 0	0 / 0
TOTAL	185 940	1 048 140	0 / 174 941	52 800	326 299 / 67 400	281 500 / 36 300	0 / 108 900	607 799 / 440 341	0 / 0
RESIDUAL STOCK (T) (%)			3 792 000 / 100	791 700 / 100	2 271 101 / 87	635 000 / 69	16 117 200 / 100	23 607 001 / 97	
RESIDUAL YIELD (T) (%)			77 959 / 30	0 / 0	0 / 0	0 / 0	309 300 / 73	387 259 / 46	

A series of empirical observations of a sample of Kenyan communities provided information for the particular sequence of allocation of biomass to user groups under two extreme scenarios. The data on social access comes from participant observation undertaken in eight sites in Kenya, spanning a range of ethnic, demographic, and agro-ecological conditions, executed as part of the field work supporting the Beijer/Ministry of Energy study during 1981-1983 (Barnes et al., 1984; Kruks et al., 1985; Wisner, 1983). The resulting series of flow mechanisms summarized in Table 16.2, are not presented as any substitute for detailed, district-by-district, participatory action-research which would reveal, in each case, a more realistic and useful set of flow mechanisms. However, as the primary aim is to demonstrate the general usefulness and desirability of this type of approach, the results of the participant-observation studies are presented as a moderately realistic (although clearly over-generalized) basis for tracing flows among social classes of users.

The two extreme scenarios used to structure the analysis of flows are called sustained yield and satisfied need. Under the assumptions of sustained yield, only annual biomass increment can be allocated. Stock cannot be touched. Under satisfied need, biomass from stock can also be allocated until need is satisfied, or until stock is exhausted, whichever occurs first.

In the case of sustained yield, a scenario that simulates the imposition of severe governmental controls on biomass extraction, the stress created could be referred to as social stress and is suggested by the values in the extreme right-hand column of the matrix (Table 16.1) under the heading residual need. The other extreme scenario, satisfied need, produces what one might call ecological stress since biomass stock often falls victim to the imperative to cover need. This is suggested in the two extreme bottom rows of the matrix, called residual stock and residual yield. Of course, in reality ecological stress quite quickly provokes social stress as deforestation, erosion, loss of agricultural land, lowering of water tables, and so forth drive on the vicious spiral of the poor person's energy crisis. The preliminary work does not take these interaction effects into account.

The numbers in Table 16.2 abstract the data gathered in the participant-observation studies mentioned above, and indicate from what land types and in what sequence each social class of user will obtain a flow of woodfuel. Numbers in the lower field of a cell refer to yield, while numbers in the upper field refer to stock. If the same number appears in various fields, this means that the corresponding social classes (to be read off in the column to the left) have identical priority or rank in the sequence of allocation, at least as far as the available data allows estimations. That is, the corresponding social groups have identical claims on the flow from

TABLE 16.2: BIOMASS FLOW MECHANISMS

SUSTAINED YIELD

	LARGE FARMS >4HA	SMALL FARMS <4HA	COMMON LAND	FOREST	OCCUPIED RANGELAND
LARGE FARMERS	1				
LANDLESS WITH NO NO ACCESS	3				
SMALL FARMERS WITH NO ACCESS	3	2			
SMALL FAR. WITH COMM. LAND		2	4		
SMALL FAR. WITH ACC. TO FOREST		2		5	
LANDLESS WITH COMM. LAND			4		
LANDLESS WITH ACC. TO FOREST				5	
FARMERS ON OCCUPIED RANGELAND					6
URBAN			4	5	

SATISFIED NEED

	LARGE FARMS >4HA	SMALL FARMS <4HA	COMMON LAND	FOREST	OCCUPIED RANGELAND
LARGE FARMERS	3 1		2		
LANDLESS WITH NO NO ACCESS	5 4				
SMALL FARMERS WITH NO ACCESS	7	8 6			
SMALL FAR. WITH COMM. LAND		6	10 9		
SMALL FAR. WITH ACC. TO FOREST		6		12 11	
LANDLESS WITH COMM. LAND			14 13		
LANDLESS WITH ACC. TO FOREST				16 15	
FARMERS ON OCCUPIED RANGELAND					16 17
URBAN			20 19	22 21	

a given land type's stock or flow. In such cases the flow is arithmetically divided in proportion to each social group's need (see third column from left in Table 16.1, labelled need and quantified in tonnes).

So, for instance, taking an example under the assumption of sustained yield, the first step taken by the computer is to try to satisfy the need of the social category "large farmers" from the annual yield of biomass available on the land category "large farms" (logically enough as this is the land directly controlled by the social group in question). The second step is to try to satisfy the need of all three subgroups of "small farmers" from annual yield on their land ("small farms"). As the third step, if there is anything left of the annual biomass yield on the category large farms, it is to be divided in proportion to the need of the social group "landless without access" (to forest or to common land) and to the group "small farmer without access" (to forest or to common land) if this group's need has not already been covered during step two. Sustained yield continues through a fourth, fifth, and sixth step, fully allocating available yield.

The scenario satisfied need requires a more complex, longer series of steps, but the internal logic is similar. Step 1 is to satisfy large farmers' need from large farms' biomass yield. Step 2 is to carry on satisfying large farmers' need (if it is not yet covered), this time from the land type common land. Note here that common land is shared in a complex way among four social groups, its yield and even its stock being allocated as flows in a certain sequence. Step 3 is to continue satisfying the large farmers' need, this time from their own land's stock. In no case was it necessary to go on to yet another category of land in order to meet large farmers' need, so the sequence now shifts to the need of the social group landless with no access (Steps 4 and 5). Since, by definition, this group has no other options, the sequence then moves on to the task of satisfying the need of the group called small farmers (Steps 6, 7, 8, 9 and 10). Note here that as regards some categories of land, the three subgroups of small farmer share identical access, while in regard to biomass from other land categories they do not. The sequence moves on through a total of 22 steps required to satisfy the need for woodfuel of all nine social classes.

DATA AND DATA SOURCES

Production Side of the Woodfuel Matrix

Thirty-two of Kenya's 41 districts were analyzed as surfaces upon which the interaction of land uses and such significant factors as rainfall (itself highly correlated with altitude) and other ecological factors produce a series of different growth conditions for woody biomass.

The map of ecological potential in the Atlas of Kenya (Government of Kenya [GOK], 1970) allowed the areas in each district of arable land to be quantified. The forested areas reported in Kenya's Statistical Abstract 1982 (GOK, 1982) were subtracted from the arable land in each district. Likewise, national parks, nature reserves, and water surfaces were quantified and subtracted from the district total of arable land.

A further step was to distinguish privately held arable land from arable land as yet not registered. Here it was impossible to get up-to-date data on the progress of official land registration, so an ecological definition of common land was adopted, and privatized land was derived by exclusion. For nearly 30 years, beginning even before Independence, land adjudication, consolidation, and registration has been taking place as a high governmental priority, beginning with the highlands and working out through the medium potential land into the rangelands. It was assumed, therefore, that really only the land surveyed as bushland in the Atlas of Kenya (GOK, 1970) is likely by now not to be either privatized or to be in process of becoming privatized, or to be near enough to another area undergoing privatization so that local, informal preparations are being made of a sort that would certainly affect social access to biomass.

Privately held arable land was further divided into the amount held in units of more than 4 ha and that held in units smaller than this threshold between large and small farms, using data from Kenya's Integrated Rural Surveys 1976-1979 (GOK, 1981b) and a series of assumptions to allow for the division of provincial areas among constituent districts (Antille, 1985).

In this manner the four land categories to be found on the production side of the woodfuel matrix, namely, large farms, small farms, common land and forest were defined. The fifth, and final, category, is occupied rangeland. Here, according to Ojany and Ogendo (1973), live nomads where rainfall is less than 500 mm yearly and arable farmers up to this 500 mm threshold. Hence the term occupied rangeland. Over the last two decades an increasing number of landless peasants from the highlands have been settling in this zone, farming with considerable resilience and ability to adapt to high risk, but nonetheless representing a very poor and highly vulnerable social stratum (Bernard and Thom, 1981; Mbithi and Barnes, 1975; Porter, 1979; Wisner, 1978).

The resulting land categories are mapped in Figure 16.2. Biomass stock and yield per year in tonnes were then calculated for each of these surface areas within the districts. Coefficients of woody biomass productivity for high potential, medium potential,

222

FIGURE 16.2: LAND CATEGORIES FOR MATRIX

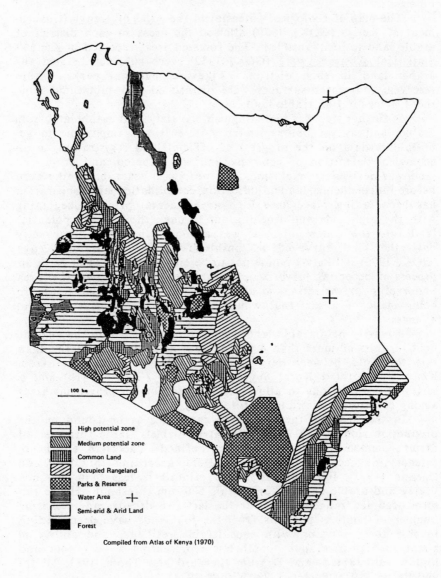

High potential zone

Medium potential zone

Common Land

Occupied Rangeland

Parks & Reserves

Water Area

Semi-arid & Arid Land

Forest

Compiled from Atlas of Kenya (1970)

common land (bushland), and occupied rangeland were taken from the literature review and field studies undertaken by the Beijer/Ministry of Energy study (O'Keefe et al., 1984). The stock and yield results are presented in Table 16.3.

It is extremely important for the reader to recall that the major objective of the exercise was to demonstrate the usefulness of a tool to be refined and calibrated at district level. The data set was constructed from information available in Zurich. This was not a substitute for district level redefinition of the social class and land types and collection of data.

Consumption Side of the Woodfuel Matrix

Since cooking is the most important domestic end use in Kenya the household was defined as the basic woodfuel consumption unit (Hosier, 1982). Further simplification resulted by assuming an average household size of five persons for all districts and social groups, despite some evidence of a certain regional and social variability in Kenya (GOK, 1981b).

Rural and urban households were distinguished in each district using the most recent population census (GOK, 1981a), but adjusted in Nyanza Province by data from district development plans. The urban/rural distinction is necessary because of the importance of charcoal in urban areas and of untransformed woodfuel in the countryside.

A next step was to distinguish in each district the number of households in rural areas living in occupied rangeland. This was done cartographically (Antille, 1985). These households are not only important to distinguish because of their significantly different patterns of access, but they are important in the production of charcoal for the urban market, a major non-farm source for households who otherwise would be even more reliant on high-risk farming.

Data available in Kenya's Integrated Rural Surveys 1976-1979 (GOK, 1981b) was used to further distinguish numbers of rural households that are landless, small farm owners, and large farm owners.

Of further critical importance is the fact that small-farmer households and landless households must depend on flows of woodfuel from land they themselves do not control. Therefore, for a start, locational access was built into a further differentiation of these classes by distance from forest and/or common land (bushland). This was done cartographically, assuming a threshold distance of 10 km (20 km round-trip). Locational access having been absorbed in the definition of user groups, social access alone would channel biomass flows according to the flow mechanisms in Table 16.2.

TABLE 16.3: VALUES FOR PRODUCTION SIDE OF MATRIX

	Large Farms (t)		Small Farms (t)		Common Land (t)		Forests (t)		Occupied Rangeland (t)		Total (t)	
	Stock	Yield	Stock	Yield	Stock	Yield	Stock	Yield	Stock	Yield	Stock	Yield
Kilifi	9566400	638100	333800	22200	11942000	386400	4930000	136000	6190100	146300	32962400	1329000
Kwale	3991700	266100	314300	20900	12332100	343700	1720600	47500	2611800	61700	20970500	739900
Lamu	14196900	946500	42300	2800	1455100	43300	192300	5300	0	0	15886600	997900
Taita	1371200	91600	74700	5000	0	0	143100	3900	4158500	98300	5747500	198800
Tana River	3407900	227600	66800	4500	1655300	53900	0	0	6210600	146800	11340600	432800
Machakos	3792000	252900	791700	52800	2597400	67400	916500	36300	16117200	418200	24214800	827600
Kitui	1337200	89400	281700	18800	3330000	86400	1203300	47200	26873100	697200	33025300	939000
Embu	1004800	66700	245000	16300	0	0	1021400	43000	6060600	157200	8331800	283200
Maru	1329600	88500	852700	56800	0	0	6319100	261000	11333100	294000	19834500	700300
Nyeri	1579700	105000	815600	54200	1249200	43200	9544600	301300	0	0	6582100	503700
Murang'a	1165300	77400	2009000	133500	0	0	3407800	107600	0	0	6582100	318500
Kirinyaga	1025600	68200	467500	31100	0	0	2690400	84900	428000	10500	4611500	194700
Kiambu	1591100	107200	1127900	76000	249800	8600	4229100	133500	0	0	7197900	325300
Nyandarua	1820000	121000	369900	24600	8369600	289400	5286400	166900	0	0	15845900	601900
Narok	10191500	682900	87400	5800	18649300	570500	8706900	226400	1203000	27900	38838100	1513500
Kajiado	5600000	375500	56700	3800	504500	11700	155500	4000	1455300	33800	7772000	428800
Nakuru	2637100	176800	192200	12800	8942100	265700	23652300	617900	0	0	35423700	1073200
Nandi	2212300	148200	150800	10000	0	0	3791300	98600	0	0	6154400	256800
Kericho	3279600	219700	310700	20600	481700	15100	12617800	328100	0	0	16689800	583500
Elgeyo/Marakwet	598800	40100	55000	3600	4691800	141400	9388600	244100	776200	18000	15510400	447200
Baringo	1459800	97900	83600	5600	10993800	300900	7207400	191300	7198900	167000	26943500	762700
Trans-Nzoia	2126400	142400	112700	7500	0	0	2691000	70000	0	0	4930100	219900
Uashin-Gishu	3228000	216200	124200	8200	0	0	6279900	163300	0	0	9631200	387700
West Pokot	3825200	256400	66000	4400	8052100	215400	4674400	121600	2367300	54900	18987000	652700
Laikipia	5065400	339600	55600	3700	10263900	314600	8675900	227100	388100	9000	24448900	894000
South Nyanza	7012300	467500	1150700	76700	894200	30200	0	0	0	0	9057200	574400
Kisii	1974100	131600	834100	55600	0	0	0	0	0	0	2808200	187200
Kisumu	2702700	180200	381000	25400	0	0	0	0	0	0	3083700	205600
Siaya	2349700	156600	767200	51100	968800	32800	0	0	0	0	4085700	240500
Kakamega	1676500	111800	1134000	76100	0	0	3866100	116700	0	0	6676600	304600
Bungoma	2042800	136200	412600	27700	0	0	6467200	195300	0	0	8922600	359200
Busia	1282400	85500	292900	19600	0	0	0	0	0	0	1575300	105100

This process produced the nine consumption groupings in Table 16.1.

Yearly woodfuel consumption in Kenya has been established by a series of large-scale, random sample surveys (Hosier, 1982; O'Keefe et al., 1984). There is surprisingly little variation in annual consumption of woodfuel per capita by social class. Households consume around 80 GJ per year. That is around 5 tonnes of air-dry wood if it is burned directly or 12 tonnes of wood if it is consumed as charcoal, because of energy loss in conversion.[3]

Table 16.4 presents the values for the consumption side by district and consumption group. Given the number of households in each group, simple multiplication by the average consumption per household per year produces this array of numbers, about which earlier caveats apply.

RESULTS

The woodfuel matrix was employed to identify allocations of wood under the two scenarios satisfied need and sustained yield. The results indicate the extent to which the fuel needs of various social groups can be satisfied and, at the district level, the use of stock and yield resources and the spatial incidence of biomass surpluses and deficits.

The Situation of Population Groups

The data presented in Tables 16.5 and 16.6 allow one to hypothesize that large farmers[4] are generally able to cover their woodfuel needs from their own land. This has tremendous implications for the women of such households, who do not have to spend very long hours in woodfuel provision. Their labour time can be spent in other ways, and this too gives such households an additional advantage over their poorer neighbours, increasing the growing stratification and socio-economic gap between larger and smaller landholders in rural Kenya. If the larger farmers are able to avoid theft of wood from their land, they are likely not to suffer environmental degradation on their land due to over-exploitation of wood, at least in the medium term.

Small farmer households, on the contrary, were not able to meet their needs from their own land in any of the 32 districts investigated. They had to direct their attention to biomass on other categories of land; common land, forest or neighbouring large farms. Case studies provided sufficient knowledge of the diversity and richness of social mechanisms by which these households secure access to biomass, that it was possible to translate a representative sample of such social relations into the mathematical language of

TABLE 16.4: VALUES FOR CONSUMPTION SIDE OF MATRIX

HOUSEHOLDS:

	Large Farm	Landless with no access	Small F. with no access	Small F. with acc. to common land	Small F. with acc. to forest	Landless with acc. to common land	Landless with acc. to forest	Farmers on occupied rangeland	Urban	Total
Kilifi	7000	1880	3900	23400	11700	11270	5640	4520	7440	76750
Kwale	5540	750	1540	12360	16990	5950	8180	380	560	52250
Lamu	750	600	1250	2500	420	1200	200	0	1750	8670
Taita	2170	5540	11500		610		290	9420	2180	31710
Tana River	1760	3560	7370	2460		1190		910	0	17250
Machakos	9570	5800	21730	32600	54330	8700	14510	21780	16920	185940
Kitui	3970	8410	31520	9010	4500	2400	1200	24210	1460	86680
Embu	1910	4640	17370		4340		1160	16460	4360	50240
Meru	8700	2640	9880		88900		23730	2510	14310	150670
Nyeri	3420	960	3260	6510	55340	1910	16240		10600	98240
Murang'a	4880	13650	46500		46500		13650		4070	129250
Kirinyaga	1960	6570	22390		14920		4380	1760	1750	53730
Kiambu	5000	11180	38120	4770	52420	1400	15380		14030	142300
Nyandarua	1550	0	0	29520		8660			3470	43200
Narok	5070	1960	2610	13010	1730	9800	1310	370	1900	37760
Kajiado	3700	8080	10740	1260	630	950	480	450	2280	28570
Nakuru	11640	0	0	29850	9950	22470	7490		33220	114620
Nandi	8130	3140	4170		23620		17770		700	57530
Kericho	16730	19380	25750	28610	2860	2150	21530		7830	124840
Elgeyo/Marakwet	2960	0	0	10120		7620		12960		33660
Baringo	5130	660	870	15790	880	11870	660	6010	870	42740
Trans-Nzoia	6070	7820	10390		10390		7820		6530	49020
Uashin-Gishu	6690	6890	9150		13730		10330		13430	60220
West Pokot	4010	2060	2740	10280	690	7740	520	1100	0	29140
Laikipia	3480	2240	2970	6540	2380	4920	1790	120	5850	30290
South Nyanza	9100	34930	178380	31480		6160			5310	265360
Kisii	6600	29780	152100						7850	196330
Kisumu	3010	13600	69490						37960	124060
Siaya	6070	20540	104930	34980		6850			1750	175120
Kakamega	9950	8330	82400		82400		8330		6660	198070
Bungoma	3620	4550	44980		14990		1520		9330	78990
Busia	2570	4310	42560						5670	55110

TABLE 16.5: RESIDUAL YIELD AND STOCK UNDER SCENARIO SATISFIED NEED

	Large Farms Residual Stock	Large Farms Residual Yield	Small Farms Residual Stock	Small Farms Residual Yield	Common Land Residual Stock	Common Land Residual Yield	Forest Residual Stock	Forest Residual Yield	Occ. Rangeland Residual Stock	Occ. Rangeland Residual Yield	Total Residual Stock	Total Residual Yield
Kilifi	100	90	100	0	100	35	100	41	100	84	100	67
Kwale	100	85	100	0	100	73	96	0	100	96	99	73
Lamu	100	98	100	0	100	12	100	46	—	—	100	94
Taita	100	0	100	0	—	—	81	0	100	52	99	25
Tana River	100	73	100	0	100	68	—	—	100	96	100	80
Machakos	100	30	100	0	87	0	69	0	100	73	97	46
Kitui	100	0	58	0	100	18	100	43	100	82	99	65
Embu	100	0	83	0	—	—	96	0	100	47	99	26
Meru	100	0	98	0	—	—	93	0	100	95	97	40
Nyeri	100	66	100	0	90	0	99	0	—	—	99	13
Murang'a	98	0	91	0	—	—	94	0	—	—	94	0
Kirinyaga	100	0	85	0	—	—	99	0	100	16	98	0
Klambu	100	0	88	0	25	0	96	0	—	—	93	0
Nyandarua	100	93	100	0	100	28	100	100	—	—	100	60
Narok	100	93	100	0	100	76	100	93	100	93	100	86
Kajiado	100	70	100	0	94	0	99	0	100	93	99	69
Nakuru	100	67	100	0	95	0	100	86	—	—	98	60
Nandi	100	48	100	0	—	—	97	0	—	—	98	28
Kericho	100	0	74	0	78	0	100	26	—	—	98	15
Elgeyo/Marakwet	100	63	100	0	100	39	100	100	93	0	99	72
Baringo	100	66	100	0	100	52	100	96	100	82	100	71
Trans-Nzoia	100	17	100	0	—	—	96	0	—	—	98	11
Uashin-Gishu	100	48	100	0	—	—	98	0	—	—	98	27
West Pokot	100	83	100	0	100	59	100	95	100	89	100	77
Laikipia	100	87	100	0	100	60	100	91	100	93	100	78
South Nyanza	100	0	49	0	76	0	—	—	—	—	91	0
Kisii	97	0	15	0	—	—	—	—	—	—	73	0
Kisumu	100	0	40	0	—	—	—	—	—	—	92	0
Siaya	100	0	39	0	80	0	—	—	—	—	84	0
Kakamega	100	0	68	0	—	—	90	0	—	—	89	0
Bungoma	100	0	73	0	—	—	100	3	—	—	98	2
Busia	100	0	51	0	—	—	—	—	—	—	90	0

flow mechanisms. While obviously distorting and insufficiently representing the richness of reality, kinship, theft, barter, sale, wages-in-kind, gift relationships and fringe benefits of rural employment were all taken into account in designing Tables 16.1 and 16.2. It is possible therefore to be reasonably confident that the poor person's energy crisis in Kenya is not being exaggerated, and nor are the resilience and social imagination of adaptation to the crisis. Of course, one should also not underestimate the very real costs of such adaptation. Whatever category of land they choose outside of their small farms, these households, in particular the women and children, must divert labour time from other important activities and/or cash in order to make use of these social mechanisms and continue the flow of woodfuel they need for daily cooking needs.[5]

TABLE 16.6: RESIDUAL YIELD AND RESIDUAL NEED UNDER SCENARIO SUSTAINED YIELD

District	RESIDUAL YIELD						RESIDUAL NEED									
	Large Farms	Small Farms	Common Land	Forest	Occ. Rangeland	Total	Large Farmers	Landless No Access	Small Farmers No Access	Small Farmers Common Land	Small Farmers Forest	Landless Common Land	Landless Forest	Farmers on Occ. Rangeland	Urban	Total
Kilifi	90	0	35	41	84	67	0									0
Kwale	85	0	73	0	96	73	0				50		58			25
Lamu	98	0	12	46		94	0									0
Taita	73	0		0	52	25	0				79		87		87	15
Tana River	30	0	68		96	80	0									0
Machakos	0	0		0	73	46	0	62	57	74	83	82	92	0	76	57
Kitui	0	0	18	43	82	65	0	41	34		37		43		43	26
Embu	0	0		0	47	26	0	20	18		54		61		61	26
Meru	66	0		0	95	40	0				21		25		18	50
Nyeri	0	0		0		13	0	77	55	61	44	73	61		61	23
Murang'a	0	0	0	0	16	0	0	53	44		15		19		19	52
Kirinyaga	0	0		0		0	0	61	52		59		70		67	31
Kiambu	0	0	0	0		0	0									59
Nyandarua	0	0	28	100		60	0			80		95				0
Narok	93	0	76	93	93	86	0									17
Kajiado	93	0	0	48	93	69	0			65	78	69	83		57	18
Nakuru	70	0	0	0		38	0			55	48	59	52		52	37
Nandi	48	0		1		28	0									14
Kericho	0	0	0	100		0	0	37	34	80		87				27
Elgeyo/Marakwet	63	0	39	96		72	0				53		57	72	57	0
Baringo	66	0	52	0	82	71	0									32
Trans-Nzoia	17	0		0		11	0									28
Uashin-Gishu	48	0		95		27	0									0
West Pokot	83	0	59	91	89	77	0				38		40		40	0
Laikipia	87	0	60		93	78	0									0
South Nyanza	0	0	0			0	0	57	53	81		87			87	57
Kisii	0	0				0	0	88	81						100	81
Kisumu	0	0	0			0	0	57	53						100	76
Siaya	0	0				0	0	78	72	78		84			84	72
Kakamega	0	0	0	0		0	0	85	77		69		76		76	70
Bungoma	0	0		3		2	0	47	43							23
Busia	0	0				0	0	66	60						100	66

Under these circumstances, a pressure toward over-exploitation of woody biomass on the land of smallholder households would be likely. At present, little is known about the management by women of hedgerows that separate these small plots in many parts of Kenya. The results reinforce other calls for the study of such agro-forestry practices (Fortmann and Rocheleau, 1985).

The situation of the landless varies from district to district. Results here suggest that some landless households are able to cover their fuel needs from the land of large farmers, usually those for whom they work as permanent or casual agricultural labourers. International recession, depression of the price of export crops, and the fiscal crisis mentioned at the beginning of this paper are likely to reduce flows of biomass to landless through this flow mechanism, as large farmers cut back on employment of landless. In other districts, the landless categories are thrown back on common land and forest, either through direct extraction or market purchase. They are particularly vulnerable to the present tendency to extend private ownership even into the bushland and rangeland land types (Campbell, 1981). As they have no legal rights, convention alone protects their access, and in a situation of very rapid social as well as economic change, their conventional rights can be easily eroded. They are also vulnerable to increased governmental vigilance in protecting gazetted forests, on the one hand, and to price speculation on woodfuel provided legally to such landless (as irrigation scheme members) by contractors who exploit some government forest areas under official supervision (Wisner, 1983). Landless is a category of household about which the case study data, insufficient and pushed to the limit of over-generalization at best, is particularly weak. Little is known about how the landless cope (Ghai et al., 1979). Further research with groups of landless on their situation is therefore an urgent priority. Already in such districts as Kiambu, Kajiado, Kericho, South Nyanza, and Siaya there is very little common land or forest left, a situation that must fall very heavily on the landless (Tables 16.3 and 16.6).

The urban population had their needs covered under both extreme scenarios. This mirrors the guarded acceptance of the widespread view that urban bias, an historical inheritance of Africa's colonial past, gives the urban classes more political visibility and voice as well as purchasing power in a situation of inequality of urban-rural terms of trade (Lipton, 1977; Sandbrook, 1982). The flow mechanisms built urban bias into the provision of woodfuel (as charcoal) since it was assumed:

1. that the rural poor, especially in the occupied rangeland, will continue to produce cheap charcoal as a cash crop because they have few other options, and

2. that the present economic crisis will not wipe out the purchasing power of vast numbers of marginally employed in the regional towns.

Both these assumptions are, in fact, open to question as the full depth of the economic crisis is as yet unclear, nor can one rule out rapidly accelerating desertification in the occupied rangelands, which would cut off charcoal provision. Results do suggest that already some districts must be importing charcoal from other districts in order to provide for their lower order urban centres. The most that can be safely said about the urban population at this time is that the urban question is urgent and should be further researched.

The Situation of Districts

Figure 16.3 is a composite of residual yield and residual need columns and rows from each district matrix. In the words of one Kenyan colleague, they map wood mountains and empty bowls in this particular cartographic representation (Juma, 1984). Several results are striking. The reader is referred back to Figure 16.1 for the identification of districts by name.

First, the surplus yield of woody biomass in the north is striking, although interpretation requires care. In the extreme north, technical and locational factors preclude access (Turkana, Marsabit, Wajir, Mandera Districts).[6] On the other hand, districts with surplus yield in the near north (Samburu, Baringo, Laikipia, Isiolo) already provide commercial charcoal to national markets, and there is discussion among planners concerning the desirability of formally defining some of these areas as commercial charcoal producing areas on a project basis (Winiger, 1985). Similarly, surplus biomass in the east (Kitui, Tana River, Garissa) has in the past provided considerable charcoal, even for international export to the Middle East, before the government moved in to control export.

The fact that Figure 16.3 shows both residual yield and residual need in Kwale District, neighbouring Mombasa, suggests the hypothesis that large-scale charcoal production for the Mombasa market is taking place alongside the unmet need of some small holder or landless groups. This may also be the case in Nakuru and Machakos, historically two districts that have provided the Nairobi market.

Large-scale irrigation settlement on the lower Tana River, where most of Kenya's unused irrigation potential lies, is bound to generate woodfuel need by the landless irrigation scheme participants. The very large Bura irrigation scheme, presently being implemented, only considered the domestic fuel needs of participants at a very

FIGURE 16.3: RESIDUAL YIELD AND RESIDUAL NEED, SUSTAINED YIELD

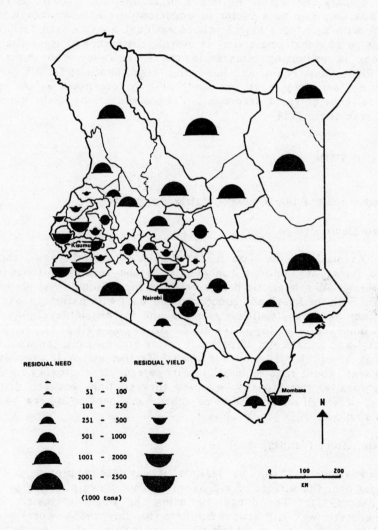

RESIDUAL NEED

	1 — 50
	51 — 100
	101 — 250
	251 — 500
	501 — 1000
	1001 — 2000
	2001 — 2500

(1000 tons)

RESIDUAL YIELD

N

0   100   200
KM

late stage of planning. Woodlots are being planted, but considerable local deforestation of the unique gallery forest along the Tana is also bound to take place (Hughes, 1983).

There are reports of increased charcoal production in Narok and Kajiado, although further research is needed to determine how much is going to Nairobi and how much to Kisumu and the deficit, high density districts of Western Kenya. Imports of charcoal from Uganda may also be a factor in understanding how Western Kenya copes with such very high levels of residual need. Given technical limits to charcoal production in Narok, distance and legal complications in exploiting biomass in the Rift Valley, the slopes of Mt. Elgon (West Pakot) and importing large quantities from Uganda, it is not surprising that Western Kenya is recognized as the most critical zone of rapid deforestation (stock reduction) in the country (O'Keefe et al., 1984).

DISCUSSION

Possible Uses of the Woodfuel Matrix Approach

Micro-Macro Bridge

As crude as the data is, the results already discussed should raise issues and options for debate in the fora of district-level planning. As a heuristic bridge between the national-level planners, armed with the LEAP and concerned above all with national financial solvency and urban political pressure, and the district-level planners, who must represent the needs of the district as well as the environmental and social costs of national policy and projects, the woodfuel matrix approach may find a niche. Effective use of the matrix in this way would require localizing its categories, improving its data base locally, and probably working through links between district flows of woodfuel and flows of other basic need satisfiers: water and staple foods.

Participatory Planning Tool

Participation can be real or it can easily provide a thin veneer over the surface of a conventional top-down planning process (Kruks, 1983). The danger of using the woodfuel matrix in a technocratic way will always be there (Bradley, 1985). Local people will invest the time in meaningful participation, refining categories in the matrix and gathering data, only when they recognize benefits for themselves. Other preconditions for participatory planning would include a local perception that there is a problem. As

Bradley (1985,) remarked: "The difficulty is to get the men to acknowledge that the women have a problem, and to be prepared to help them (or allow the women themselves) to do something about it". On the other hand, some sort of district-level planning is definitely underway in Kenya (Juma, 1984; Mutiso, 1985) and the involvement of non-governmental organizations in district planning committees may provide the opening required to represent basic need consequences of policy and projects in a more meaningful way. The process underway of preparing District Operational Master Plans for Rural Tree Development under Kenya's Ministry of Natural Resources might provide another concrete opportunity (Zimmermann, 1985).

Limitations of the Woodfuel Matrix

Problems with data have been mentioned frequently enough. It has been emphasized that on the ground they would be resolved by further refinements of categories, flow mechanisms, and more gathering of data. However, there are some conceptual lacunae that must be pointed out, and the elimination of which is probably a precondition to a future for the matrix approach.

Some early commentators on the approach have suggested that conditions can change very rapidly (Bradley, 1985) and certainly vary from season to season (Rölings, 1985). Others emphasized the extreme spatial variability of the flow mechanisms and of ecological productivity conditions (Bradley, 1985; Rocheleau, 1985; Ssennyonga, 1984; Whyte, 1985), some even suggesting the administrative location (much smaller than the district) as the more appropriate planning unit (Rocheleau, 1985).

Another difficult problem is a special case of the general theoretical problem of system closure in human ecology. Rural-urban, interdistrict, or international flows have not been dealt with at all adequately, even at the conceptual level (Porter, 1985; Sulzer, 1985; Whyte, 1985).

CONCLUSION

The fuelscape is not immediately perceptible as if it were a landscape. Rather this unseen landscape of class-stratified scarcity and abundance (Wisner, 1984) requires reflection and discussion in order to see it. Howes (1985a and 1985b) recently reviewed more than 150 rural energy studies, but found almost none that dealt with this socio-environmental aspect of the fuelscape. In other words, the matrix approach may fill a gap, despite its deficiencies. It represents a beginning. The final tool must, however, be developed by the people themselves in districts where they themselves define woodfuel as a major problem. Ssennyonga (1984) describes an old widow in Western Kenya asking a neighbour for the privilege of digging up the roots of a recently felled tree. At the other extreme, Hosier (1982) subtitles his recent study of domestic fuel use "Something to Buy Parafin With". Privatization, commercialization, and marginalization are three interrelated processes that have been at work in Kenya for at least 30 years (Wisner, 1984). The resulting energy crisis of the poor therefore presents very complex and variable aspects. Solutions are more likely to lie in the direction of equity and ecodevelopment (Sachs, 1984) than enrichment of progressive farmers through comparative advantage (World Bank, 1981) and growth (Clausen, 1985). Whether, under these circumstances, one can or should design a single methodology for providing a district diagnosis (Zimmermann, 1985) is doubtful. At best one can provide guidelines and open questions. The landless, small farmers, urban squatters, and widows will teach the rest.

NOTES

1. Kuni is Swahili for firewood.
2. From a formal point of view, this task is similar to the estimation of flows in interaction matrices using information theoretical methods (Schwartz, 1981; Wilson 1981).
3. Empirically established consumption does not necessarily establish need, but it was necessary to overlook this problem.
4. Of course, large farmers would be redefined in each district. Four ha is hardly a large holding in medium potential land. This very low threshold was adapted in order to focus on the basic needs of the very poorest smallholders in the country, those who have been by-passed by virtually all development efforts since Independence (Burrows, 1975; Ghai et al., 1979; Livingstone, 1981).
5. The dietary and social costs of not maintaining the flow of domestic energy is only just beginning to be documented, but certainly appears to be great. Where the main protein source is legumes, long simmering time is often necessary to make them digestible, especially by weanling children. Insufficient woodfuel can, therefore, directly provoke protein malnutrition (Cecelski, 1984; Wisner, 1983).
6. Small diameter of biomass is ill-suited to charcoal production (O'Keefe et al., 1984). Distance to markets are very great. High altitude in some cases (Mt. Marsabit) further complicates access. Also, biomass productivity coefficients for such land are less certain and could have been over-estimated.

REFERENCES

Antille, N., 1985, Bois de Chauffage au Kenya. Zürich: Institut de Géographie, ETH (Travail de diplome au department des sciences naturelles de l'EPFZ).

Barnes, C., J. Ensminger and P. O'Keefe (eds.), 1984, Wood, Energy, and Households: Perspectives on Rural Kenya. Uppsala: Scandinavian Institute of African Studies.

Bernard, F. and D. Thom, 1981, "Population Pressure and Human Carrying Capacity in Selected Locations of Machakos and Kitui Districts", Journal of Developing Areas, 15, pp. 381-406.

Bradley, P., 1985, "Kenya Woodfuel Development Programme", Letter commenting on Woodfuel Matrix Progress Report.

Brandão, C.R. (ed.), 1984, Repensando a Pesquisa Participante. São Paulo: Brasiliense.

Burrows, J., 1975, Kenya: Into the Second Decade. Baltimore: John Hopkins University Press.

Campbell, D.J., 1981, "Land-use Competition at the Margins of the Rangelands". In G. Norcliffe and T. Pinfold (eds.), Planning African Development. London: Croom Helm, pp. 39-61.

Cecelski, E., 1984, The Rural Energy Crisis, Women's Work and Family Welfare. Geneva: Working Papers, WEP 10/WP., 35, International Labour Office, World Employment Programme Research.

Chambers, R., 1983, Rural Development: Putting the Last First. London: Longman.

Clausen, A.W., 1985, Poverty in the Developing Countries - 1985. San Francisco: The Hunger Project Papers, No. 3, The Hunger Project.

Dubell, F., T. Erasmie and J. de Vries (eds.), 1981, Research for the People, Research by the People. Linköping: Report LiU-PEK-R-70, Department of Education, Linköping University.

Eckholm, E., 1976, Losing Ground. New York: Norton.

Eckholm, E., G. Foley, G. Barnard and L. Timberlake, 1984, Fuelwood: The Energy Crisis That Won't Go Away. London: Earthscan.

Epp, H., J. Agatsiva, N. Ochanda and D. Lantieri, 1983, "Applications of Remote Sensing in Earth Resources Monitoring in Kenya", ITC Journal, 2, pp. 148-153.

Fortmann, L. and D. Rocheleau, 1985, "Women and Agroforestry: Four Myths and Three Case Studies", Agroforestry Systems, 2, pp. 253-272.

Geiser, U. and M. Sommer, 1983, "Monitoring Deforestation in Sri Lanka Through Visual Interpretation of Landsat Imagery". In Proceedings of the Fourth Asian Conference on Remote Sensing. Colombo.

236

Ghai, D., M. Godfrey and F. Lisk (eds.), 1979, Planning for Basic Needs in Kenya. Geneva: International Labour Office.
GOK, 1970, Atlas of Kenya. Nairobi: Survey Department/Government Printer.
GOK, 1981a, Kenya Population Census. Nairobi: Central Bureau of Statistics/Government Printer.
GOK, 1981b, Integrated Rural Surveys 1976-1979. Nairobi: Central Bureau of Statistics/Government Printer.
GOK, 1982, Statistical Abstract 1982. Nairobi: Central Bureau of Statistics/Government Printer.
Greeley, M., 1985, Letter commenting on Woodfuel Matrix Progress Report, Institute of Development Studies at the University of Sussex.
Hosier, R., 1982, Something to Buy Parafin With: An Investigation into Domestic Energy Consumption in Rural Kenya. Worcester: Unpublished Ph.D. Thesis, Graduate School of Geography, Clark University.
Howes, M., 1985a, Review of Rural Energy Studies. Ottawa: Unpublished, International Development and Research Centre.
Howes, M., 1985b, Letter commenting on Woodfuel Matrix Progress Report, Institute of Development Studies at the University of Sussex.
Hughes, F., 1983, "Helping the World Conservation Strategy? Aid Agencies in Kenya", Area, 15 (3), pp. 177-184.
Juma, C., 1984, Personal communication, commenting on Woodfuel Matrix Preliminary Presentation, Zürich, Science Policy Research Unit, University of Sussex.
Kassam, Y. and K. Mustafa (eds.), 1982, Participatory Research: An Emerging Alternative Methodology in Social Science Research. New Delhi: Society for Participatory Research in Asia/African Adult Education Association.
Kruks, S., 1983, Notes on the Concept and Practice of Participation in the KWDP. Nairobi/Stockholm: Discussion Paper, Kenya Woodfuel Development Programme/Beijer Institute.
Kruks, S., B. Wisner and P. O'Keefe (eds.), 1987, Working On Wood With Women: Background and Further Studies of Rural Kenya. Uppsala: Scandinavian Institute of African Studies, forthcoming.
Lipton, M., 1977, Why Poor People Stay Poor. London: Temple Smith.
Livingstone, I., 1981, Rural Development, Employment and Incomes in Kenya. Report prepared for the International Labour Offices's Jobs and Skills Programme for Africa. Addis Ababa: International Labour Office/JASPA.
Mbithi, P. and C. Barnes, 1975, The Spontaneous Settlement Problem in Kenya. Kampala: East African Literature Bureau.

Miller, H., 1985, Letter commenting on Woodfuel Matrix Progress Report, Mennonite Central Committee, Nairobi.

Mutiso, G., 1985, Letter commenting on Woodfuel Matrix Progress Report, Mutiso Consultants Ltd., Nairobi.

Ojany, F. and R. Ogendo, 1973, Kenya: A Study in Physical and Human Geography. Nairobi: Longman.

O'Keefe, P., P. Raskin and S. Bernow, 1984, Energy and Development in Kenya: Opportunities and Constraints. Uppsala: Scandinavian Institute of African Studies.

Openshaw, K., n.d., Costs and Benefits of Proposed Tree Planting Programme for Satisfying Kenya's Wood Energy Requirements, Stockholm: Parts 1 and 2, The Beijer Institute.

Porter, P., 1979, Food and Development in the Semi-Arid Zone of East Africa. Syracuse: Maxwell School of Citizenship and Public Affairs, Syracuse University.

Porter, P., 1985, Letter commenting on Woodfuel Matrix Progress Report, Department of Geography, University of Minnesota.

Rocheleau, D., 1985, Letter commenting on Woodfuel Matrix Progress Report, International Council for Research in Agro-forestry, Nairobi.

Rölings, N., 1985, Letter commenting on Woodfuel Matrix Progress Report, Department of Extension Education, Wageningen Agricultural University.

Sachs, I., 1984, Développer les Champs de Planification. Paris: Université Cooperative Internationale.

Sachs, I., 1985, Letter commenting on Woodfuel Matrix Progress Report, International Center for Research on Environment and Development (CIRED), Paris.

Sandbrook, R., 1982, The Politics of Basic Needs: Urban Aspects of Assaulting Poverty in Africa. London: Heinemann.

Schwartz, R., 1981, Informationstheoretische Methoden. Schoning: Paderborn.

Ssennyonga, J., 1984, Personal communication, commenting on preliminary presentation of the Woodfuel Matrix, Institute of African Studies, Nairobi.

Sulzer, P., 1985, Die Brennholzmatrix. Zurich: Geographisches Institut ETHZ (Diplomarbeit).

Whyte, A., 1985, Letter commenting on Woodfuel Matrix Progress Report, United Nations Educational, Scientific and Cultural Organization, Division of Ecological Sciences.

Wilson, A., 1981, Geography and the Environment: Systems Analytical Methods. Chichester: John Wiley.

Winiger, M., 1985, Personal communication in discussion of the Woodfuel Matrix and Swissaid Work in Kenya, Institute of Geography, University of Bern.

Wisner, B., 1978, <u>The Human Ecology of Drought in Eastern Kenya</u>. Worcester: Unpublished Ph.D. Thesis, Graduate School of Geography, Clark University.

Wisner, B., 1983, <u>Energy and Self-Reliant Struggle in African Development</u>. Stockholm: The Beijer Institute.

Wisner, B., 1984, "Energy-Agriculture Conflicts and Complementarities in African Development: Experience with Method", Presented to International Seminar on Ecosystems, Energy and Food. Brasilia: National Scientific Research Council.

World Bank, 1981, <u>Accelerating Development in Sub-Saharan Africa: An Agenda for Action</u>. Washington, D.C.: World Bank/Oxford University Press.

Zimmermann, R., 1985, Letter commenting on Woodfuel Matrix Progress Report, Rural Forestry Advisor, Ministry of Natural Resources, Nairobi.

17

RATING AGRICULTURAL LAND: SOME NEW MEASURES OF IMPORTANCE

Mark Flaherty and Barry Smit

INTRODUCTION

A major land-use issue in both developed and developing nations is whether sufficient agricultural land will be available to meet future food needs (Beaubien and Tabacnik, 1977; Hopkins et al., 1982; Woods, 1981). This concern has arisen in the face of many factors, including the rising world demand for food, the conversion of agricultural land to urban and other nonagricultural uses, and growing scepticism over the ability to increase crop yields through the adoption of more intensive production strategies (Pimmentel and Pimmentel, 1980; Timmons, 1979). Many now argue that high quality agricultural land is a strategic resource and thus it is crucial that areas as large as possible be reserved for agriculture. Indeed, the preservation of agricultural land is now the focus of contemporary land policy in several nations including Japan (Cathelinaud, 1980), Egypt (Parker and Coyle, 1981), and the Netherlands (Miner and Chorich, 1979), as well as the United States and Canada (Bryant and Russwurm, 1982).

Although many agricultural land preservation policies have now been implemented, substantial disagreement continues to exist among investigators as to the severity of the land supply problem (Fischel, 1982; Lapping, 1980). One of the major factors fueling this controversy is the lack of a suitable procedure for assessing how important the existing stock of agricultural land is in meeting expected food needs. To date, farmland preservation advocates have relied upon land capability for agriculture and other land rating systems as a means of identifying important agricultural land areas. This paper briefly reviews the use of conventional land rating systems in rural land-use planning and presents some recently developed methods for rating the importance of land for agricultural use.

LAND RATING FOR AGRICULTURE

Land rating may be defined as the process of assigning classes, categories or values to areas of the earth's surface. In the recent past, considerable effort has been devoted to the design and application of a variety of land rating systems. This interest stems, in part, from a growing concern over the use of land resources and the expressed needs of policy makers and planners for better information about land-use opportunities (Bailey et al., 1978; Hoffman, 1976; Swinnerton, 1974). Conventional land rating systems identify homogeneous parcels of land and assess these parcels according to their potentials for an assumed use. Depending upon the use for which the rating is undertaken, the criteria for selecting and evaluating land characteristics may be highly varied. The specific information required to develop a rating of land for agriculture, for example, may be quite different from that needed to rate land for aggregate extraction, wildlife habitat, housing or other urban uses. Nevertheless, the fundamental principles for rating land parcels may be shared in all applications.

The common feature of all land rating systems is that they delimit areas that are of high quality for their respective uses. Most land rating schemes are based entirely upon the physical properties of land (Davidson, 1980). Although it is recognised that an understanding of the resource base is an essential component of land-use planning, the role of land rating systems in the design of land-use policy continues to be a source of disagreement (Dumanski et al., 1979; Flaherty and Smit, 1982; Smit, 1981). From a physical standpoint, particular parcels of land may be equally well-suited to several different uses (Langkamp, 1985). Although conventional land rating systems are convenient for summarizing the potential agricultural use of specific areas, they do not identify areas that are strategically important for agriculture. As a result, they are of limited utility, by themselves, in addressing the fundamental issue of whether agriculture should have priority over other land uses. In order to establish land-use priorities it is necessary to know how important it is that land be allocated to different uses. This concept of importance, rather than simply suitability, underlies much of the discussion of agricultural land rating (Orbell, 1977; Reganold and Singer, 1979). However, the concept of importance is used rather loosely in the land-use planning literature. For agricultural lands, importance seems to be related most commonly to the degree to which an area of land is critical for agricultural activities if the supply of certain products is to be maintained. Using this production-related concept, it is proposed here that the importance of land for a given use might be established on the basis of three criteria:

1. the suitability of the land for the given use,
2. demand for the use, and
3. opportunities elsewhere for satisfying the demand for the use.

These principles for assessing the importance of land for a given use can be readily illustrated by the controversy surrounding the use of specialty croplands such as the Niagara Fruit Belt in Ontario, Canada. Many argue that these lands represent a unique resource and should therefore be reserved for agriculture (see, for example, Krueger, 1977 and 1978). Uniqueness is related to criteria 1 and 3: the lands in question are well-suited to tender fruit production and there are few equally suitable areas for fruit production elsewhere in Canada. However, it might be questioned whether uniqueness alone is a sufficient basis for preserving these lands for agricultural use. Implicit in the argument advanced for preserving the Niagara Fruit Belt is the assumption that there is a demand or need for fruit to be grown in Canada. If there was no demand for fruit then it could be argued that despite their unique suitability, these lands are not important for fruit production.

Accepting the three criteria proposed for establishing the importance of land for a use is still only part of the issue. The question then arises as to how important is the land, taking into consideration the level of demand for fruit, the suitability of these lands for fruit production, and the extent to which the demand can be fulfilled elsewhere. Are there land areas that are critical in meeting the demands? How can this criticalness be measured?

LAND-USE CRITICALNESS MEASURES

The criteria which determine the extent to which particular types of land are of critical importance for agriculture can be represented by two sets of factors. One set consists of those factors that determine the level of demand for food, such as population growth and consumer tastes. The other set consists of factors that limit agriculture's capacity for responding to food needs as, for example, the area and productivity of the land base. A measure of criticalness is needed that would indicate whether there are land areas of critical importance for agriculture in the sense that the fulfillment of agricultural commodity demands hinges upon particular types and areas of land being available for food production.

The question of how important different types of land are in meeting specified crop needs, subject to constraints on such factors as crop productivity, energy use and land availability, is consistent with mathematical programming techniques. These methods have been widely applied in the analysis of resource allocation problems, as they provide a framework for identifying the conditions under which different levels of demand can be met and those under which a resource scarcity problem arises (Buckwell and Thompson, 1978; Heady and Nicol, 1976).

Conventional applications of mathematical programming techniques, however, have not directly investigated the issue of land-use criticalness as defined in this paper. For example, in their study of the impact of nonagricultural demands for land upon the capacity to produce food in the continental United States, Spaulding and Heady (1977) acknowledge that some land areas may be of critical concern from an agricultural perspective because of unique site characteristics. They note that the production of specialty crops cannot be readily relocated because of unique climatic requirements and that the loss of some agricultural areas to other uses could have a detrimental impact on production capacity. Nevertheless, their study does not provide information about how important these lands are in meeting given levels of demand.

The question of whether some resource allocations are especially important in meeting specified demands has only recently emerged as a concern in agricultural land-use programming studies (Smit, 1981; Smit et al., 1983). One of the more innovative approaches to the analysis of critical allocations is that developed by Chapman et al. (1984). They define criticalness in resource use as the degree to which the attainment of specified demands depends upon particular resource-use allocations, and suggest alternative interpretations and measures of criticalness within a linear programming framework. The general methodology seems well-suited to the problem of assessing the importance of assigning particular land areas to given agricultural uses in meeting specified demands. The remainder of this paper examines the analytical methods and properties of the measures, incorporates some recent technical improvements suggested by Flaherty et al. (1986), and indicates their interpretation in an agricultural land-use context.

To set the notation for the ensuing review of alternative measures of land-use criticalness, consider the following rudimentary set of constraints:

$$\sum_i a_{ij} \leq A_j \qquad (1 \leq j \leq m), \qquad (1)$$

$$\sum_j a_{ij} y_{ij} \geq Q_i \qquad (1 \leq i \leq n), \qquad (2)$$

$$a_{ij}, \, y_{ij} \geq 0, \qquad (3)$$

where A_j is the amount of land type j available,

Q_i is the amount of crop i required,
y_{ij} is the productivity of crop i on land type j,
a_{ij} is the amount of land of type j allocated to crop i.

The vectors $(a_{11}, ..., a_{mn})$ that satisfy the above constraints form a convex set in mn-dimensional space, commonly called the feasible region, which is denoted as R. Any number of constraints could be specified in a similar manner to reflect more accurately a given land-use system. The overriding considerations in specifying the number and form of the constraints are the nature of the land-use system being examined, and the particular research questions for which the set is developed. This simple constraint set is sufficient for investigating the properties of the measures, and for illustrating how alternative assumptions about future conversions of agricultural land to urban uses or changes in food production requirements could be incorporated into the analysis.

Depending upon the degree of aggregation of land uses, the importance of land in meeting given demands can be specified in different ways. One option is to rate the necessity of assigning individual crops to each land type so as to meet given crop demands. The second option is to specify a more general measure of criticalness by rating the importance of each land type in meeting a set of crop demands; that is to assess the criticalness of each land type for agriculture generally. Both types of measures are examined in the following sections.

ABSOLUTE MINIMUM ALLOCATION

An area of land can be considered to be of critical importance for a given crop if the attainment of specified crop production targets requires that a large proportion of it be allocated to that crop. One measure of the critical importance of a land type (j) for a given crop (i), then, is the smallest value of a_{ij} found in the entire feasible region R. This value is the area of land type j that must be allocated to crop i in order to satisfy the constraints. Expressing the absolute minimum value of each decision variable as a proportion of the total area of the respective land type available, this measure of land-use criticalness can be specified as:

$$C_{ij} = (\min a_{ij})/A_j. \tag{4}$$

This ratio provides a measure of requisiteness of particular crop assignments. A zero value indicates that it is not necessary to assign any of a given land type to a particular crop in order to satisfy the constraints. A non-zero value indicates the proportion of a particular land type that *must* be assigned to a given crop in order to satisfy the constraints. A value of 1.0, for example, indicates that the demands cannot be met unless all land of that type is allocated to the particular crop being considered. Thus the measures are specific to the i's and j's, have a known range (0.0-1.0), and are readily interpreted. Another appealing feature of this measure of criticalness is that it is additive over the crops. This means that a measure of importance for each land type in meeting the demand for all crops can be expressed as:

$$C_j = \sum_i C_{ij}, \tag{5}$$

where C_j is the proportion of land type j that must be available in order to meet the demands.

The minimum values for the set of decision variables are readily calculated via linear programming and are conceptually appealing as measures of land-use criticalness. Nevertheless, the interpretation of these measures requires some circumspection. One of the limitations of these measures of land-use criticalness is that the smallest value of each decision variable is identified without reference to the other decision variables in the model. Under some conditions a particular minimum allocation may hold only if one or more of the other decision variables are set at extreme values. For example, consider the case of two types of land and demand for one crop. This yields two decision variables. Assume that one option for meeting the demand is to allocate 100 per cent of Land Type A to the crop and none of Land Type B. Alternatively, the demand could be met by assigning 80 per cent of Land Type B to the crop and none of Land Type A. The value of the criticalness measure for both decision variables is 0.0, since, with the two alternatives available, it is not requisite that an area of either land type be assigned to production in order to meet demand. This value, however, takes no account of the fact that it is dependent upon a large allocation of the other land type to the crop. Thus, the sum of the minimum allocations may not satisfy the constraints. This means, then, that the absolute minimum value of each decision variable considered independently of the others may understate the importance of some crop assignments in meeting the demands. The following section examines a method of overcoming this problem.

CONDITIONAL MINIMUM ALLOCATION

An alternative approach to measuring how critical different types of land are in meeting the demand for specific crops is to identify minimum assignments for each decision variable that do not rely upon extreme values of other decision variables. Chapman et al. (1984) suggest that this can be done by determining the minimum value of each decision variable conditional upon the remaining decision variables being held at their average values. In a linear programming context, the average values of the decision variables, are given by the coordinates of a central point in the feasible region. A central point T in region R can be defined as:

$$T = (t_1, t_2, ..., t_{mn} \in R). \tag{6}$$

The general form of a conditional minimum allocation measure of criticalness can be expressed as:

$$C^*_{ij} = min [a_{ij}; (t_1, t_2, ..., a_{ij}, ..., t_{mn} \in R)]/A_j, \tag{7}$$

where C^*_{ij} is the proportion of land type j that must be allocated to crop i in order to satisfy the constraints, conditional on other decision variables being set at central values given by the coordinates of point T.

This measure is equivalent to setting all the decision variables, except the one of interest, to the value of the designated interior point (T). The smallest feasible value that the selected decision variable can assume while the others are held at their central values is then found. Geometrically, this corresponds to drawing a straight line through point T, parallel to the a_{ij} axis, and finding the lowest value for the point of intersection with the boundary of region R. The conditional minimum values of the decision variables can be found using a simple iterative process, often called the bisection method (Jamieson, 1983). Given a point A outside region R and a point B inside region R, the method undertakes to decrease the interval between these points by finding the midpoint $M = (A + B)/2$ of the line segment A, B. If M is inside region R, set B = M, otherwise set A = M. Apply the same process to the new line segment and repeat to the required accuracy.

A measure of criticalness calculated using the above noted procedure has a somewhat different interpretation than one based on the absolute minimum value of a decision variable. Rather than indicating how much of a given land type must be allocated to each crop in order to meet the demands, it identifies crop assignments that are important in meeting the demands. These measures are also additive over the crops, which provides a measure of importance for each land type in meeting the demands. That is:

$$C^*_j = \sum_i C^*_{ij}, \tag{8}$$

where C^*_j is the importance of land type j in meeting the demands conditional on the decision variables being held at their central values.

The minimum value that each decision variable can take when other decision variables are held at their average values is appealing as a measure of criticalness in land use as it takes into account the interdependence of the variables. This measure of criticalness, however, requires that a central point within the feasible region defined by a linear set of inequalities be found. Chapman et al. (1984) suggest two alternative central points, which they call the centroid and epicentre respectively, and present procedures for identifying both points. Flaherty et al. (1986) have identified several technical shortcomings in these procedures for finding the central points, and have defined a new central point called the average epicentre which overcomes the noted problems. It is this point that is used in the present analysis. A discussion of the technical problems associated with identifying a unique central point in the feasible region defined by a set of linear inequalities is provided by Flaherty et al. (1986).

EMPIRICAL ILLUSTRATION OF SELECTED
LAND-USE CRITICALNESS MEASURES

This paper uses a small hypothetical problem to illustrate the two measures of land-use criticalness. The set of constraints employed is represented by inequalities (1) to (3). The hypothetical problem consists of three types of land of varying productivity for four different crops. The numerical description of the problem is presented in Table 17.1. This table specifies the yields of each crop on each of the land types, two levels of demand for the different crops, and the amount of each type of land available. The analysis illustrates how the measures of criticalness could be used to assess the importance of particular crop allocations under alternative levels of demand, or as other conditions change, by reducing the amount of Land Type 2 available.

The first measure of land-use criticalness examined is based on the absolute minimum value of the decision variables. Table 17.2 presents the values of C_{ij} for each demand scenario and as the area of Land Type 2 is reduced.

In the base scenario (Land Type 2 = 5,000 ha) and given low demands, all the criticalness values are zero. Under these conditions, then, none of the three land types can be considered critically important for any one crop. Of course, some land would have to be assigned somewhere in the system to each of the crops in order to meet the demands. However, there is apparently sufficient crop

TABLE 17.1: LAND-USE SCENARIO DATA

CROP YIELDS (TONNES PER HECTARE)

	Land Type 1	Land Type 2	Land Type 3
Crop 1	12.1	7.0	0.0
Crop 2	9.8	8.1	4.9
Crop 3	8.0	5.8	3.6
Crop 4	2.7	2.5	1.0

CROP DEMANDS (TONNES)

	Crop 1	Crop 2	Crop 3	Crop 4
Low	2000	5000	7500	9000
High	7000	10000	12000	17000

LAND AVAILABILITY (HECTARES)

	Land Type 1	Land Type 2	Land Type 3
Base	2000	5000	12000

production capacity within the system so that it is not absolutely necessary that any particular allocation of crop to land type be non-zero.

As the area of Land Type 2 is decreased under the low demand scenario the criticalness values remain at zero until only 1,000 ha of Land Type 2 are available (Table 17.2). Under these conditions the criticalness value for Crop 4 on Land Type 3 (i.e., C_{43}) is .13, indicating that the demands cannot be met unless at least 13 per cent of Land Type 3 is devoted to Crop 4. Recall that in the example, the demand for Crop 4 is relatively high and that its productivity on each land type is relatively low (Table 17.1). Once all Land Type 2 is removed, C_{43} increases to .34, and C_{11} becomes .08. This latter result is explained by the fact that under the specified conditions Land Type 1 is the only land remaining for which Crop 1 has non-zero yields.

TABLE 17.2: CRITICALNESS MEASURES BASED ON ABSOLUTE MINIMUM VALUES OF DECISION VARIABLES

AREA OF LAND TYPE 2 (HECTARES)

	5000		4000		3000		2000		1000		0	
	L	H	L	H	L	H	L	H^1	L	H^1	L	H^1
C_{11}	.0	.0	.0	.0	.0	.0	.0	-	.0	-	.08	-
C_{21}	.0	.0	.0	.0	.0	.0	.0	-	.0	-	.0	-
C_{31}	.0	.0	.0	.0	.0	.0	.0	-	.0	-	.0	-
C_{41}	.0	.0	.0	.0	.0	.0	.0	-	.0	-	.0	-
C_{12}	.0	.0	.0	.0	.0	.0	.0	-	.0	-	-	-
C_{22}	.0	.0	.0	.0	.0	.0	.0	-	.0	-	-	-
C_{32}	.0	.0	.0	.0	.0	.0	.0	-	.0	-	-	-
C_{42}	.0	.0	.0	.02	.0	.62	.0	-	.0	-	-	-
C_{13}	.0	.0	.0	.0	.0	.0	.0	-	.0	-	.0	-
C_{23}	.0	.0	.0	.0	.0	.0	.0	-	.0	-	.0	-
C_{33}	.0	.0	.0	.0	.0	.0	.0	-	.0	-	.0	-
C_{43}	.0	.05	.0	.26	.0	.47	.0	-	.13	-	.34	-

[1] No feasible solution

Note: L = Low Demands
H = High Demands
Criticalness Measure: C_{ij} is the proportion of land type j that must be allocated to crop i in order to satisfy the constraints

Under high crop demand conditions (Table 17.2), the importance of the demand for Crop 4 in placing restrictions on the use of available land is again apparent. Even under the base scenario (Land Type 2 = 5,000 ha), C_{43} has a non-zero value. With the area of Land Type 2 reduced to 3,000 ha, C_{42} = .62 and C_{43} = .47, indicating that the opportunities for using Land Types 2 and 3 are quite limited if the demands are to be met. If the area of Land Type 2 is reduced to 2,000 ha under high demands, then the demands cannot be met under any allocation of crops. There is simply not enough land available to produce the specified target levels.

Under the high demand scenario with Land Type 2 set at 3,000 ha, it is intuitively obvious that the assignment of Crop 4 to Land Types 2 and 3 respectively are not the only crop allocations that are necessary if the set of demands are to be met. For example, substantial proportions of Land Types 1 or 2 must also be available for the production of Crop 1 so that the demand for this crop can be met. Yet this need is not indicated by the absolute-minimum allocation measure of land-use criticalness.

Table 17.3 presents the results using the conditional minimum measure of criticalness for the same scenarios used above. In the base scenario (with low crop demands), two crop assignments are identified as important. As the area of Land Type 2 is reduced, the value of C^*_{43} increases, the value of some other allocations become non-zero, and some values (including that of C^*_{42}) decrease. This apparent inconsistency of some values decreasing is explained by the fact that the measures are based on a central point in region R known as the average epicentre. As the area of Land Type 2 is reduced, which has the effect of reducing the size of region R, the coordinates of the average epicentre also change. That is, as the area of Land Type 2 is reduced, the face of region R corresponding to this constraint moves closer to the original central point which can no longer be considered central to the entire feasible region. Thus, in this example, the average epicentre shifts its location away from the approaching face which in turn affects the values of the criticalness measures. This example demonstrates the type of interdependence that exists in the land-use system. Whereas it may be tempting to expect the importance of Land Type 2 in meeting the demands to increase as its area is reduced, the criticalness measures indicate that Land Type 3 becomes increasingly important for Crop 4.

In the high crop demand scenarios, the demand for Crop 4 is again identified as a major factor affecting the importance of particular crop allocations. In the base scenario each land type is identified as important for Crop 4, and the values of the criticalness measures increase as the area of Land Type 2 is reduced.

Under the high demand scenario and Land Type 2 = 3,000 ha the highest criticalness value is C^*_{42}, with the other non-zero values, in descending order, being for C^*_{41}, C^*_{43}, C^*_{11}, C^*_{33}, and C^*_{23}. This measure gives quite different results from those associated with land productivity. Land Types 2 and 3 are not especially productive, nor are they the most limited in extent, and none of the areas is especially productive for Crop 4, yet it is Crop 4 which seems to restrict options most in meeting the full set of demands. By this measure, the allocation of Crop 4 to Land Types 2, 1 and 3 are as critical to meeting the demands as any other allocation. This approach to measuring criticalness demonstrates the need to consider production opportunities relative to demands. The approach does not yet yield a neat, readily interpretable value, but its heuristic contribution remains.

TABLE 17.3: CONDITIONAL MEASURES OF CRITICALNESS BASED ON AVERAGE EPICENTRE

	AREA OF LAND TYPE 2 (HECTARES)										
	5000		4000		3000		2000		1000		0
	L	H	L	H	L	H	L	H^1	L	H^1	L	H^1
C^*_{11}	.0	.23	.0	.26	.0	.28	.0	-	.03	-	.08	-
C^*_{21}	.0	.0	.0	.0	.0	.0	.0	-	.0	-	.02	-
C^*_{31}	.0	.0	.0	.0	.0	.0	.0	-	.10	-	.13	-
C^*_{41}	.0	.11	.0	.36	.0	.61	.0	-	.0	-	.09	-
C^*_{12}	.0	.0	.0	.0	.0	.0	.0	-	.0	-	-	-
C^*_{22}	.0	.0	.0	.0	.0	.0	.0	-	.0	-	-	-
C^*_{32}	.0	.0	.0	.0	.0	.0	.0	-	.0	-	-	-
C^*_{42}	.07	.03	.03	.81	.0	.92	.0	-	.0	-	-	-
C^*_{13}	.0	.0	.0	.0	.0	.0	.0	-	.0	-	.0	-
C^*_{23}	.0	.11	.0	.13	.0	.16	.0	-	.0	-	.02	-
C^*_{33}	.0	.21	.0	.24	.01	.27	.07	-	.06	-	.08	-
C^*_{43}	.44	.47	.51	.50	.57	.54	.60	-	.64	-	.66	-

[1] No feasible solution

Note: L = Low Demands
H = High Demands
Criticalness Measure: C^*_{ij} is the proportion of land type j that must be allocated to crop i in order to satisfy the constraints, conditional on other decision variables being set at central values given by the coordinates of the average epicentre

CONCLUSION

An important public issue today centres upon the adequacy of land to produce sufficient food in the future. This issue emanates from the awareness that there is enough uncertainty surrounding the many factors that affect land supply and productivity to warrant careful consideration of policies for the use of agricultural land. Land rating systems have been developed in many nations to provide policy makers and planners with information about the extent of the agricultural land base and its variability in terms of selected physical factors that affect productivity. This information about the supply of land of different degrees of suitability for agriculture is intended to provide direction for policy relating to lands which are important enough for agriculture to preserve for that use. However, the measures by themselves tend not to provide a means of identifying important agricultural lands. This paper has argued that in order to assess the importance of land for agricultural uses, the supply of land for agriculture must be related to the lands' productivities and to the level of demand for agricultural products. These principles provide a framework within which the degree to which particular areas or types of land are critically important for agriculture can be assessed.

The assessment of land-use criticalness subject to constraints on crop productivity, land availability, crop demand, energy use and so forth is consistent with mathematical programming techniques. While these methods have traditionally been used to analyze the conditions under which different levels of demand can be set, the issue of whether critical allocations exist in meeting specified demands has only recently attracted attention. This paper has outlined the need for such measures and has examined the interpretation of some proposed measures in a hypothetical agricultural land-use context.

The methods examined in this paper require that many complex factors affecting land productivity, supply and demand be considered. As in any model-based approach to problem solving, there are inevitably many trade-offs that must be made between the realism of the representation and the tractability of the resulting model. In applying the measures of land-use criticalness, a major task is to identify and quantify the major variables that delineate food production capacity. Perhaps one of the most formidable tasks is to anticipate the level of demand for food that is likely to develop in the future. However, any land rating system intended to contribute to land-use planning assumes, at least implicitly, something about the nature of demand or need for agricultural commodities. This is not simply an interesting factor which might be considered in rating the importance of land for agricultural uses, but rather it is a necessary precursor to the development of any useful rating scheme.

REFERENCES

Bailey, R., R. Pfister and J. Henderson, 1978, "Nature of Land and Resource Classification: A Review", Journal of Forestry, 76 (10), pp. 650-655.

Beaubien, C. and R. Tabacnik, 1977, People and Agricultural Land. Ottawa: Science Council of Canada.

Bryant, C. and L. Russwurm, 1982, "North American Farmland Protection Strategies in Retrospect", Geojournal, 6 (6), pp. 501-511.

Buckwell, A. and K. Thompson, 1978, "A Linear Programming Model of the Agricultural Sector of Great Britain", European Review of Agricultural Economics, 5 (3/4), pp. 313-324.

Cathelinaud, Y., 1980, "Land Constrained Economies: Some Answers from the Western European Countries and Japan". In Resource Constrained Economies: The North American Dilemma. Arkeny: Soil Conservation Society of America, pp. 37-46.

Chapman, G., B. Smit and W. Smith, 1984, "Flexibility and Criticality in Resource Use", Geographical Analysis, 16 (1), pp. 54-62.

Davidson, D., 1980, Soils and Land Use Planning. New York: Longman.

Dumanski, J., I. Marshall and E. Huffman, 1979, "Soil Capability Analysis for Regional Land-Use Planning - A Study of the Ottawa Urban Fringe", Canadian Journal of Soil Science, 59 (4), pp. 363-379.

Fischel, W., 1982, "The Urbanization of Agricultural Land: A Review of the National Agricultural Lands Study", Land Economics, 58 (2), pp. 236-259.

Flaherty, M., G. Chapman and B. Smit, 1986, "Land-Use Criticalness Measures Based on An Interior Point in a Convex Polytope", Unpublished manuscript. Guelph: Land Evaluation Group, University School of Rural Planning and Development, University of Guelph.

Flaherty, M. and B. Smit, 1982, "An Assessment of Land Classification Techniques in Planning for Agricultural Land Use", Journal of Environmental Management, 15 (3), pp. 332-333.

Heady, E. and K. Nicol, 1976, "Models of Agricultural Water, Land Use and the Environment". In R. Thrall, E. Heady, T. Schad, A. Schwartz and R. Thompson (eds.), Economic Modeling for Water Policy Evaluation. New York: North Holland, pp. 29-56.

Hoffman, D., 1976, "Soil Capability Analysis and Land Resource Development in Canada". In G. McBoyle and E. Summerville (eds.), Canada's Natural Environment: Essays in Applied Geography. Toronto: Methuen, pp. 140-167.

Hopkins, R., R. Paarlberg and M. Wallerstein, 1982, Food in the Global Arena. Toronto: Holt, Rinehart and Winston.

Jamieson, M., 1983, Elementary Numerical Methods. Toronto: Copp Clark Pitman.

Krueger, R., 1977, "The Preservation of Agricultural Land in Canada". In R. Krueger and B. Mitchell (eds.), Managing Canada's Renewable Resources. Toronto: Methuen, pp. 119-131.

Krueger, R., 1978, "Urbanization of the Niagara Fruit Belt", Canadian Geographer. 22 (3), pp. 179-184.

Langkamp, P., 1985, "Potential Conflict Between the Coal and Arable Land Resources in Australia: A Case for Corporate Responsiveness", Environmental Management, 9 (1), pp. 49-60.

Lapping, M., 1980, "Agricultural Land Retention: Responses, American and Foreign". In A. Woodruff (ed.), The Farm and The City. Englewood Cliffs: Prentice Hall, pp. 145-178.

Miner, D. and M. Chorich, 1979, "The European Experience with Farmland Protection: Some Inferences". In M. Schneph (ed.), Farmland, Food and the Future. Arkeny: Soil Conservation Society of America, pp. 203-209.

Orbell, G., 1977, "The Soil Parameter as a Tool in Regional Planning", Town Planning Quarterly, 47 (1), pp. 45-48.

Parker, J.B. and J.R. Coyle, 1981, Urbanization and Agricultural Policy in Egypt. Washington, D.C.: Foreign Agricultural Economic Report No. 169, Economic Research Service, International Economic Division, United States Department of Agriculture.

Pimmentel, D. and S. Pimmentel, 1980, "Ecological Aspects of Agricultural Policy", Natural Resources Journal, 20 (3), pp. 555-585.

Reganold, J. and M. Singer, 1979, "Defining Prime Farmland by Three Land Classification Systems", Journal of Soil and Water Conservation, 34 (2), pp. 172-176.

Smit, B., 1981, "Prime Land, Land Evaluation and Land Use Policy", Journal of Soil and Water Conservation, 36 (4), pp. 209-212.

Smit, B., S. Rodd, D. Bond, M. Brklacich, C. Cocklin and A. Dyer, 1983, "Implications for Food Production Potential of Future Urban Expansion in Ontario", Socio-Economic Planning Sciences, 17 (3), pp. 109-119.

Spaulding, B. and E. Heady, 1977, "Future Use of Agricultural Land for Nonagricultural Uses", Journal of Soil and Water Conservation, 32 (1), pp. 88-93.

Swinnerton, G., 1974, "Land Classification and Environmental Planning". In Land Capability Classification, Technical Bulletin No. 30, Ministry of Agriculture, Fisheries and Food. London: Her Majesty's Stationery Office, pp. 109-124.

Timmons, J., 1979, "Agricultural Land Retention and Conversion Issues: An Introduction". In M. Schneph (ed.), Farmland, Food and the Future. Arkeny: Soil Conservation Society of America, pp. 1-11.

Woods, R., 1981, Future Dimensions of World Food and Population. Boulder: Westview Press.

18

ASSESSING THE IMPACTS OF ACID RAIN ON REGIONAL AGRICULTURAL PRODUCTION IN ONTARIO

Laurie Ludlow and Barry Smit

INTRODUCTION

Acid rain is recognized as a serious pollution problem in many industrial areas of the world. In Ontario, and elsewhere, the effects on aquatic and forest ecosystems are well documented. Considerably less attention, however, is devoted to assessing the impacts of acid rain on agriculture, despite evidence that acid rain may affect the growth and yields of some crops. This paper provides an assessment of the possible implications of acid rain for regional agricultural production in Ontario.

Assessing the effects of acid rain on production requires information on both the levels of rain acidity in a region and on the amount by which current production may change in the region at the specified acid rain levels. In Ontario, the county level is chosen as the scale at which to assess the effects of acid rain on regional production. Data on agricultural production are available for each county, and rain acidities can easily be identified at this scale.

The paper describes the sources and current distribution patterns of acid rain in Ontario and the effects of acid rain on aquatic and terrestrial systems. The possible impacts on selected crop yields are discussed and estimates of the effects of acid rain on regional agricultural production are presented.

ACID RAIN IN ONTARIO

Acid rain results when pollutants such as sulphur dioxide (SO_2) and nitric oxides (NO_x) are emitted into the atmosphere from anthropogenic sources. Most sulphur dioxide emissions originate from non-ferrous smelting and from the combustion of fossil fuels, such as coal and oil, to produce electricity. Nitric oxides result primarily from power generation and from vehicle exhausts (Johnston and Finkle, 1983; Rhodes and Middleton, 1983). These emissions are chemically transformed in the atmosphere by hydrolysis and oxidation to form sulphuric and nitric acids, before returning to the earth in precipitation (Galloway and Likens, 1981; Ontario Ministry of the Environment [OME], 1981).

The regional transport of human-generated sulphur and nitrogen oxides over hundreds or even thousands of kilometres from their sources before returning to the earth as acids in precipitation is documented by several researchers (Heidorn, 1979; Lyons et al., 1978). These studies suggest that large quantities of sulphur and nitrogen pollutants are being carried by prevailing winds from the eastern United States to Ontario. Galloway and Whelpdale (1980), for example, calculated the sulphur budget for eastern North America and concluded that about half the anthropogenic sulphur in the atmosphere in eastern Canada originates from transboundary flow from the United States. The flux of sulphur in the opposite direction was calculated to be much smaller (by a factor of one-third) in comparison. Although the nitrogen budget for eastern North America is not documented, long range transport studies of individual storm events suggest that large quantities of nitrogen oxides may also be transported into Ontario from the United States (Heidorn, 1979; OME, 1981).

Human-generated sulphur dioxide and nitric oxides which contribute to acid precipitation in Ontario originate locally and are also transported by prevailing winds from the eastern United States. The major emitting areas of these pollutants in Ontario are located in the highly populated and industrial regions of the province - the London, Sudbury, Hamilton and Toronto areas, as well as the Niagara Peninsula (Johnston and Finkle, 1983; Memorandum of Intent on Transboundary Air Pollution [MOI] Work Group, 1983; OME, 1981). The major source areas in the eastern United States which contribute to acid precipitation in Ontario are in Michigan, Illinois, Indiana, and the Upper Ohio River Valley, where high sulphur coal is used to produce electricity with little or no control over emissions (Galloway and Whelpdale, 1980; MOI Work Group, 1983; OME, 1981).

A common measure of the acidity of a solution is pH. The pH scale ranges from 0 to 14, with a value of 7 representing a neutral solution, values below 7 indicating higher acidity and values above 7 indicating higher alkalinity. A pH of 5.6, which is the pH of distilled water in equilibrium with atmospheric carbon dioxide (CO_2), is generally accepted as a convenient reference value for unpolluted or pure precipitation (Altshuller and McBean, 1979; Coote et al., 1981; Likens et al., 1979; OME, 1981). Precipitation with pH values below 5.6 is considered to be abnormally acidic and termed acid precipitation.

There is evidence which suggests that precipitation falling in eastern North America prior to the Industrial Revolution generally had pH values greater than 5.0 (Langway et al., 1965; Likens et al., 1979; Matveev, 1970). By the 1950s evidence revealed that precipitation may have already become highly acidic (Cogbill and Likens, 1974; Junge and Gustafson, 1956), and it is believed by some that this acidity has been spreading and intensifying over eastern North America ever since (Cogbill, 1976; Likens, 1976; Likens et al., 1979). This increase in the acidity of precipitation corresponds with increased sulphur and nitrogen emissions (MOI Work Group, 1983; OME, 1981).

Recent concern about acid precipitation in North America has led to the establishment of sampling networks across Canada and the United States which regularly monitor the chemical composition and pH of precipitation. The Canadian federal government began operating a long-term nationwide program known as the Canadian Network for Sampling Precipitation (CANSAP) in 1976, while in the United States the National Acidic Deposition Program (NADP) was initiated in 1978. In addition, many provincial and state networks have been established. The most extensive network in Ontario, which began operating in 1981, is the Acidic Precipitation in Ontario Study (APIOS). These networks have begun to provide information on the range, extent and strength of acid precipitation in all regions of the United States and Canada.

Results from the monitoring activities reveal that highly acidic precipitation is prevalent over most of eastern North America. The highest precipitation acidities are centred over the New England and middle Atlantic states, and the provinces of Ontario and Quebec. Most of Ontario now receives average annual precipitation with pH less than 5.6 (OME, 1981). Monitoring activities have also shown that there are seasonal trends in precipitation acidities. In Ontario, sulphate, and to a lesser extent nitrate, concentrations in precipitation tend to be higher in the summer than in the winter, resulting in higher summer precipitation acidities. Some authors believe this is a function of the air masses which dominate the weather in the province (Bloxam et al., 1984; Raynor and Hayes, 1982). In the summer months, prevailing winds are generally from the south and carry pollutants from industrial areas in the United States into Ontario, while in the winter months unpolluted Arctic air frequently moves in from the north or northwest (Summers and Whelpdale, 1976).

Given that precipitation acidities vary seasonally and that the interest here is on implications for agricultural crops, pH values for the growing season, rather than average annual pH values, were used in the analyses. Utilizing average 1981 monthly rainfall pH values collected from the APIOS monthly sampling network, the current distribution pattern of acid rain over the growing season for Ontario has been identified (Figure 18.1). Figure 18.1 indicates that, generally speaking, the highest rain acidities occur in the southwest and southeast portion of Ontario (pH 3.98 to 4.05), while central Ontario experiences lower rain acidities (pH 4.07 to 4.19). Rain acidity also decreases toward the north. This distribution pattern is a reflection of both the industrial activity in Ontario and the prevailing wind patterns.

The pH values identified in Figure 18.1 represent the averages for the growing season. It must be realized that pH values as well as sulphate and nitrate concentrations also vary from storm to storm within the growing season. For example, daily precipitation pH values measured at Longswood, Ontario, near to the city of London, ranged from 3.32 to 4.54 during the 1982 growing season (OME, 1984).

EFFECTS OF ACID RAIN ON AQUATIC AND TERRESTRIAL SYSTEMS

In Ontario, acid precipitation has had adverse consequences for many ecological systems. Studies reveal that at present, approximately 150 lakes in the province do not support fish life and are classified as acid lakes, and many thousands more with valuable fish populations are in the early stages of acidification (Rutherford, 1985). These lakes are located in Northern Ontario in areas of Precambrian Shield rock and little soil cover, providing insufficient buffering capacity to neutralize even small amounts of acid (OME, 1980). As a result, the runoff water in these areas is acidic. In addition, runoff water contains high concentrations of toxic metals, such as aluminum and iron, which are released from the Precambrian rock upon contact with acids. Spring meltwater is the most acidic, contains the highest concentrations of toxic metals, and is consequently the most harmful to aquatic life (Altshuller and McBean, 1979; OME, 1981). Recently hatched fish spawn are the first to be destroyed upon contact with the spring meltwater. After many decades of exposure to acid runoff, a lake eventually becomes acidified to the extent that major disruption occurs to its entire biological community (OME, 1980).

It is not only aquatic systems in Ontario that are adversely affected by acid rain. Evidence suggests that the decrease in forest productivity that has been occurring over the last 20 to 30 years may also be attributable to acid rain (Crocker and Forster, 1985). For example, it has been shown that nutrients are leached and that toxic metals are mobilized in soils that have been exposed to long-term acid deposition (OME, 1980). These processes are believed to be one reason for the reductions in tree growth that

FIGURE 18.1: ACID RAIN IN SOUTHERN ONTARIO, 1981

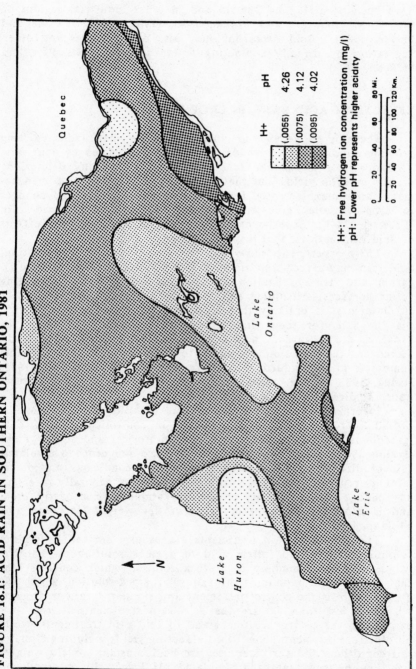

H+: Free hydrogen ion concentration (mg/l)
pH: Lower pH represents higher acidity

have been occurring in Ontario and in other industrial regions of the world (Johnston and Finkle, 1983; OME, 1980; Wetstone and Foster, 1983). Acid deposition may also damage trees and other vegetation by directly contacting foliar surfaces (Altshuller and McBean, 1979).

EFFECTS OF ACID RAIN ON CROP YIELDS

There is as yet no conclusive evidence that under existing growing conditions crop yields are adversely affected by acid rain. This does not mean that acid rain has not had any deleterious effects on crop yields, but that factors such as better crop management techniques, increased fertilizer and pesticide use, and changes in crop varieties may be offsetting the effects of acid rain (Forster, 1984). Experiments which attempt to isolate the effects of acid rain indicate that this may indeed be the case.

These experiments show that, like forests and other vegetation, acid rain may affect crop yields in two ways: indirectly by acidification and demineralization of soils, and directly by contacting foliar surfaces (Altshuller and McBean, 1979; Coote et al., 1981). In Ontario it is unlikely that crops will be affected by acid rain via the soils for some time since most agricultural soils in the province are calcareous and hence capable of neutralizing acids. Moreover, the addition of acids to soils by rain is negligible compared to that added through fertilization (Evans et al., 1981; Irving, 1983; McFee, 1980). For these reasons, this study focuses upon the direct effects of acid rain on crops.

Information on the direct effects of acid rain on crops is provided from experiments conducted in controlled environments (greenhouses, growth chambers and laboratories) and in the field (Irving, 1983). These experiments involve exposing crops to simulated rain of different pH levels, under monitored conditions, and determining crop yield response. Crop yield response generally refers to any change in the quantity of the marketable portion of the crop, and is expressed in terms of fresh or dry weight (Jacobson and Troiano, 1983).

The simulated rain treatments are usually derived by adding sulphuric acid and/or nitric acid to a stock solution of distilled water, or more commonly to a stock solution which contains ions that approximate unpolluted rainfall. This stock solution, which has a pH of 5.6, is the control treatment and simulated rain treatments with pHs less than 5.6 are the acid rain treatments. Crops are exposed to the control treatment and to acid rain treatments, while all other environmental conditions affecting yields including climate, soil conditions and fertilizer use, are held constant. Yield weights are then measured at each simulated pH level. By interpolating between these simulated rain pH levels it is possible to estimate yield weight over a wide range of pH values.

The experiments performed to develop these yield-pH relationships vary slightly in design (Evans and Thompson, 1984). The nature of the simulated rain event (e.g., droplet size, rate, number and duration of the event), chemical composition of the simulated rainfall, climatic conditions, and types of soil and fertilizer applications may vary from experiment to experiment. It has been suggested that these variations in experimental design do not limit the validity of the results, but fall within the range of conditions normally encountered (Jacobson, 1980). There are, however, some discrepancies between experimental and actual conditions that must be noted. One major discrepancy is that the chemical composition of the simulated rain events differs from the rain events occurring naturally; simulated rain tends to have higher concentrations of sulphuric and/or nitric acids than ambient rain. Furthermore, ambient rain pH levels and chemical composition are usually held the same in the experimental environment, while in nature rain pH and chemical composition may vary substantially from storm to storm. The effects on yield at a particular experimental pH may therefore differ from the effects on yield from ambient rain at the same average pH level.

Another discrepancy between experimental and actual conditions is often in the type of cultivar studied. Frequently, cultivars used in the experimental situation differ from cultivars grown in the particular area under consideration, in this case Ontario. Since it has been shown that crop cultivars within the same species may respond differently to acid rain (Forsline et al., 1983a and 1983b; Kuja and Enyedi, 1983), yield responses of one cultivar may not necessarily represent species response.

Despite these differences between experimental and actual conditions, the experiments provide a useful means of estimating yield-pH relationships since they isolate the effects of acid rain by controlling all other factors which may affect crop yields. Information provided by these experiments was reviewed in order to identify yield responses for 17 selected field, fruit and vegetable crops. Since many experiments have been performed, differing in design and approach and sometimes producing inconsistent results, criteria were needed for selecting the experiments which provide the most likely crop yield responses. The type of experimental approach adopted provided the initial criterion. When crop response data derived from field experiments were available, these were chosen in favour of those derived from controlled environmental experiments, regardless of the location of the field experiments. This is because field experiments are considered to be a more realistic means of estimating actual effects than controlled environmental experiments (Irving, 1983; Lee, 1982).

A further basis for distinguishing between experiments was whether simulated sulphuric-nitric acid rain treatments or sulphuric acid rain treatments were applied to crops. Since ambient rainfall in Ontario has sulphate-to-nitrate concentrations of about two-to-one (OME, 1981), simulated sulphuric-nitric acid rain, usually of about the same ratio, was assumed to be most like ambient rainfall, and chosen, where possible, ahead of other concentrations.

Finally, when available, yield responses were selected for cultivars grown in Ontario rather than in some other location. For example, McIntosh and Concord are the most produced apple and grape cultivars in Ontario, respectively. Since experimental information on these crop cultivars is available, this information was utilized in this research (Forsline et al., 1983a and 1983b). Where data were lacking, it was assumed that experimental results on any one cultivar were representative of species' response for other selected crops grown in Ontario. For those crops for which there have been no reported experiments, it was assumed that they respond to acid rain in the same manner as related crops for which data were available.

The experimental data on crop responses indicate that as simulated rain pH decreases from the control level of 5.6, yields of the selected crops exhibit one of the following responses (Figure 18.2):

a) no change in yield weight,
b) a steady decrease in yield weight,
c) an increase in yield weight until a threshold rain acidity level is reached, after which yields begin to decrease, or
d) a decrease in yield weight until a threshold rain acidity level is reached, after which yields begin to increase.

Barley, oats and wheat are reported to be resistant to acid rain by many researchers (Cohen et al., 1981; Evans et al., 1982; Harcourt and Farrar, 1980; Lee et al., 1981) and exhibit no change in yield weights as acid levels vary from the control treatment (Figure 18.2a). Alternatively, other experiments (Evans et al., 1984; Forsline et al., 1983a and 1983b) show that yields of crops such as soybeans and fruits (apples, grapes and peaches) steadily decrease as rain acidities increase (Figure 18.2b). Decreases in yields of these crops are attributed to the fact that acid rain alters the physiological processes of the crop and also interferes with the development and survival of the crop's reproductive systems (Evans et al., 1981; Proctor, 1983).

Crop yields may also be beneficially affected if nutrients found in the rain are absorbed by plant foliage in limited amounts (Jacobson, 1980 and 1984a). Since limited amounts of sulphur and nitrogen are essential to plant nutrition, it is reasoned that

FIGURE 18.2: CROP RESPONSES TO ACID RAIN

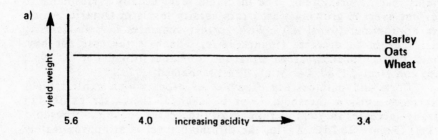

a) yield weight / increasing acidity → / 5.6 / 4.0 / 3.4 — Barley, Oats, Wheat

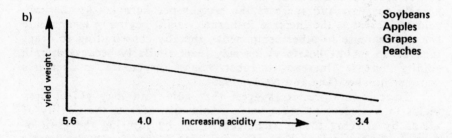

b) yield weight / increasing acidity → / 5.6 / 4.0 / 3.4 — Soybeans, Apples, Grapes, Peaches

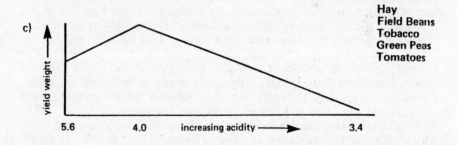

c) yield weight / increasing acidity → / 5.6 / 4.0 / 3.4 — Hay, Field Beans, Tobacco, Green Peas, Tomatoes

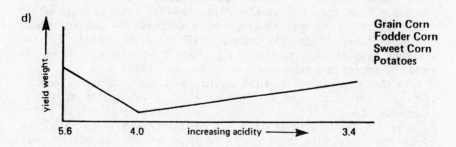

d) yield weight / increasing acidity → / 5.6 / 4.0 / 3.4 — Grain Corn, Fodder Corn, Sweet Corn, Potatoes

moderately acidic rain acts as a fertilizer stimulating the growth and yield of certain crops (Irving, 1983; Irving and Miller, 1981). As the acidity of the rainfall increases to the threshold level, crop yields reach a maximum. The threshold level usually corresponds to current average growing season rain acidity levels in Ontario, which are approximately pH 4.0. With further increases in rain acidity, yields begin to decrease (Figure 18.2c). Such is the case for hay, field beans, tobacco, green peas and tomatoes (Cohen et al. 1982; Lee and Neely, 1980; Lee et al., 1981; Mohamed, 1979).

Corn and potatoes are examples of crops which exhibit yield decreases until a threshold level is reached, thereafter exhibiting steady increases in yield as rain acidity increases above the threshold levels (Figure 18.2d). Again, the threshold level is at approximately pH 4.0. Lee (1982) notes that in the case of corn, acid rain tends to decrease the number of ears per plant, decrease the number of kernels per ear, and increase the weight per kernel. As the rain acidity increases, the increase in kernel weight begins to compensate for the decrease in other components, thereby contributing to a net increase in yield. Potato yields may react similarly because as rain acidity increases, increases in tuber weight compensate for decreases in tuber number (Lee and Neely, 1980).

Experimental results suggest that acid rain may affect crop yields in a variety of other ways. Acid rain affects the quality of yields by altering the nutrient content or by injuring the fruit of crops. Experiments show, for instance, that the carbohydrate and/or protein content of crops such as apples, soybeans and beans decreases as rain acidity increases (Ferenbaugh, 1976; Forsline et al., 1983a and 1983b; Proctor, 1983). Lesions on fruits such as apples and tomatoes caused by simulated rain are often severe enough to affect marketability (Forsline et al., 1983b; Lee et al., 1981; Proctor, 1983). Crop yields may also be affected indirectly by acid rain. Extensive foliar injury to apple trees is believed to affect yields by triggering an early ripening process which enhances red colouring of the fruit and causes premature fruit drop (Proctor, 1983). Acid rain may also inhibit or stimulate the growth of microorganisms which live on the surfaces of crops (Evans, 1982; Linthurst et al., 1982; Shriner, 1980), or remove commercially used fungicides and pesticides from crop foliage (Jacobson, 1984b). Such impacts affect yields indirectly by making crops more sensitive to disease, insects and other forms of gaseous pollutants (Evans et al., 1981). Finally, evidence suggests that acid rain may have long-term effects on the yields of apples and other perennials (Proctor, 1983).

Although changes in yield quality and the indirect effects of acid rain on yields are worth noting, it is impossible as yet to determine the extent to which they may change marketable yields. As a result, these impacts have not been included in the analyses, which deal only with the impacts on yield weights. Similarly, any

long-term cumulative effects incurred by the perennials have not
been included because they are also largely unknown. This research
focuses then on the effects acid rain may have on crops during a
single growing season.

ASSESSING THE EFFECTS OF ACID RAIN
ON REGIONAL AGRICULTURAL PRODUCTION

Several studies have estimated the impacts of air pollution
problems, including acid rain, on agricultural production, both at the
macro-scale (e.g., province, state or country) and at the farm level
(Adams et al., 1982; Brown and Smith, 1984; Forster, 1984;
Pearson, 1982). Studies at the macro-scale provide broad but
necessarily crude estimates of impacts since spatial variations in
the levels of pollution, as well as variations in crop response, are
not considered. Studies at the farm level, on the other hand, have
the advantage in that they allow for variations in crop choice and
in the levels of pollution, but it is difficult to aggregate impacts in
these studies over larger spatial areas, such as the province. The
approach adopted here is similar to those employed in other macro-
scale studies, but allows for spatial variations and the variations in
crop responses noted in the previous section.

Assessing the effects of acid rain on regional agricultural
production required that the rain pH for each county be identified
and the impacts of acid rain on crop yields at these pH levels be
estimated. The average growing season rain pH values for 1981
were determined from Figure 18.1, and range from pH 4.00 to 4.46
across Southern Ontario. Experimental data were used to identify
yield response estimates for selected crops at these pH levels.
Since pH 5.6 is assumed to represent the acidity level of unpolluted
rain, yield response estimates were determined assuming that rain
pH changed from current levels to a pH of 5.6. In other words,
yield response estimates indicate the amount crop yields might
change if acid pollutants no longer affected rain pH.

The range of response estimates that might be expected across
Southern Ontario if acid pollution is eliminated are presented in
Table 18.1. They indicate the proportion by which yields for a
specific crop differ from those currently achieved. A negative
value indicates the proportion by which yields are expected to
decrease from current yields, while a positive value indicates that
crop yields are expected to increase. For example, crops such as
grain corn and fodder corn would exhibit the largest proportional
increases in yields. These increases range from .030 to .099 (or
from 3.0 to 9.9 per cent). Conversely, crops such as hay and
tobacco would exhibit proportional decreases in yields, if rain was
unpolluted, of .013 to .036 and .010 to .029, respectively.

TABLE 18.1: YIELD RESPONSES OF SELECTED CROPS IN SOUTHERN ONTARIO

CROPS	YIELD RESPONSES (if rain was unpolluted by acids)
FIELD	
Barley	0
Field Beans	−.025 to −.069
Fodder Corn	+.030 to +.099
Grain Corn	+.030 to +.099
Hay	−.013 to −.036
Mixed Grain	0
Oats	0
Potatoes	+.011 to +.031
Soybeans	+.016 to +.038
Tobacco	−.010 to −.029
Winter Wheat	0
FRUIT	
Apples	+.004 to +.012
Grapes	+.001 to +.004
Peaches	+.004 to +.012
VEGETABLE	
Green Peas	−.025 to −.069
Sweet Corn	+.030 to +.099
Tomatoes	−.024 to −.065

Note: − indicates a decrease
+ indicates an increase

The response estimates presented in Table 18.1 may also be interpreted as indicators of the degree to which crop yields are currently affected by acid rain, since all other factors which affect yields are held constant. Grain corn and fodder corn, for example, are not presently achieving the yield levels which they might if it was not for acid rain; these crops are among those most adversely affected at current acid rain levels. Tobacco and hay, on the other hand, are actually benefitting from acid rain at current levels.

Crops affected by acid rain exhibit a similar spatial pattern of yield response across the counties in Southern Ontario, but the magnitude and direction of the response varies. This spatial pattern of crop response reflects the present rain pH pattern. Grain corn and fodder corn, for example, would show the greatest proportional increases in yields in the counties which currently experience the highest rain acidity levels, and would exhibit the smallest proportional increases in those counties currently experiencing lower rain acidities. Hay and tobacco would show the largest proportional decreases in yields in counties with the highest current rain acidities and the smallest proportional yield decreases in the counties with lower current rain acidities. Alternatively, the greatest losses in corn yields are presently occurring in counties in the southwest, while at the same time these counties are experiencing the greatest increases in tobacco and hay yields.

Not only may the crop response estimates presented in Table 18.1 be interpreted as the proportion by which yields would change from those currently achieved across Ontario if rain was unpolluted; they may also represent the extent to which production would change assuming land-use patterns, inputs, and other factors remain constant. In order to estimate the changes in production attributable to acid rain, these estimates may be applied to the present production levels of each crop in each county (Ludlow, 1986). Effects on levels of production are then a function of both yield response, which varies spatially, and the pattern of production of the specific crop under consideration. These possible effects on regional production, if acid pollution was eliminated are described for selected crops by Ludlow (1986), and form the basis of the assessment of effects on overall crop production.

To estimate the effects of acid rain on total combined production requires that production values be in comparable units, so they can be summed. This was achieved by estimating changes in total farm value of production (in 1981 dollars), rather than using tonnes of production. Estimates of the changes in value of production of each crop in each county were then calculated and summed, and expressed as a proportion of total farm value of production in each county to provide measures of the regional impacts expected if acid pollution was eliminated:

$$\nabla V_j = \sum_i \Delta P_{ij} \frac{v_{ij_2}}{V_j} \tag{1}$$

where ∇V_j is the proportional change in farm value of production of all selected crops in county j expected if acid pollution was eliminated,

ΔP_{ij} is the change in production of crop i in county j if acid pollution was eliminated,

v_{ij} is the current (1981) farm value per unit weight of crop i in county j,

V_j is the current (1981) farm value of production of all selected crops combined in county j.

These regional impacts for total agricultural production are illustrated in Figure 18.3. The magnitude and direction of the proportional change is dependent upon the mix of crops grown in the county and their various responses to the specified acid rain levels. To facilitate comparisons between the pattern of proportional changes and the pattern of current total farm value of production, the current (1981) total farm value estimates of all 17 crops combined (V_js) were also mapped.

The map shows that if rain was unpolluted by acids, most counties would exhibit increases in total farm value of production. The greatest increases would generally occur in counties of the south and southwest parts of the province, which is also the region with the greatest farm value of production. A notable exception is Haldimand-Norfolk County (located in south-central Ontario), which displays a relatively large decrease in total farm value of production. This decrease reflects the fact that Haldimand-Norfolk is the largest tobacco producing county in Ontario, and tobacco yields would decrease if rain was unpolluted (Table 18.1). Tobacco also has the highest farm value per unit weight of all selected crops (Ontario Ministry of Agriculture and Food [OMAF], 1982). A number of counties located in south-central Ontario would also exhibit decreases in total farm value of production, but these are negligible compared to that estimated for Haldimand-Norfolk.

Reciprocally, these results indicate that counties in the south and southwest are incurring losses in total farm value of production at current levels of acid rain. In other words, in terms of current total farm value of production, these counties are the most sensitive to acid rain. Again, Haldimand-Norfolk County is an exception; the current total farm value of production in Haldimand-Norfolk is actually higher than would be expected if there was no acid rain because of the high level of tobacco production.

Finally, the impacts of acid rain on provincial production have been estimated for each crop in terms of both tonnes and dollar value. These values are presented in Table 18.2. Positive values indicate that crop production would increase from current levels if there was no acid rain and negative values indicate that production would decrease. For example, increases in provincial grain corn production of 420,000 tonnes (47 million dollars) annually and soybean production of 23,000 tonnes (6 million dollars) annually

FIGURE 18.3: IMPACTS OF ACID RAIN ON REGIONAL PRODUCTION

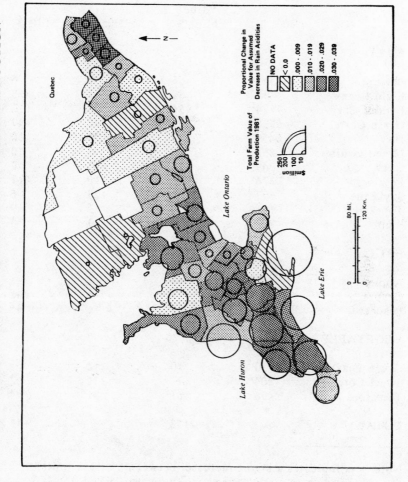

**TABLE 18.2: CHANGE IN PRODUCTION AND FARM
VALUE OF PRODUCTION OF SELECTED
CROPS IN SOUTHERN ONTARIO**

CROPS	1981		IF RAIN WAS UNPOLLUTED BY ACIDS	
	Total Production	Total Farm Value	Change in Production	Change in Farm Value
	000s T	Mills $	000s T	Mills $
FIELD				
Barley	545	66	0	6
Field Beans	94	64	−5	−3
Fodder Corn	7724	154	+605	+12
Grain Corn	5232	591	+420	+47
Hay	6459	325	190	10
Mixed Grain	854	106	0	0
Oats	209	28	0	0
Potatoes	376	51	+10	+1
Soybeans	607	160	+23	+6
Tobacco	101	338	−3	−9
Winter Wheat	702	102	0	0
FRUIT				
Apples	136	43	+1	+s
Grapes	62	23	+s	+s
Peaches	18	11	+s	+s
VEGETABLE				
Green Peas	30	10	−2	−s
Sweet Corn	204	20	+16	+2
Tomatoes	496	61	−31	−4
TOTAL		2153		+43

Note: +s indicates a slight increase (between 0 and .5 units)
       -s indicates a slight decrease (between -.5 and 0 units)
       Totals may not agree due to rounding

would be expected if rain was not polluted by acids. Conversely, the provincial production of tobacco would be expected to decrease by 3,000 tonnes (9 million dollars) annually.

By summing over both crops and counties, a measure of change in provincial farm value of production for all crops combined was obtained (Table 18.2). It was estimated that in the absence of acid rain, the total provincial farm value of production of all selected crops combined would increase above the current annual level (of about 2 billion dollars) by approximately 43 million dollars. This increase is attributed to the large increase in total provincial farm value of grain corn. This result may also be interpreted another way: at current rain pH levels the province is incurring a loss in total farm value of production of 43 million dollars annually.

CONCLUSIONS

In Ontario, acid rain has had adverse effects on aquatic systems and perhaps on forest ecosystems. Evidence also suggests that acid rain may damage the growth and yields of many of the major field, fruit, and vegetable crops grown. This paper has provided an assessment of the possible implications of acid rain for regional agricultural production in the province.

The results of this study reveal that acid rain has a differential effect, with the production of some crops increasing and some decreasing, while others are unaffected by acid rain. The impacts of acid rain vary regionally across the province as well. In terms of total agricultural production, findings indicate that if rain was unpolluted by acids, the province could expect an increase in production of more than 43 million dollars annually. Alternatively, at present acid rain levels the province is incurring a 43 million dollar loss annually in agricultural production.

By itself, an annual loss of 43 million dollars in agricultural production is hardly significant, representing only about a 2 per cent loss in total provincial farm value of production. Of course, on a crop-by-crop and regional basis impacts are more pronounced. In addition, other effects of acid rain on crop yields, such as long-term effects incurred by perrennials, indirect impacts and changes in yield quality have not been addressed here due to lack of available data.

It must be stressed that the numerical results presented in this paper must be treated with caution, and that they represent only rough estimates of the impacts of acid rain on production. This is because, although yield responses derived from experiments represent the best information to date on the effects of acid rain on crop yields, these data are far from ideal. Further research is needed in order to provide better estimates of the effects of acid rain on crop yields. As these data become available they can easily be accommodated in the method described in this paper.

ACKNOWLEDGMENTS

The authors gratefully acknowledge the support and assistance of the Land Evaluation Group at the University of Guelph, the Land Resource Research Centre of Agriculture Canada, the Ontario Ministry of Agriculture and Food, Chris Cocklin and Marie Puddister.

This paper is based in part on the article "Assessing the Implications of Environmental Change for Agricultural Production: The Case of Acid Rain in Ontario, Canada", in Journal of Environmental Management, forthcoming 1987.

REFERENCES

Adams, R., T. Crocker and N. Thanavibulchai, 1982, "An Economic Assessment of Air Pollution Damages to Selected Annual Crops in Southern California", Journal of Environmental Economics and Management, 9, pp. 42-58.

Altshuller, A. and G. McBean, 1979, The LRTAP Problem in North America: A Preliminary Overview. United States-Canada Research Consultation Group on the Long-Range Transport of Air Pollutants.

Bloxam, R., J. Hornbeck and C. Martin, 1984, "The Influence of Storm Characteristics on Sulfate in Precipitation", Water, Air, and Soil Pollution, 23, pp. 359-374.

Brown, D. and M. Smith, 1984, "Crop Substitution in the Estimation of Economic Benefits Due to Ozone Reduction", Journal of Environmental Economics and Management, 11, pp. 347-362.

Cogbill, C., 1976, "The History and Character of Acid Precipitation in Eastern North America", Water, Air, and Soil Pollution, 6, pp. 407-413.

Cogbill, C. and G. Likens, 1974, "Acid Precipitation in the Northeastern United States", Water Resources Research, 10, pp. 1133-1137.

Cohen, C., L. Grothaus and S. Perrigan, 1981, "Effects of Simulated Sulfuric Acid Rain on Crop Plants". Corvallis: Special Report 619, Agricultural Experimental Station, Oregon State University.

Cohen, C., L. Grothaus and S. Perrigan, 1982, "Effects of Simulated Sulfuric and Sulfuric-Nitric Acid Rain on Crop Plants: Results

273

of 1980 Crop Survey". Corvallis: Special Report 670, Agricultural Experiment Station, Oregon State University.

Coote, D., D. Siminovitch, S. Shah and C. Wang, 1981, The Significance of the Acid Rain Problem to Agriculture in Eastern Canada. Ottawa: Research Branch, Agriculture Canada.

Crocker, T. and B. Forster, 1985, "Some Economic Implications of Alternative Biological and Chemical Explanations of the Impacts of Acidic Deposition on Forest Ecosystems", Presented at the International Symposium on Acidic Precipitation, Muskoka.

Evans, L., 1982, "Biological Effects of Acidity in Precipitation on Vegetation: A Review", Environmental and Experimental Botany, 22 (2), pp. 155-169.

Evans, L. and K. Thompson, 1984, "Comparison of Experimental Designs Used to Detect Changes in Yields of Crops Exposed to Acidic Precipitation", Agronomy Journal, 76, pp. 81-84.

Evans, L., K. Lewin and M. Patti, 1984, "Effects of Simulated Acidic Rain on Yields of Field-Grown Soybeans", New Phytologist, 96, pp. 207-213.

Evans, L., N. Gmur and D. Mancini, 1982, "Effects of Simulated Acidic Rain on Yields of Raphanus Sativus, Lactuca Sativa, Triticum Aestivum and Medicago Sativa", Environmental and Experimental Botany, 22 (4), pp. 445-453.

Evans, L., K. Lewin, C. Conway and M. Patti, 1981, "Seed Yields (Quantity and Quality) of Field-Grown Soybeans Exposed to Simulated Acid Rain", New Phytologist, 89, pp. 459-470.

Ferenbaugh, R., 1976, "Effects of Simulated Acid Rain on Phaseolus Vulgaris L. (Fabaceae)", American Journal of Botany, 63 (3), pp. 283-288.

Forsline, P., R. Musselman, R. Dee, and W. Kender, 1983a, "Effects of Acid Rain on Grapevines", American Journal of Enology and Viticulture, 34 (1), pp. 17-22.

Forsline, P., R. Musselman, W. Kender and R. Dee, 1983b, "Effects of Acid Rain on Apple Tree Productivity and Fruit Quality", Journal of the American Society of Horticultural Science, 108 (1), pp. 70-74.

Forster, B., 1984, "An Economic Assessment of the Significance of Long-Range Transported Air Pollutants for Agriculture in Eastern Canada", Canadian Journal of Agricultural Economics, 32, pp. 498-525.

Galloway, J. and G. Likens, 1981, "Acid Precipitation: The Importance of Nitric Acid", Atmospheric Environment, 15 (6), pp. 1081-1085.

Galloway, J. and D. Whelpdale, 1980, "An Atmospheric Sulfur Budget for Eastern North America", Atmospheric Environment, 14, pp. 409-417.

Harcourt, S. and J. Farrar, 1980, "Some Effects of Simulated Acid Rain on the Growth of Barley and Radish", Environmental

Pollution (Series A), 22, pp. 69-73.

Heidorn, K., 1979, "Synoptic Weather Patterns Associated with Nitrates in Suspended Particulate in Southern Ontario", Water, Air, and Soil Pollution, 11, pp. 225-235.

Irving, P., 1983, "Acidic Precipitation Effects on Crops: A Review and Analysis of Research", Journal of Environmental Quality, 12 (4), pp. 442-453.

Irving, P. and J. Miller, 1981, "Productivity of Field-Grown Soybeans Exposed to Acid Rain and Sulphur Dioxide Alone and in Combination", Journal of Environmental Quality, 10 (4), pp. 473-478.

Jacobson, J., 1980, "The Influence of Rainfall Composition on the Yield and Quality of Agricultural Crops". In D. Drablos and A. Tollan (eds.), Ecological Impact of Acid Precipitation, Proceedings of an International Conference, Sandefjord, Norway, pp. 41-46.

Jacobson, J., 1984a, "Effects of Acidic Aerosol, Fog, Mist and Rain on Crops and Trees", Philosophical Transactions of the Royal Society of London B, 305, pp. 327-338.

Jacobson, J., 1984b, Personal communication. Boyce Thompson Institute for Plant Research, Ithaca, New York.

Jacobson, J. and J. Troiano, 1983, "Dose-Response Functions for Effects of Acidic Precipitation on Vegetation", Water Quality Bulletin, 8 (2), pp. 67-71.

Johnston, D. and M. Finkle, 1983, Acid Precipitation in North America: The Case for Transboundary Cooperation, Canadian Institute of Resources Law.

Junge, C. and P. Gustafson, 1956, "Precipitation Sampling for Chemical Analysis", Bulletin of the American Meteorology Society, 37, pp. 244-245.

Kuja, A. and A. Enyedi, 1983, "Effect of Simulated Acid Rain on Agricultural Crops", Proceedings of Agrometeorological Workshop on the Role of Long Range Transport and Weather in Agriculture, Arboretum Centre, University of Guelph.

Langway, C., H. Oeschger, B. Alder, and B. Renaud, 1965, "Sampling Polar Ice for Radiocarbon Dating", Nature, 206, pp. 500-501.

Lee, J., 1982, "The Effects of Acid Precipitation on Crops". In F. D'Itri (ed.), Acid Precipitation: Effects on Ecological Systems. Michigan: Ann Arbor Science Publishers, pp. 453-468.

Lee, J. and G. Neely, 1980, "CERL-OSU Acid Rain Crop Study Progress Report". Corvallis: Air Pollution Effects Branch, Environmental Research Lab.

Lee, J., G. Neely, S. Perrigan, and L. Grothaus, 1981, "Effect of Simulated Sulfuric Acid Rain on Yield, Growth and Foliar Injury of Several Crops", Environmental and Experimental Botany, 21 (2), pp. 171-185.

Likens, G., 1976, "Acid Precipitation", Chemistry and Engineering News, 54, pp. 29-44.

Likens, G., R. Wright, J. Galloway and T. Butler, 1979, "Acid Rain", Scientific America, 241, pp. 43-51.

Linthurst, R., J. Baker and A. Barthuska, 1982, "Effects of Acidic Deposition: A Brief Review". In E. Frederick (ed.), Proceedings of Atmospheric Deposition Specialty Conference, pp. 82-113.

Ludlow, L., 1986, "Assessing the Implications of Acid Rain for Regional Agricultural Production in Ontario". Guelph: M.A. Thesis, Department of Geography, University of Guelph.

Lyons, W., J. Dooley and K. Whitby, 1978, "Satellite Detection of Long-Range Pollution Transport and Sulphate Aerosol Hazes", Atmospheric Environment, 12, pp. 621-631.

McFee, W., 1980, "Effects of Atmospheric Pollutants on Soils". In T. Toribara, M. Miller and P. Morrow (eds.), Polluted Rain. New York: Plenum Press, pp. 307-323.

Matveev, A., 1970, "Chemical Hydrology of Regions of East Antarctica", Journal of Geophysical Resources, 75, pp. 3686-3690.

Mohamed, M., 1979, "Response of Vegetable Crops to Acid Rain Under Field and Simulated Conditions". New York: PhD. Dissertation, Cornell University.

MOI Work Group, 1983, Memorandum of Intent on Transboundary Air Pollution (United States-Canada), Executive Summaries Work Group Reports, Submitted to the Coordinating Committee in fulfillment of the requirements of the Memorandum of Intent on Transboundary Air Pollution signed by Canada and the United States on August 5, 1980.

OMAF, 1982, Agricultural Statistics for Ontario. Toronto: Ontario Ministry of Agriculture and Food.

OME, 1980, The Case Against the Rain, A Report on Acidic Precipitation and Ontario Programs for Remedial Action. Toronto: Ontario Ministry of the Environment.

OME, 1981, "A Submission to the United States Environmental Protection Agency on Interstate Pollution Abatement by the Province of Ontario". Toronto: Docket No. A-81-09, Ontario Ministry of the Environment.

OME, 1984, Acidic Precipitation in Ontario Study Precipitation Concentration and Wet Deposition Fields of Pollutants in Ontario, September 1981 to December 1982. Toronto: Atmospheric Research and Special Programs Section, Air Resources Branch, Ontario Ministry of the Environment.

Pearson, P., 1982, Oxidant Effects on Agricultural Crops in Ontario. Toronto: Ontario Ministry of the Environment.

Proctor, J., 1983, "Effect of Simulated Sulfuric Acid Rain on Apple Tree Foliage, Nutrient Content, Yield and Fruit Quality", Environment and Experimental Botany, 23 (2), pp. 167-174.

276

Raynor, G. and J. Hayes, 1982, "Concentrations of Some Ionic Species in Central Long Island, New York Precipitation in Relation to Meteorological Variables", Water, Air, and Soil Pollution, 17, pp. 309-335.

Rhodes, S. and P. Middleton, 1983, "Public Pressures, Technical Options: The Complex Challenge of Controlling Acid Rain", Environment, 25 (4), pp. 6-37.

Rutherford, G., 1985, "The Influence of Acid Precipitation on the Canadian Biosphere". In K. Atkinson and A. McDonald (eds.), Planning and the Physical Environment in Canada, A Conference Held at Leeds, March 1985, Regional Canadian Studies Centre, University of Leeds.

Shriner, D., 1980, "Vegetation Surfaces: A Platform for Pollutant/Parasite Interactions". In T. Toribara, M. Miller and P. Morrow (eds.), Polluted Rain. New York: Plenum Press, pp. 259-272.

Summers, P. and D. Whelpdale, 1976, "Acid Precipitation in Canada", Water, Air, and Soil Pollution, 6, pp. 447-455.

Wetstone, G. and S. Foster, 1983, "Acid Precipitation: What is it Doing to Our Forests?", Environment, 25 (4), pp. 10-12.

19
PROGRAM EVALUATION OF RURAL RESOURCE IMPROVEMENT
Willem van Vuuren and George W. McCaw

INTRODUCTION

Canadian agricultural development in certain regions has been impaired through adverse drainage conditions. Programs have been developed mutually by the federal and provincial governments to stimulate growth in those regions with little natural drainage, through subsidizing the construction of outlet drains which collect and dispose of water from surface and subsurface drains. In Ontario this was attempted initially under the federal-provincial Agricultural Rehabilitation and Development Administration (ARDA) program, which was initiated in 1966 and expired in 1979. More recently, the Eastern Ontario Development (EOD) program was aimed at stabilizing, diversifying and expanding the economic base of the region, assisting in the development of the natural resources of the area and promoting private investment in the region (Government of Ontario, n.d.). Twenty-eight per cent of the funds available under this program were devoted to agriculture, the greater part ($11 million) for the construction of outlet drains on farmlands. The program agreement was signed in 1979 and expired in 1984.

The aim of the agreement between the federal and the provincial government was to provide for development programs for the improvement of the economic and social well-being of Eastern Ontario residents (Government of Ontario, 1979). For the agricultural drainage component this was accomplished by subsidizing the construction and maintenance of outlet drains. For most regions in Ontario, the Drainage Act calls for a provincial subsidy of one-third of the cost of installing and maintaining outlet drains. The EOD program supplied an additional subsidy of one-third from the federal government. As a consequence, under the agreement two-thirds of the cost of installing and maintaining outlet drains was subsidized.

This paper evaluates the agricultural drainage component of the programs. More specifically, it evaluates how drainage has contributed to the improvement of economic well-being of Eastern Ontario farmers. In addition, an assessment is made as to whether or not outlet drainage is making a positive contribution to the overall national economy, although this was not an explicit objective of the program.

A problem in the evaluation is how to interpret the major program objective; the improvement of the economic and social well-being of Eastern Ontario residents [farmers]. Is the emphasis on the individual farmer or on the aggregate of all farmers? If the emphasis is on the individual farmer, the distribution of income among farmers is an important yardstick to evaluate the program. On the other hand, if the purpose of the program is the advancement of total or average economic well-being in the region, the increase in total or average income emanating from the program becomes the criterion for evaluating the program. The program objectives are not clear on this point. However, the evaluation incorporates both points of view, since the program could be successful from one point of view but not from the other.

TIMING, AREA AND METHOD OF EVALUATION

In areas with little natural drainage, excess water often appears on undrained land at crucial periods during the planting, growing and harvesting seasons. This precludes cultivation of high-value crops and reduces agricultural productivity of low-value crops. As a consequence, agricultural incomes may be lower than elsewhere. The problem can be alleviated through the installation of surface and subsurface drains, provided that water from these drains can be collected and disposed of in natural or human-made outlet drains. Human-made drainage canals, in turn, deposit their water in rivers and lakes.

Increasing agricultural productivity in these areas by changing from low-value to high-value crops, and by increasing output per hectare, through the installation of surface and subsurface drains on farms is conditional on the presence of outlet drains. Where no natural outlets exist, they can be dug. Outlet drains by themselves may have some effect on agricultural productivity by decreasing flood hazards. In general, however, the construction of outlet drains will only contribute to increased agricultural productivity and improved economic well-being if farmers make adjustments such as installing subsurface drainage and subsequently changing from low to high-value crops; for example, from rough pasture to corn.

For an appropriate evaluation of the drainage component, there must be a considerable lapse of time between the evaluation and the construction of the outlet drain, since on-farm adjustments may be initiated long after the outlet drain was dug.

In order to evaluate the impact of outlet drainage on economic well-being of farmers, a drainage area in Eastern Ontario was chosen where the outlet drain was dug in the mid-seventies under the ARDA program: the evaluation was undertaken in 1983. It was assumed that by 1983 all on-farm adjustments had taken place. It was also assumed that outlet, surface and subsurface drainage were totally depreciated fifty years from the construction of the outlet, while every ten years major maintenance costs were required for the outlet drain.

The drainage area chosen for the investigation was reasonably representative of the entire region in terms of soil types and pre-drainage cropping patterns. The method used to evaluate changes in economic well-being resulting from outlet drainage and from on-farm adjustments made possible by outlet drainage was cost-benefit analysis. The data for the analysis were obtained from ten interviews and from published statistics (Ontario Ministry of Agriculture and Food [OMAF], various years). The ten farms constituted a representative sample of the drainage area.

The valuation of crop output resulting from drainage is dependent on the purpose for which the crop is grown. The output could be sold, but it could also replace feed purchases or it could be used to expand livestock production. The value in all three cases is different, because the purchasing price of feed exceeds the selling price received by the producer, and feed converted into livestock products usually results in a value for the crop different from its purchasing or selling price. An *ex post* evaluation makes it possible to observe what is done with the output resulting from drainage. In an *ex ante* analysis, the additional output is usually valued at the selling price that the farmer is expected to receive. This can result in an underestimation of drainage benefits.

EVALUATION FROM DIFFERENT VIEWPOINTS

The evaluation can be performed from two major viewpoints: from that of private firms affected by the program, and from that of society at large. As indicated, evaluation of private benefits can look at total and average benefits from outlet drainage or at the distribution of benefits among those affected.

Subsidies and taxes are the major causes for the discrepancy between private and public benefits. From the public point of view, these are transfer items and should be excluded from the analysis. From the private point of view, they are true benefits and costs and should be included in the analysis. Another reason for the discrepancy is the divergence between the social and private discount rates. A social discount rate of 4 per cent was used (McCaw, 1984; Randall, 1981). The private rate was a blended average of the actual private costs of the various capital sources. Accordingly, the private rate differed among farmers. Since the entire analysis was done in constant 1983 dollars, the discount rate used was a real rather than a nominal rate.

A difference between private and public benefits can also exist for those products whose output is curtailed by a supply management program, such as milk. Where quotas are transferable, output expansion on one farm is accompanied by a corresponding output reduction on other farms. A public benefit occurs only if output expands on cost-efficient farms and declines on cost-inefficient farms. Assuming similar costs on farms where output expands and on farms where output contracts, no public benefits of output expansion in the drainage area are apparent. On the other hand, there could be a private benefit for a farmer in the drainage area from buying quotas and expanding production.

It is important that the analysis be performed from both points of view. The outcome of the private analysis indicates how farm incomes are affected by the outlet drain. If the analysis is disaggregated to the farm level, it will also show what the distribution of the total benefits is among farmers in the drainage area. The outcome of the public analysis, on the other hand, indicates whether or not society is becoming better off; that is whether or not national income will increase as a result of installing outlet drains. In addition, the public analysis will also disclose whether or not the subsidies paid by the governments provide any pay-off. If the outlet would not have been installed without the subsidy, society is better off paying the subsidy whenever the net present value in the public evaluation is positive. If it is negative, society would have been better off transferring the subsidy directly to farmers in the form of income transfers rather than through investment in outlet drainage, if the aim is to increase depressed farm incomes.

RESULTS AND DISCUSSION

Private Benefits

Significant private benefits have been gained from investment in drainage within the area of outlet drainage. For the ten farms, the average net present value per hectare was $1,208, while the discounted drainage investment cost per hectare (for outlet, surface and subsurface drainage) was $685. Thus, on average, for every dollar invested in drainage, farmers received $1.77 net in return. This amounts to a 17 per cent real rate of return, which is high.

Although the average return on drainage investment in the drainage area is high, there is a large discrepancy in returns among farmers. Table 19.1 provides some relevant information regarding the ten properties. According to the table, the net present value per hectare varies from -$330 to +$2,200. Closer scrutiny reveals that negative returns are always associated with a deficiency in farm adjustments. The lack of subsequent subsurface drainage and consequently the lack of a cropping pattern change renders the investment in outlet drainage on these farms uneconomic. On the other hand, the highest returns were obtained on farms where subsurface drainage was installed subsequent to outlet investment and where the change in cropping patterns was from a low-value to a high-value crop, such as from unproductive pasture to corn.

In some cases the outlet and surface drainage reduced flooding. This resulted in increased yields and in some minor changes in cropping patterns, such as from pasture to hay and from pasture to mixed grains (Farms 4 and 6).

Where high-value crops were grown prior to outlet investment, and subsurface drainage was installed subsequently to increase yields of those crops, the returns on such investments were low or negative. Farms 1 and 5 are two examples. On both farms, flood reduction benefits were attained from outlet and surface drainage, while subsurface drainage was installed to increase yields. On Farm 1, flood reduction benefits were small, rendering the total investment in drainage negative. On the other hand, on Farm 5 flood reduction benefits were high. However, the yield increase resulting from subsurface drainage by itself was too small on both farms to justify its outlay. Simulating zero flood reduction benefits, but allowing for yield increases resulting from subsurface drainage, made the present value of drainage investment on both farms negative. The high net present value on Farm 5 originates from flood reduction. The negative return on Farm 1 is amplified by the fact that it is a dairy farm where additional output requires the purchase of production quota.

Social Benefits

On average, there is a positive pay-off on drainage investment for society at large (Table 19.2). There is slightly more than one dollar net gain for every dollar invested. However, the public pay-off varies greatly among farms, ranging from a loss of $1,085 per hectare to a gain of $2,470 per hectare.

TABLE 19.1: SUMMARY OF PRIVATE BENEFITS DERIVED FROM AND COSTS OF INVESTMENT IN DRAINAGE OVER 50 YEARS

Farm	Ha in Drainage Area	Ha Tiled	Outlet or Surface Drainage Benefit	Tile Drainage Benefit	Use of Increased Production	NPV Discount Rate	NPV Amount	IRR	NPV/ha	Discounted Investment Cost/ha
1	32.4	32.4	Flood reduction benefit- barley	Yield increase: mostly hay and barley	LE dairy	4.0	−3513	2.8	−108	800
2	75.7	75.7	0	Wasteland to corn and barley	Sale	4.5	154302	22.0	2038	828
3	8.5	0	9	0	—	4.5	−963	—	−113	113
4	12.1	0	Pasture to hay	0	FPR	4.5	4840	15.0	400	252
5	42.5	30.4	Flood reduction benefit—corn and barley	Yield increase: corn and barley	Sale	4.0	56451	21.8	1328	788
6	13.8	0	Pasture—mixed grain	0	FPR	4.5	2664	8.3	193	237
7	2.0	0	0	0	—	4.5	−659	—	−330	330
8	17.8	17.8	0	Pasture-barley	LE beef and sale	4.3	34456	17.6	1936	724
9	21.4	0	0	0	—	4.5	−4268	—	−199	200
10	30.4	30.4	0	Wasteland-corn and barley	Sale	4.0	66886	20.9	2200	951
Total/ Average	256.8	186.6					310196	17.0	1208	685

Note: NPV=Net Present Value, IRR=Internal Rates of Return, LE=Livestock Expansion, FPR=Feed Purchase Replacement, Wasteland=Unproductive Pasture

TABLE 19.2: SUMMARY OF PRIVATE AND PUBLIC BENEFITS AND COSTS OF DRAINAGE OVER 50 YEARS

Farm	Private Benefits and Costs[1]		Public Benefits and Costs[2]	
	Net Present Value per Hectare	Present Value Investment Cost per Hectare	Net Present Value per Hectare	Present Value Investment Cost per Hectare
	$	$	$	$
1	−108	800	−1085	1085
2	2038	828	2470	1198
3	−113	113	−348	348
4	400	252	−146	754
5	1328	788	1646	1112
6	193	237	−329	724
7	−330	330	−998	998
8	1936	724	1752	1216
9	−199	200	−692	692
10	2200	951	2444	1307
AVERAGE	1208	685	1174	1065

[1]Discounted at the relevant private rate, ranging from 4% to 4.5% among farmers
[2]Discounted at the 4% social rate

Comparison Between Private and Social Benefits

Table 19.2 compares the private and public net present values of drainage investment for various farms. On seven out of ten farms, the public net benefits were lower than the private benefits. Subsidies on output and on drainage investment, tax write-offs, and production under a quota system tend to depress public compared to private benefits. On the other hand, income taxes and a social discount rate smaller than private rates tend to raise public relative to private benefits. Where private net benefits were negative or low, the subsidies and tax write-offs were not offset by increased taxes, resulting in lower public than private benefits.

Three farms which realized high gains from drainage (Farms 2, 5 and 10) paid relatively high income taxes, thus reducing the private gain and making public benefits greater than private benefits. It is interesting to note that although Farm 8 also had a relatively high private net present value per hectare, its public net present value was nevertheless lower. This farm has only 17.8 hectares in the drainage area and the real increase in total income was therefore considerably smaller than that on Farms 2, 5 and 10. Moreover, due to a smaller total income, Farm 8 faced a lower marginal tax rate than the latter. The additional tax resulting from increased production on Farm 8 was therefore not sufficient to offset the subsidies and tax write-offs.

On Farm 1, the private loss was considerably smaller than the investment cost incurred by the farmer, while from a public point of view the social loss was identical to total investment cost. This discrepancy is due to the fact that under a quota system, additional milk production on this farm is matched by a corresponding decrease on another farm, thus eliminating any social gain, given equal production costs on both farms.

One might conclude that outlet drainage investment installed for farmers who neither adjust their farming practices nor benefit from the outlet through flood reduction, lowers farm as well as national income (Farms 3, 7 and 9). The same can be said for Farm 1 which produces under a quota system. Farmers who do not install subsurface drainage subsequent to outlet investments, or who install it without adjusting cropping patterns, but who benefit from the outlet through flood reduction, allowing for minor cropping pattern changes and gains in yields, realize some increase in income from outlet drainage (Farms 4 and 6). However, outlet drainage investment on these farms leads to a decrease in national income. On the other hand, Farm 5 gained large benefits through flood reduction, resulting in large private and public benefits. Farmers who make major adjustments through subsurface drainage and cropping pattern changes realize large increases in income (Farms 2, 8 and 10). These investments are also justified from the nation's point of view.

SUMMARY AND CONCLUSIONS

As indicated, the evaluation can be performed from a public and two private viewpoints. A public evaluation of the drainage program gives an indication of whether or not society is becoming better off by investment in outlet drainage and by providing drainage subsidies. A private evaluation gives an indication of whether or not the farmers in the area are becoming better off, either in the aggregate or individually, by investment in outlet drainage.

Although, on average, drainage investment in the area investigated paid off both from a private and from a public point of view, not all farmers benefited equally; some gained, others lost. Farmers receiving the greatest proportion of the benefits were those who adjusted their farm operation by installing subsurface drainage and by introducing high-value crops. The losers and those who gained little tend to be farmers who did not make these adjustments. In general, they were low income farmers who might have lacked the funds to do so.

For farmers who were negatively affected by the outlet drain, the subsidies were insufficient to nullify this effect, although they played an important role in reducing the losses for them. For these farms, the public losses were considerably larger than the private ones. Public losses were even associated with farms making relatively small gains. Whenever a public loss from outlet drainage is involved on individual farms, drainage subsidies are a poor instrument to raise incomes of these low income farmers. These farmers would have been better off if the subsidy had not gone into drainage, but if instead an equivalent amount had been directly transferred to these low income farmers without any strings attached.

Farmers who made large gains from drainage investment tend to farm the largest holdings and be situated in higher income brackets. One could argue that they do not need the subsidy to increase their income. As a matter of fact, the subsidy was a relatively small proportion of their returns. They could have paid the full cost and still have been better off.

Many farmers would have been better off if they had received the subsidies in cash rather than through outlet investment. As a consequence, drainage subsidies were a poor instrument to improve the incomes of those in the lowest income brackets. On the other hand, to increase national income, drainage subsidies are justified if the total investment provides a net overall public benefit and would not have been undertaken without the subsidy. This is quite plausible. Since all farmers in the drainage area are affected by the drain, outlet construction requires agreement among owners.

The Ontario Drainage Act requires that for the construction of a petition drain, approval is needed from a majority of owners or from owners holding 60 per cent of the land in the area requiring drainage.

Six of the ten farms in the sample benefited from the outlet, while only four would have benefited if no subsidies were provided. Moreover, at the time of petition there was great uncertainty about future benefits. For this reason, risk-averse farmers may have voted against the petition, in spite of the fact that with hindsight they would have benefited. One of the questions asked of farmers was whether they would have approved the petition if no subsidies were provided. It turned out that neither of the two criteria for approval required by the Drainage Act were met. If no subsidies had been provided, the drain would not have been installed, although national income increased through the investment. The subsidy was also important for those who voted against the petition and whose income declined. The subsidy reduced their losses substantially and consequently reduced bad feelings that may have been created for the farmers who had to pay for something they did not want.

Whether or not drainage subsidies benefit farm incomes in certain designated regions, depends on the objective being pursued. If advancement of total or average farm income in the region is aimed for, then evidence provided here suggests this is possible. However, if advancement of low incomes in the region is the objective, then drainage subsidies are likely not the most appropriate strategy to adopt. This study has demonstrated that distribution of income among farmers has deteriorated through the subsidy program. Those at the lower end of the income scale became worse off and those at the higher end became better off.

Those in low income brackets who became worse off probably lacked the funds to make the necessary farm adjustments, and low equity prevented them from borrowing money. It also appears that those who did not make adjustments were older than those who did, and were likely more conservative and risk-averse. Moreover, institutional factors such as prevailing tax provisions (e.g., tax write-offs for tile drainage) are less favourable for those in low income brackets than for those in high income brackets. And finally, short-term lease contracts prevented tenants from making the necessary adjustments.

Factors inhibiting necessary farm adjustments detract from the profitability of outlet drainage. To obtain an optimal result from outlet drainage, government policies must be coordinated. Additional policies are needed to counteract these inhibiting forces, such as the provision of credit, improving the tenancy system, and directing farm extension work towards low-income farmers. However, even these additional instruments, combined with drainage subsidies, may be insufficient or too costly to improve incomes of low-income farmers. Since these coordinated policies have not been executed, evaluating their effect is as yet impossible.

REFERENCES

Government of Ontario, n.d., <u>Eastern Ontario Development Program</u>. Toronto: Government of Ontario.

Government of Ontario, 1979, <u>Eastern Ontario Subsidiary Agreement</u>. Toronto: Government of Ontario.

McCaw, G.W., 1984, "Cost-Benefit Analysis of Public Investment in Outlet Drainage in Eastern Ontario". Guelph: Unpublished M.Sc. Thesis, Department of Agricultural Economics and Business, University of Guelph.

OMAF, various years, <u>Crop Budgeting Aids</u>. Toronto.

Randall, A., 1981, <u>Resource Economics, An Economic Approach to Natural Resource and Environmental Policy</u>. Columbus: Grid Publishers Inc.

20
THE DYNAMICS OF THE URBAN FIELD
Ian Moffatt

INTRODUCTION

One of the characteristic features of contemporary urbanization in western industrial countries has been the rapid sprawl of urban land uses and occupations into hitherto rural areas. In the last two decades (1961-1981), for example, large central urban areas in Britain have continued to decline in both the number of inhabitants and job opportunities. This decline of the urban core has been accompanied by growth in the metropolitan peripheries as well as in the remote rural areas (Goddard and Champion, 1983; Hugo and Smailes, 1985). The changing pattern of urbanization is not confined to Britain. In the United States of America it has been noted that counter-urbanization has replaced urbanization as the dominant form of settlement. Similarly, in Australia and Canada the past trend of concentration in the major urban areas has been reversed with more urban growth in the medium sized cities and small centres adjacent to the large metropolitan regions (Beesley and Russwurm, 1981; Berry, 1976). The incidence of scattered non-farm populations around cities in the developed world "is likely to remain a significant feature of the landscape and society of the urban field for a long time to come" (Russwurm and Bryant, 1984, p. 134). These important changes in both urban and rural areas need to be examined in an integrated fashion so that the socio-economic and ecological consequences of these recent movements can be explained. It is the purpose of this chapter to review the ways in which the dynamics of the urban field can be simulated on a computer.

There are several reasons for developing an integrated approach to dynamic computer-based models of the urban field. First, empirical studies have merely described the changes in the urban field. The point, however, is to understand the processes underlying these changes. Second, these studies inevitably demand some form of explanation, and this might be accomplished by way of computer models. It will be shown below that there are at least five different approaches to building computer-based models of the dynamics of the urban field. Third, the ecological and socio-economic problems of an increasingly large population spreading out onto good quality rural land needs careful management, at least if society wishes to avoid some resource problems in the future. Fourth, several of the policy issues relating to the current and future use of land within the urban field raise ethical questions concerned with long-term changes to the environment. Rather than ruin the resource base of the urban field, is there a genuine concern with developing models to simulate and promote socially desirable, sustainable futures as noted in the recent United Kingdom response to the World Conservation Strategy (World Wildlife Fund, 1983)?

These recent changes in the dynamics of the urban field raise several conceptual, technical and policy-oriented issues, which have not been addressed by researchers adopting a conventional "urban" or "rural" approach. In the following section a broad definition of the urban field is given, drawing upon recent work on urbanization in Canada, the United States and Britain. After discussing some of the conceptual problems of defining the urban field, five distinctive approaches to dynamic modelling are identified. These five approaches are termed cybernetic or systems theory models, neo-classical, neo-Keynesian, neo-Marxist, and models of self-organization or dissipative structures. Several examples of these approaches are discussed in the context of the urban field in Britain. The penultimate section of the paper briefly considers the role of positive and normative modelling in understanding and managing the urban field. It is argued that too little attention has been given to the relationships between modelling and the dominant political views of the day. Finally, on the basis of this review of the dynamics of the urban field, some new directions for research are noted.

DEFINING THE URBAN FIELD

Since the 1950s, the pattern of urbanization in Britain has been marked by two distinct stages. First, there was gradual decline in population and employment opportunities in the old core of the large cities. Next, the rapid expansion of the suburbs has been slowed down and the more remote rural areas have begun to grow. As Davidson and MacEwen (1983, p. 117) note: "Overall, the decade up to 1981 saw a 1.9 per cent decline in the urban population and a 9.7 per cent increase in rural areas". These changes are shown graphically in Figure 20.1.

The changes in the distribution of people in Britain can be termed broadly urban decline and rural growth. Yet it is exceedingly difficult to monitor and model these changes given a persistence in

FIGURE 20.1: PERCENTAGE POPULATION CHANGE 1961-1971 AND 1971-1981 IN URBAN AND RURAL AREAS

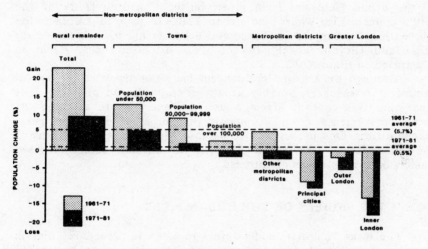

(After Craig, 1982)

use of standard urban and rural classifications by census administrators.   Fortunately, in Britain for the period 1931-1971, urban
areas have been defined broadly as Standard Metropolitan Labour
Areas (SMLA) and Metropolitan Economic Labour Areas (MELA).
The SMLA is defined as an urban core consisting of a contiguous
belt of local authority areas with job densities of over 5 per acre
or a total employment of over 20,000.   Around these cores the
MELA was defined as a metropolitan ring which had more than
15 per cent of the economically active population commuting to the
core.   This enlarged area was used in a detailed study of the 1971
census and extended to Scotland (Goddard and Champion, 1983;
Hall, 1973; Spence et al., 1982).

While the SMLA and MELA are extremely useful definitions
for analyzing socio-economic changes in British urbanization they
do not capture the varied land uses in these extensive areas.   An
alternative framework for examining socio-economic and ecological
change is to employ the concept of the urban field.

The concept was first proposed in 1965 (Friedmann and Miller,
1965), when the urban field was identified as a spatially extended
pattern of functional interaction and a multicentred form of spatial

organization; as a field of different population densities related to each other by a complex network of communications, transport and energy flows; and characterized also by permanent and periodic uses of land-extensive environmental resources for recreational, residential and economic activity. Perhaps the clearest definition of the urban field has been given in the Canadian study of the city's countryside, where the urban field is seen to embrace the conventional urban core, suburbs and urban fringe as well as a rural hinterland (Bryant et al., 1982). This dispersed urban field is illustrated in Figure 20.2.

Although the urban field concept has been discussed by several groups of researchers, notably urban geographers and planners, it is clear that this concept offers a useful framework to examine the recent movements from essentially urban areas into the rural communities. One useful way to explain these changing patterns of the dynamics of the urban field is to develop computer-based models of these systems of interest.

COMPUTER MODELS OF THE URBAN FIELD

The term computer model refers to a set of procedures that in some way represent and replicate the behaviour of a system of interest using a set of mathematical equations (Ayeni, 1979). The use of computers offers social and physical scientists a "laboratory" for analyzing and verifying their models of a specific system of interest. In dynamic models of the urban field the trajectories of these systems can be simulated on a computer. Furthermore, relevant policies can be run on computer-based models of a system before translating these policies into real world action. It must always be remembered, however, that computer models only mimic part of the behaviour of the real world. Furthermore, any model is only as good as the assumptions incorporated within it as well as the data it uses. This section re-examines the theoretical assumptions implicit in a variety of models of the dynamics of the urban field used in Britain in the last 20 years. Such a re-examination obviously cannot cover the entire field of enquiry nor can it enter into the detailed empirical work in each study. Nevertheless, the "grab" sample of studies indicates the rich diversity of theoretical approaches to modelling the dynamics of the urban field.

Systems Theory

While systems theory has been used in military operations since the 1940s, it was only in the 1960s that this approach was used to model and control complex urban and regional systems.

FIGURE 20.2: THE URBAN FIELD

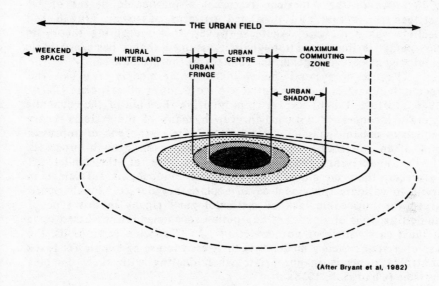

(After Bryant et al, 1982)

One of the earliest attempts to simulate urban growth was Forrester's (1969) model of urban dynamics. Like other systems engineers, Forrester claimed that his model was a theory of urban dynamics, but unfortunately no theory is given and this is not helped by ignoring the urban economic literature then available. His model consists of three major components, namely population, housing and industry. Each of these components is subdivided into three groups to produce nine state variables. These nine state variables are interconnected by a series of feedback loops to generate a "life cycle" of urban growth over 250 years. This pioneering model did not attempt to compare the model with reality, although researchers have subsequently attempted to do this for urban growth in the United States. Schroeder (1974), in particular, reported that by making nine parameter changes in the original model of urban dynamics a reasonable fit between the predicted and actual patterns of urban growth of Lowell, Massachusetts over the period 1800-1970 was obtained. While this result appears to be convincing at first sight, the minor variables demonstrate an extremely poor fit with the relevant observed minor variables in Lowell (Madden, 1977). Furthermore, there are major weaknesses in the structure of the migration equations in both these models (Madden and Moffatt, 1980).

In Britain, the pattern of urban growth and decline of Spennymoor, Country Durham, 1901-1970 has been simulated using the techniques of system dynamics pioneered by Forrester (Brookbanks, 1973). As in the American research, a reasonable degree of fit between the actual and predicted patterns of urban growth and decline was achieved. Again, however, the underlying theory in this model is implicit, although it is assumed that a basic/non-basic employment category generates changes in the urban area.

The use of systems theory in computer models of urban and regional dynamics has generated a huge amount of criticism (Batty, 1976; Moffatt, 1983b). Apart from ignoring the bulk of the economic literature concerned with urban growth, many of the systems theory models of urban dynamics contain many, often hundreds, of unproven and often untestable hypotheses concerning the growth processes. If the underlying assumptions and structure of the model are incorrect, then no amount of empirical evidence is sufficient in itself to validate the model as an explanatory device. Furthermore, given the noticeable lack of methodological rigour in this type of modelling, it is obvious that any policy recommendations based upon it must carry little or no conviction. As Chadwick reminds us, the use of systems theory models which stress the use of simple feedback control systems is inappropriate when dealing with these complex systems (Chadwick, 1978).

Neo-Classical Theory

Like the classical predecessor, neo-classical economic theory is primarily concerned with the problems of static equilibrium and growth at full employment. One of the many assumptions common to these two sets of economic theory is that the market is atomistically competitive (i.e., no producer or consumer is able to influence the prices paid for, or quantities purchased in the markets). Under these and other neo-classical assumptions at least two distinct approaches to computer modelling of urban and regional systems have been developed, namely entropy maximizing methods and dynamic simulation (Batty, 1976; Wilson, 1975 and 1981).

At the heart of both these models lies the well-known Garin-Lowry model (Lowry, 1964). This model is essentially two gravity-type models, one for residential location and one for service location, coupled together through an economic base mechanism. This latter mechanism assumes that an exogenous input of basic employment generates total population of the urban area and this in turn generates service employment. The exact specification of total population and service employment hinges upon the precision of the regional multipliers involved. There is also the thorny problem of defining basic and non-basic employment in this model (Massey, 1973; Sayer, 1976). Despite these criticisms, the Garin-Lowry model forms the basis of the entropy maximizing and dynamic simulation computer models which will be described briefly below.

The entropy maximizing model, or class of models, has been pioneered and developed by Wilson and his co-workers at Leeds (Wilson, 1967 and 1974). Entropy maximization is a method of reasoning which ensures that no unconscious arbitrary assumptions have been introduced into a model of a system of interest. Basically, this method is used to calculate the most probable distribution of, say, journeys to work which satisfies all the known constraints acting on the system. In the context of the general urban model being developed at Leeds University, the individual state variables include spatial, demographic and economic inputs and associated subsystems. Thus for population activities, the subsystems include residence, workplace, utilization of services and transport facilities. The economic subsystems include housing, basic jobs, service employment and transport facilities. One of the constraints on the economic subsystems is the availability of land in each zone within the urban region (for details see Wilson, 1974). The entire model is interconnected by a series of entropy maximizing models which link flows of people with various urban activities. While this research effort is based on a firm neo-classical theoretical foundation, the general model has not, as yet, been fully calibrated or tested with the relevant data.

A somewhat similar approach to dynamic urban modelling has been attempted by Batty (1976) using simulation techniques together with entropy maximizing methods. Again, basic employment is exogenous to the model and then all the other inputs such as transport, services, residential floor space and population are endogenous to the system. The model consists of 71 equations and incorporates time-lags and feedback loops which operate in the model within and between time periods. This simulation model has been run with data from the Reading area in Central Berkshire for the period 1951-1966 in one year time periods. The statistical tests, such as linear regression of the observed and predicted values for each activity, reveal "that the performance of the model is fair in the light of the major assumptions" (Batty, 1976, p. 338).

Despite the reasonable performance of this dynamic simulation model, both these broadly neo-classical based models have been criticized. Critics argue that basic employment, service employment and population may be empirically related, but could be caused by other factors in the urban system (Sayer, 1976). Similarly, the model assumes no unemployment, which is hardly a realistic assumption. Furthermore, most of the models have been designed to simulate urban or regional growth and are not well-suited to simulating no growth or decline. They are also unable to accommodate population growth and decline simultaneously, which is a characteristic of the urban field. Despite these criticisms, this type of modified Garin-Lowry modelling has been used in a variety of real studies in Britain, such as Bedfordshire (Cripps and Foot, 1969), Cheshire (Barras et al., 1971) and in Reading, Cambridge and Stevenage (Echenique et al., 1969), as well as abroad (Foot, 1981).

Neo-Keynesian Theory

Unlike the neo-classical scholars, Keynes and the neo-Keynesians are concerned with the behaviour of the economic system as a whole, focussing attention on, for example, aggregate employment and aggregate investment rather than on the employment or investment and savings of individuals (Keynes, 1936). This focus on macroeconomics topics has influenced civil servants and politicians in Britain for many years. In Britain, these macroeconomic policies have often been translated into urban and regional policies by stressing the effect of the Keynesian multiplier in creating further employment in an area after an initial injection of capital by the government into a depressed region.

By 1973, the famous Lowry "model of metropolis" was used as the basis for a broadly Keynesian model of the United Kingdom's Northern Economic Region. The main purpose of this model, known as REG2, was to evaluate the impact of proposed major regional development policies in the area. One of the model's characteristic behavioural modes was to forecast massive outmigration of the unemployed from the region, which gradually reached a state of dynamic equilibrium between the number of people in employment and the number of jobs available. This dynamic equilibrium was achieved largely through massive out-migration of the unemployed. Hence, in 1976, a revised model (REG3) was built in order to make the model's behaviour more credible (Brookbanks et al, 1973; Telford, 1976). REG3 was able to simulate endogenously generated business or trade cycles which would, of course, have an impact on industry and employment. Despite this methodological improvement, the problem of massive out-migration of the unemployed was not resolved. In fact REG3 is more akin to a macroeconomic national model than to a demographic-economic model or a model of the urban field.

One of the major problems in modelling the urban field is that most researchers have treated exogenous inputs and constraints as acting independently of the modelled system. Thus, in the case of REG2 and REG3 dynamic equilibrium in, say, employment can be achieved by allowing the out-migrants to move elsewhere. It is obvious that there are interregional links between one area and the rest of the country in which it is embedded. It is therefore essential that interregional movements of people and capital must be considered if model builders are to mirror the structure of the real world as accurately as possible before introducing policies for the urban field.

In 1977, Madden developed an interregional demographic-economic model for Great Britain for all ten economic regions (Madden, 1977). While the model is extremely crude, it is acknowledged that some state variables in the model do reflect the real data accurately. Using Thiel's coefficient of inequality, the fit between the simulated data and the 1971 census data is quite good, although the migration aspect again is poor. This latter component has been re-examined and a more reasonable model is now used (Madden and Moffatt, 1980).

One of the uses of computer models is that the researchers can introduce policy alternatives into the model in order to examine the impact that these policies may have on the real system. In the case of the interregional demographic-economic model, a regional multiplier was switched on in the model in order to stimulate economic growth and employment in several depressed regions. It is difficult to test this aspect of the model predictions until the relevant data is available. Unfortunately, changes in urban and regional policy by the current (1987) Conservative government prevent any such meaningful empirical work from being undertaken. This raises the question of the role of policy in relation to urban field dynamics, which will be discussed later.

Neo-Marxist Theory

Several researchers in the 1970s expressed dissatisfaction with the type of explanations proposed in urban geography, regional science and urban economics (Holland, 1976; Sayer, 1976). Harvey (1973, p. 302) has argued that "the only method capable of uniting disciplines in such a fashion that they can grapple with issues such as urbanization, economic development and the environment, is that founded in a properly constituted version of dialectical materialism as it operates within a structured totality in the sense that Marx conceived it". This resurgence of interest in the writings of Marx is primarily motivated by the apparent failure of orthodox economics to resolve the persistent economic problems such as high unemployment and stagflation in Western economies. Not all urban geographers, economists or model builders are convinced that Marx's economics offers a better explanation of urban and regional problems (Chisholm, 1975). Nevertheless, it is instructive to examine the way in which Marx's method can be used as a theoretical basis for simulating urban growth.

In order to explore the possibility of linking Marxian political economic theory with an operational, testable model of urban growth, a model of a hypothetical British city has been developed (Jenson-Butler, 1979; Moffatt, 1983a and 1986). This model uses the technique of system dynamics but, unlike the systems theory models, this model is based on Marxian political-economic theory. The model consists of seven sectors, namely a Marxian economic base; a demographic sector divided into three classes; a migration component; industrial and housing sectors; employment, including an unemployed category; and urban land area. These sectors are interconnected by a series of feedback loops and the entire model consists of 63 equations.

In order to test the model, 18 British cities were chosen and the model was initialized for each city in 1801. The predicted patterns of urban growth were then compared to the actual population data for the period 1801-1971. The model yields reasonable predictions for all the urban areas, and the simulations for Bristol, Portsmouth, Hull, Stoke-on-Trent, York, Wigan, Aberdeen and Dundee are all within 10 per cent of the actual data. In a more detailed study of Wigan the population growth, total housing stock and areal expansion of the town in the nineteenth century shows a close correspondence with the actual historical data. This approach to dynamic modelling is clearly as empirically valid as other economic approaches and deserves to be developed further (Moffatt and Jackson, 1986).

Self-Organizing Systems

The four approaches outlined above have their friends and foes but they are not the only way of modelling the dynamics of the urban field. In fact a form of methodological pluralism reigns as new approaches using alternative conceptual frameworks are attempted (Massey and Batey, 1977). The following three approaches give some flavour of the current research into the development of general dynamic models of an urban or regional area. Although these three approaches use different techniques, they are all characterized by systems which exhibit self-organizing behaviour.

According to Wilson (1975, p. 261) "the ultimate goal of the scientist analyst is the construction of a general and comprehensive model of a city". Over the past nine years Wilson and his co-workers at Leeds University have made considerable progress in developing a general model of a city using a modified Garin-Lowry model and entropy maximizing techniques (Wilson, 1967). The general model consists of a Lowry model with an exogenous input of basic employment and host of sophisticated submodels. It is anticipated that these submodels will eventually include detailed housing structure and residential location, retailing, industrial and agricultural sectors, as well as transport network evolution and spatial interaction. At present the numerical simulation produces a dynamic spatial structure that qualitatively resembles many western cities. As this general model has been developed, however, it is clear that bifurcations are taking place in some of the non-linear relationships. These bifurcations can often lead into new structures growing during the simulation of a hypothetical urban system. Further research into applying this general model to real world data has yet to be undertaken. In the retail sector some preliminary results have been obtained but it is recognized that in developing a comprehensive, general urban model "there is clearly a long way to go" (Birkin et al., 1984, p. 19).

An alternative way of examining the dynamics of the urban field has been established at the Free University of Brussels. The focus of this research centres on the development and application of the principle of self-organizing systems or dissipative structures in order to understand the long-term implications of policy decisions concerning transport and land use. Dissipative structures occur when exogenous inputs of energy drive a system which is already far from one equilibrium position into a new structure. Originally these structures were discovered in chemistry but Prigogine has extended this intriguing concept to urban and regional modelling (Nicholis and Prigogine, 1977; Prigogine, 1967). In this context Allen and his researchers have examined the inter-urban as well as the intra-urban interactions. Using a relatively simple model, preliminary empirical work indicates that the model is sufficient to describe correctly the evolution of tertiary employment and of residential structure in the Bastogne region of Belgium, 1947-1970 (Allen et al., 1981).

A third approach to the problem of developing a comprehensive dynamic model of the urban field has adopted an aspatial framework but has attempted to incorporate economic and ecological activity within the same model. The ecological sector consists of inputs such as solar energy and precipitation, which have an impact on the agricultural, forest, grassland and wildlife of a hypothetical urban field. The economic sector of the model includes non-solar energy inputs, as well as housing, industry, demography, employment and land-use allocation. This preliminary model attempts to predict the magnitude and the rates at which proposed changes in land use can affect the economy and ecology of an area. It is envisaged that by integrating the ecology and economy of an urban field into a coherent, commensurate framework then objective evaluations of proposed land-use changes can be made. Again this research endeavour is still in its infancy (Moffatt, 1983c).

There are, of course, several other approaches to understanding the dynamics of urban and regional systems, such as the use of Sraffa's economics (Scott, 1980; Sraffa, 1963) or the development of structuralist models (Sayer, 1976). Nevertheless, these three new approaches indicate that some researchers are examining structural changes in dynamic models of the urban field. These research efforts contain a common theme, namely the prediction of qualitatively similar behaviour to real world systems of interest before more quantitative work is undertaken. As this research is very new, it is perhaps prudent to depart from this methodological review to examine some of the policy implications embedded in these diverse modelling research programs.

THE ROLE OF POSITIVE AND NORMATIVE MODELLING

All models are simplifications of the real world and in scientific enquiry a model can be regarded as a formal expression of a theory. It should be noted, however, that many different models can be built to represent some aspect of the same theory. In the case of modelling the dynamics of the urban field, a neo-Marxist model differs fundamentally from a neo-classical one with regard to both the concept used as well as policy recommendations emanating from the model. At the heart of the debate between different model builders is the epistemological question concerning the role between positive and normative models (Munton and Goudie, 1984).

The positivistic mode of explanation attempts to demonstrate logically, and test empirically, how a particular system of interest operates. The operation of a system may be explained by functionalist, historical or systematic modes of argument. The normative mode of argument, however, is concerned with how the system ought to operate. This implies some preselection of an objective function or functions for the system which, in turn, is based on individual or social value judgements.

Given then some observations about the performance of an urban or regional system of interest, these perceptions are translated into a conceptual model. This conceptual model is often, but not always, related to a body of theory. In urban and regional economics a whole variety of theories are implicit, or occasionally explicit, in many dynamic models. This conceptual model is then translated into a mathematical model, which in turn may be built into a computer-based model. Often these computer models are written in a general purpose language such as FORTRAN or BASIC, or specialized simulation languages like DYNAMO or CSMP are used. The simulated data is compared with the relevant data and the observed discrepancies are then used to refine the conceptual, mathematical and computer models. This refinement is achieved by careful sensitivity tests (i.e., trying to ascertain sensitive parameters in the model as well as by calibrating the model using an independent data set). Results of this positivistic approach to modelling the urban field, if successful, can explain the behaviour of a particular system of interest (Figure 20.3).

FIGURE 20.3: THE RELATIONSHIP BETWEEN MODELLING AND MANAGING THE URBAN FIELD

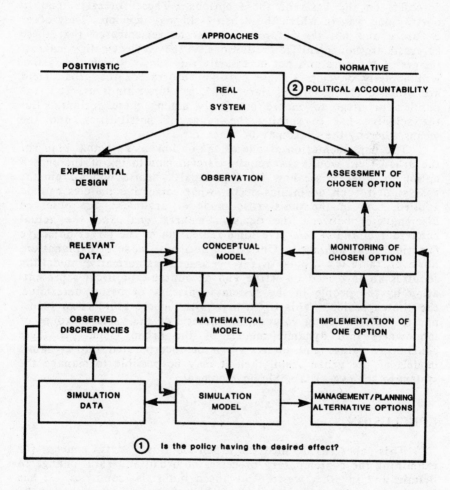

Note: There are two feedback loops:

1. is the policy having the desired effect on measured parameters of the modelled system?
2. do the people want this option?

In the normative use of models in studying the dynamics of the urban field, however, the explanation of the operation of a specific system of interest often leads into suggesting managerial and/or planning policies. In many computer-based models it is possible to build in various management options and make limited forecasts on the basis of these options. These forecasts tend to portray one way in which the urban field may develop. They offer *a* future and not *the* future. It must be remembered that these forecasts are not scientific predictions, as they reflect policy makers' images of a future and not necessarily the way in which the system will actually develop. These possible futures for the urban field are worth defining but, as Hare (1985, p. 136) reminds us, "it is the public's privilege to choose politically among these options. But the scientist has to specify the range of possibilities, and the means whereby the goals may be reached".

The implementation of one of the options as an actual plan for the urban field would also require careful monitoring of the chosen option in order to see how far the actual system deviates from the goal and, if such deviations occur, what corrective policies can be applied. As in the positivistic mode of argument, the observed discrepancies between the decision makers' goal and the actual behaviour of the system give some indication of the target objective function being achieved. Unlike the positivist mode of explanation, however, there is a crucial difference insofar as normative modelling requires an informed objective and accountable political representation by the people in the system to discuss, or better determine, the chosen option. This in turn requires model builders to incorporate the conflicting values and interests of the various groups of landowners into dynamic models of the urban field. If these conflicting values and interests can be incorporated into dynamic models of the urban field, then it may be possible to manage the system to achieve sustainable development.

CONCLUSION

This paper has defined the urban field as a useful concept for examining the contemporary processes of urban and rural change in Britain and in other western advanced industrial countries. It has been suggested that an understanding of these processes can be enhanced by developing dynamic computer-based models of these systems of interest. From a review of the literature it is clear that neo-classical, neo-Keynesian, neo-Marxist, systems theory and theories of self-organization could form the basis of a robust dynamic model of the urban field. There are, however, several problems which need to be resolved if incisive research is to be made in this area of dynamic modelling.

First, it is quite clear that the building of dynamic models of the urban field requires data sets containing, as a minimum, consistently defined state variables over a reasonable time series. Unfortunately, the changes in the way in which the urban and regional systems have been defined and the different classifications used to collect the relevant data ensures that dynamic modelling is hampered by woefully inadequate data for these purposes. Nevertheless, in several cases cited above the models have been calibrated using the available data and then further simulations have been undertaken in an attempt to verify the models' forecast.

A second related issue that needs further attention is to develop robust techniques to verify the models' output. Generally, a dynamic model is accepted as a reasonable empirical fit if it is able to replicate the major and minor state variables with regard to both their magnitude and amplitude. Very few of the dynamic models' output have been subjected to more rigorous statistical tests to ascertain the degree of correspondence with the real world. Thiel's coefficient has been used along with some of the other more familiar quantitative techniques, like multiple linear regression, but more sophisticated techniques have not been used and are clearly needed.

Many of the models described in this review have tended to ignore the rest of the socio-economic system in which they are embedded. It is quite clear that the evolution of any urban field can never be disassociated from the rest of the socio-economic system. An attempt to model the entire dynamics of the capitalist system would be a worthwhile but gargantuan task. At a formal level, one approach to this problem is to interconnect world models with national and then urban/regional models. This approach has been termed hierarchical dynamics (Isard, 1977). However, this formal level of modelling needs to be built on a firm theoretical base. Perhaps one way of achieving this understanding of the urban field could be achieved by integrating the dynamic macroeconomics of Marx with the structural transformations noted by the Brussels school (Marx, 1974; Nicholis and Prigogine, 1977). A noteworthy feature of such a synthesis would be the ability to link the fast dynamics of daily urban systems with the slower structural changes of the capitalist system (Wilson, 1981; Zeeman, 1977).

Finally, the ideological relationships between government decisions and urban field policies need to be subject to closer scrutiny. It is painfully obvious that the free movement of capital and labour in a market economy has resulted in numerous urban and regional problems. It is also abundantly clear that many of the dynamic models have been concerned merely with the spatial manifestation of these deep-seated structural issues. If these "slow" dynamics could be uncovered, then ways could be identified in which the more obvious "fast" dynamics could be used for social welfare and sustainable developments rather than individual greed in the urban field. Unfortunately, it is precisely this problem that most planners and model builders have ignored.

REFERENCES

Allen, P.M., M. Sanglier, F. Boon, J.L. Deneubourg and A. De Palma, 1981, Models or Urban Settlement and Structure as Dynamic Self-Organizing Systems. Washington, D.C.: DOT/RSPA/DPB-10/6, United States Department of Transportation.

Ayeni, B., 1979, Concepts and Techniques in Urban Analysis. London: Croom-Helm.

Barras, R., T.A. Broadbent, M. Cordey-Hayes, P.B. Massey, K. Robinson and J. Willis, 1971, "An Operational Urban Development Model of Cheshire", Environment and Planning, 3, pp. 115-234.

Batty, M., 1976, Urban Modelling: Algorithms, Calibrations, Predictions. Cambridge: Cambridge University Press.

Beesley, K.B. and L.H. Russwurm (eds.), 1981, The Rural-Urban Fringe: Canadian Perspectives. Toronto: Geographical Monographs, 10, York University.

Berry, B.J.L. (ed.), 1976, Urbanization and Counter-Urbanization. Beverly Hills: Volume 11, Urban Affairs Annual Reviews, Sage University.

Birkin, M., M. Clarke and A.G. Wilson, 1984, "Interacting Fields: Comprehensive Models for the Dynamic Analysis of Urban Spatial Structure". Leeds: Working Paper 385, Department of Geography, University of Leeds.

Brookbanks, E., 1973, "The Dynamics of Growth, Decline and Renewal in an Urban System". Newcastle Upon Tyne: Unpublished M.Sc. Thesis, University of Newcastle Upon Tyne.

Brookbanks, E., R.W. Coursey, K. Telford and A. Yule, 1973, "A Dynamic Simulation Model for Regional Planning: A Case Study of the Northern Region", IBMUKSC, 47.

Bryant, C.R., L.H. Russwurm and A.G. McLellan, 1982, The City's Countryside. Toronto: Methuen.

Chadwick, G.F., 1978, A Systems View of Planning. Oxford: Pergamon Press.

Chisholm, M., 1975, Human Geography: Evolution or Revolution? London: Pelican.

Craig, J., 1982, "Town and Country: Current Changes in Distribution of Population in England and Wales". In Town and Country: Home and Work. London: Royal Scottish Academy.

Cripps, E.L. and D.H.S. Foot, 1969, "A Land Use Model for Sub-Regional Planning", Regional Studies, 3, pp. 243-268.

Davidson, J. and A. MacEwan, 1983, "The Livable City". In World Wildlife Fund, The Conservation and Development Programme for the U.K.. London: Kogan Page, pp. 95-170.

Echenique, M., D. Crowther and W. Lindsay, 1969, "A Spatial Model of Urban Stock and Activity", Regional Studies, 3, pp. 281-312.

Foot, D., 1981, Operational Urban Models: An Introduction. London: Methuen.

Forrester, J.W., 1969, Urban Dynamics. Massachusetts: Wright-Allen.

Friedmann, J. and J. Miller, 1965, "The Urban Field", Journal of the American Institute of Planners, 31 (4), pp. 312-320.

Goddard, J.B. and A.G. Champion (eds.), 1983, The Urban and Regional Transformation of Britain. London: Methuen.

Hall, P. (ed.), 1973, The Containment of Urban England. London: Volumes 1 and 2, George Allen & Unwin.

Hare, F.K., 1985, "Future Environments: Can They be Predicted?", Transactions of the Institute of British Geographers New Series, 10 (2), pp. 131-137.

Harvey, D., 1973, Social Justice and the City. London: Edward Arnold.

Holland, S., 1976, Capital Versus the Regions. London: Macmillan.

Hugo, G.J. and P.J. Smailes, 1985, "Urban-Rural Migration in Australia: A Process View of the Turnaround", Journal of Rural Studies, 1 (1), pp. 11-30.

Isard, W., 1977, "On Hierarchical Dynamics". In D.B. Massey and P.W.J. Batey (eds.), Alternative Frameworks for Analysis. London: 7, London Papers in Regional Science, pp. 125-133.

Jensen-Butler, C., 1979, "Capital Accumulation, Regional Development and the Role of the State: A Marxist Approach", Unpublished paper, Institute of British Geographers, University of Lancaster, Annual Conference, 1980.

Keynes, J.M., 1936, The General Theory of Employment, Interest and Money. London: Macmillan.

Lowry, I.S., 1964, A Model of Metropolis. Santa Monica: RM-4035, R.C. Rand Corporation.

Madden, M., 1977, "Simulating Interregional Interaction: A Demographic-Economic Model for Great Britain", Simulation, 28 (6), pp. 161-170.

Madden, M. and I. Moffatt, 1980, "The Modelling of Migration in Urban and Regional Systems". In L. Dekker, G. Savastano and G.C. Vansteenkiste (eds.), Simulation of Systems '79. Holland: North Holland Publishers, pp. 115-125.

Marx, K., 1974, Capital. London: Volumes I, II and III, Lawrence & Wishart.

Massey, D.B., 1973, "The Basic Service Categorisation in Planning", Regional Studies, 7, pp. 1-15.

Massey, D.B. and R.W.J. Batey (eds.), 1977, Alternative Frameworks for Analysis. London: London Papers in Regional Science, 7.

306

Moffatt, I., 1983a, "A Political-Economic Model of Urban Growth in Britain, 1801-2001". In J.D.W. Morecroft, D.F. Anderson and J.D. Sterman (eds.), The 1983 International System Dynamics Conference. Boston: Volume 1, Massachusetts Institute of Technology, pp. 40-74.

Moffatt, I., 1983b, "Some Methodological and Epistemological Problems Involved in Systems Dynamics Modelling". In J.D.W. Morecroft, D.F. Anderson and J.D. Sterman (eds.), The 1983 International System Dynamics Conference. Boston: Volume 1, Massachusetts Institute of Technology, pp. 339-358.

Moffatt, I., 1983c, "Modelling the Environment as a Dynamic System", Environmental Conservation, 10, 4, pp. 348-349.

Moffatt, I., 1986, "A Political-Economic Model of Urban Growth in Britain, 1801-1971". In B. Hutchinson and M. Batty (eds.), Advances in Urban Systems Modelling. Amsterdam: Volume 15, Studies in Regional Science and Urban Economics.

Moffatt, I. and J.T. Jackson, 1986, "The Dynamic Modelling of Two Nineteenth-Century Lancashire Towns", Tijdschrift voor Econmische en Sociale Geografie, LXXVII (2), pp. 123-131.

Munton, R.J.C. and A.S. Goudie, 1984, "Geography in the United Kingdom 1980-84", Geographical Journal, 83, pp. 27-47.

Nicholis, G. and I. Prigogine, 1977, Self Organization in Non Equilibrium Systems: For Dissipative Structures to Order Through Fluctuations. New York: Wiley.

Prigogine, I., 1967, Introduction to the Thermodynamics of Irreversible Processes. New York: Interscience.

Russwurm, L.H. and C.R. Bryant, 1984. "Changing Population Distribution and Rural-Urban Relationships in Canadian Urban Fields, 1941-1976". In M.F. Bunce and M.J. Troughton (eds.), The Pressure of Change in Rural Canada. Toronto: Geographical Monographs, 14, York University, pp. 113-137.

Sayer, R.A., 1976, "A Critique of Urban Modelling: From Regional Science to Urban and Regional Political Economy", Progress in Planning, 6 (3), pp. 187-154.

Schroeder, W.W., 1974, "Lowell Dynamics: A Preliminary Application of the Theory of Urban Dynamics". Boston: Unpublished M.Sc. Thesis, Massachusetts Institute of Technology.

Scott, A.J., 1980, The Urban Land Nexus and the State. London: Pion.

Spence, N.A., A. Gillespie, J. Goddard, S. Kennett, S. Pinch and A.M. Williams, 1982, British Cities: Analysis of Urban Change. Oxford: Pergamon.

Sraffa, P., 1963, The Production of Commodities by Means of Commodities. Cambridge: Cambridge University Press.

Telford, K. (ed.), 1976, Economic Models and Regional Planning. IBMUKSC, 82, pp. 1-63.

Wilson, A.G., 1967, "A Statistical Theory of Spatial Distribution Models", Transportation Research, pp. 253-269.

Wilson, A.G., 1974, Urban and Regional Models in Geography and Planning. London: John Wiley & Sons.

Wilson, A.G., 1975, "Cities, Planners, People and Computers", New Society, May, pp. 258-261.

Wilson, A.G., 1981, "Catastrophe Theory and Bifurcation". In N. Wrigley and R.G. Bennett (eds.), Quantitative Geography. London: Routledge & Kegan Paul, pp. 192-201.

World Wildlife Fund, 1983, The Conservation and Development Strategy for the U.K.: A response to the World Conservation Strategy. London: Kogan Page.

Zeeman, E.C., 1977, Catastrophe Theory. Reading: Addison Wesley.

21

FARM SIZE AND LAND USE IN THE URBAN FRINGE IN SCOTLAND
Andrew H. Dawson

INTRODUCTION

Studies of the problems of agriculture in the urban fringe have usually suffered from two grave weaknesses. Descriptions of the problems have generally been anecdotal, rather than the subject of careful measurement on comparable bases, and the boundaries of the areas which have been designated as urban fringe, or which have been chosen for fringe studies, have been fixed arbitrarily. Attention was drawn to these weaknesses in a previous paper (Dawson, 1982), where an attempt was made to subsume the detailed character of the agricultural problems of the urban fringe within a simple spatial model of the von Thünen-Sinclair type (Sinclair, 1967). That theoretical presentation is extended in the first part of this paper with the help of the neo-classical model of the firm at equilibrium. Particular attention is given to farm size, at least as it can be indicated by output, and to its relationship with land idling. Conclusions are drawn about the policies which should be adopted by the authorities with respect to farmland in the urban fringe. The second part describes the changing size of the farm, as measured by the area of improved land in use, in the more important urban fringes of Scotland over the last twenty years. It also reports upon the detailed interaction of public policy and agricultural retreat in one of the most dynamic of them, that around Glenrothes New Town.

A THEORY OF FARM SIZE AND LAND USE IN THE URBAN FRINGE

The literature on agriculture in the urban fringe lists a wide variety of problems which farmers face including dogs, arson, dumping, the fragmentation of holdings, rising land taxes, thefts, trespass and vandalism (Dent, 1981; Feaver, 1982), and also some advantages (Blair, 1980; Bryant, 1981), but no general statement has been made about them. It was for this reason that an attempt was made (Dawson, 1982) to produce a synthesis of their effects. Figure 21.1 indicates that while the farmer on the edge of the city may enjoy some advantages from this location, his costs of production will rise with proximity to the city as a result of the problems listed above. In such a situation the outer boundary of the urban fringe would seem to be marked by the point at which the net benefits for the farmer begin to increase. If the two curves intersect at any point before the edge of the built-up area is reached, that most obvious manifestation of the pressures on farming - idle land - might be expected to occur. An investigation was carried out on the basis of this hypothesis into the incidence of idle land in eastern Scotland at the point at which, according to Figure 21.1, it seemed most likely that it would occur, namely on the edge of the built-up area. Also, a comparison was made with areas of similar agricultural land capability, but which were distant from any major urban settlement. A slightly higher proportion of land was found to be idle on the edge of three towns of medium or large size (Edinburgh, Glenrothes New Town and Perth) than in the more distant areas, but in no case was idling widespread.

However, the approach which was used in that study took no account of the circumstances of the individual agricultural businesses which might be caught up in the process of urban growth and land conversion, or of the way in which land loss to such development and land idling might be related. These matters will be examined here within the neo-classical microeconomic framework of the equilibrium of the firm.

Under perfect competition, the output of any firm which is at equilibrium will be given by the intersection of its marginal-cost (MC) and average-cost (AC) curves at the point at which the average-cost curve is tangential to the price line (Figure 21.2). It follows that if the costs of production of farms in the urban fringe are higher than elsewhere (MC' and AC'), those farms will go out of business. It also follows that, if the size of the farm is reduced as a consequence of the development of some of its land, or if yields are reduced as a result of damage to, or interference with, crops, livestock or infrastructure by the urban population, the level of output will fall below Q. Costs will then exceed revenue and the farm will be forced out of production. Thus, it would be expected that the urban fringe, and especially land immediately adjacent to the built-up area, would be characterized by farms which have gone out of production for a variety of reasons and that their land would be lying unused. However, this suggestion was not corroborated to any great extent by the earlier study.

FIGURE 21.1: A MODEL OF LAND USE AROUND A CITY

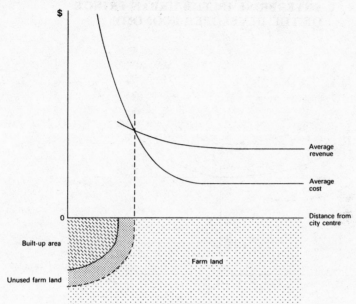

At least three reasons may account for this. Firstly, farmers do not usually operate under perfect competition. For example, in the United Kingdom and many other developed economies, the prices which they receive for their products are often artificially maintained at higher levels than would otherwise be the case, as a result of government intervention in the markets. P' represents such a price in Figure 21.2. In such circumstances farmers are able to absorb increases in costs up to P', or reductions in output down to Q', and yet remain in production. It would then be expected that more land in the urban fringe would continue to be used than would be the case under perfect competition.

Secondly, the model of the firm at equilibrium assumes that entrepreneurs are concerned to cover their costs in the long run, whereas many farmers in the urban fringe can only be assured of the continued use of their land in the short term. Thus, they will not need to maintain the farm infrastructure or soil fertility. In other words, they will be more concerned with their marginal than their average costs, and will be able to operate at any level of production down to the point at which marginal cost equals

**FIGURE 21.2: EQUILIBRIUM OF THE FARMING
ENTERPRISE IN THE URBAN FRINGE
OF THE DEVELOPED ECONOMY**

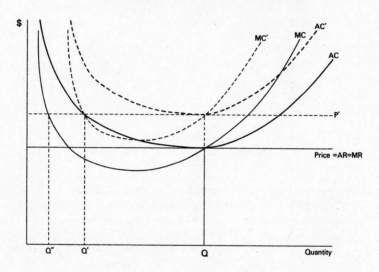

price (Q"). In this way, farms which are either very small or achieve very low yields may exist, at least in the short run, in the urban fringe, as Thomson (1981) has indicated in the case of England and Wales.

However, any such reduction in farm size, without a significant intensification of operations on the remaining land, would be contrary to the general trends of agricultural development in recent decades in developed countries. The substitution of capital for labour in these countries has raised the level of costs with the result that average and marginal-cost curves have been moving to the right, and that farmers have been encouraged to increase the scale of their operations. Indeed, so great has been this movement since the Second World War that many farmers probably now face a downward-sloping average-cost curve over any scale of production which they have been trained to undertake. Such trends work to the detriment of the urban fringe farmer who is giving up land, and are likely to increase the rate at which such farmers are forced out of business. But, in a situation in which surviving farmers may be attempting to expand their operations, if only to offset their own land losses, it does not follow that the land belonging to those who leave the industry will fall idle. Rather, it is likely to be taken over by the surviving farms.

Thus, farmers in the urban fringe in the developed market economy, especially those on the edge of the built-up area, would be expected to adopt a marginal-cost approach and, as a result, to be able to survive in business at smaller scales than otherwise. It would also seem that only very substantially increased costs of production, or reduced yields, will force farmers to abandon land when the prices of farm products are artificially high and scales of enterprise are increasing.

URBAN FRINGE POLICY OPTIONS FOR THE AUTHORITIES

If the foregoing analysis suggests that there are a variety of links between farm size and land idling in the urban fringe, it also implies the need for a range of policies on the part of those authorities which are charged with the regulation of agriculture and the preservation of the countryside around cities. In particular, policies which aim to retain land in agricultural use until the moment of development must not only ensure that farmers are protected from substantial extra costs arising out of the malign influences of urban areas, but that they are given an exact date on which their land will be required. This yields farmers the opportunity to move from average to marginal costing, and to run down their investment in a planned manner. Failure to develop such land on schedule is likely to result in it becoming idle because its early exhaustion and lack of maintenance will make it of little interest either to its original user or to other farmers. Conversely, where farmers appear to be running down land too rapidly, especially land which is not zoned for development, perhaps in the hope that it will then be released by the authorities to be sold at a greatly enhanced price, powers should be available which would allow the transfer of such land to other holdings. This would enable other farmers to take advantage of their downward-sloping average-cost curves. Such powers should be applied, *a fortiori*, to land which is designated as green belt or for some other aesthetic purpose which depends upon the continuance of agriculture for its fulfillment.

FARM SIZES IN SCOTLAND

The theoretical analysis above suggests that, in general, farmers on or close to the edge of the built-up area will probably be operating smaller than average holdings on a marginal-cost basis, and it is these hypotheses which have been tested in the case of Scotland. Since the early 1950s the built-up area, especially that of the four major cities and five new towns, has expanded substantially and much agricultural land has been converted to urban use. The effect of this expansion upon farm size has been measured in the areas adjacent or very close to these settlements, and a more detailed investigation was undertaken of individual farms on the edge of the built-up area of Glenrothes New Town.

Changes in the area of land in agricultural use, and in the number of holdings at the local scale, are available from the parish summaries of the June Agricultural Census. Table 21.1 is based upon this source. Unfortunately, the census is not ideal for this type of study for a variety of reasons (Coppock, 1955), the most serious of which is that land recorded for a parish in any year does not necessarily lie within the parish, but is that which is in use by the farmers who are based in that parish. Moreover, parish boundaries run quite independently of the edge of the built-up area. Hence, they may include not only farms which are on that edge, but others which are distant from it and which have not lost land to urban growth or are likely to do so in the near future. Third, the numbers of holdings in each parish during the 1950s are not included in the summaries, and so the description of change in Table 21.1 runs only from 1961. Nevertheless, the census is the only source which includes the necessary information about farms at a local level from past times.

Twenty-three urban fringe parishes were compared with 21 having similar land capability, but which are distant from major urban areas (Figure 21.3). In general, fringe holdings in 1983 were only about three-quarters of the size of those in other areas of Scotland, and they had been expanding slightly less rapidly since 1961. It would also appear that they had been disinvesting at a faster rate in intensive types of agricultural production - glasshouses, vegetables, soft fruit and poultry - than other farms. Also, in all these areas agriculture is less, rather than more, intensive on the edge of urban settlements. The input of labour, however, is still markedly higher. This may reflect the fact that at only 1.1 fulltime workers per holding, including farmers' families, there is little scope for further reduction unless farmers, together with sons working on their farms, go out of business. Thus, there is some evidence to suggest that, in the case of Scotland, the theoretical model of farm size and the changeover from average to marginal costing may be correct.

However, it is difficult to be certain of the reasons for such contrasts between fringe farms and other areas in the absence of more detailed investigations of the circumstances which surround farmers in fringe areas and the strategies which they pursue. Therefore, all the farmers working within the boundaries of Glenrothes New Town, one of the most rapidly expanding settlements in Scotland, were interviewed.

**TABLE 21.1:   SOME INDICATORS OF CHANGING
FARM STRUCTURE**

INDICATOR	CHANGE BETWEEN 1961 AND 1983 (1961 = 100)		1983	
	Fringe[1] Parishes	Other[2] Parishes	Fringe Parishes	Other Parishes
Average area of holding in crops and grass (ha)[3]	150.0	159.0	42.6	56.4
Fulltime workers per unit area of crops and grass (per 1000 ha of crops and grass)	56.0	53.0	26.1	17.8
Area of glass and plastic housing (per 1000 ha of crops and grass in m²)	34.0	74.0	1138.0	2236.0
Area under vegetables, soft fruits and nursery products for human consumption (per 1000 ha of crops and grass)	48.0	131.0	10.3	18.3
Poultry (per 1000 ha of crops and grass)	33.0	43.0	1946.0	2430.0

---

[1] Aberdeen, Cambuslang, Carmunnock, Cathcart, Corstorphine, Cramond, Cumbernauld, Dundee, Eastwood, Edinburgh, Glasgow, Govan, Inchinnan, Inveresk, Irvine, Kinglassie, Leith, Livingston, Mearns, Nigg (Kincardineshire), Paisley, Renfrew, Rutherglen

[2] Abercorn, Airth, Athelstaneford, Auchterarder, Belhelvie, Carluke, Craigie, Cults, Cupar, Dunnichen, Erskine, Forfar, Haddington, Houston, Kettle, Muiravonside, Oathlaw, Prestonkirk, Stair, Tarbolton, West Kilbride

[3] Measures in parentheses refer to the 1983 columns of the table

FIGURE 21.3: FRINGE PARISHES IN SCOTLAND

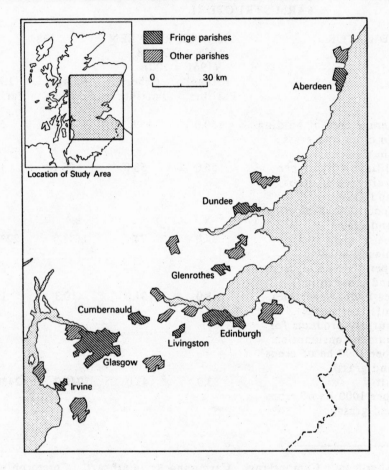

Attention was confined to the farms which hold land within the boundaries of the town for it is only these which can be affected directly by further growth of the built-up area. Out of the total of about 500 ha in 1984, approximately one-third lay in two owner-occupied farms, both of which were ring-fence holdings at some distance from the built-up area (Figure 21.4). One was separated from the built-up area by intervening fields, the other by a golf course. There was also one holding of about 70 ha under a full agricultural lease, but almost all the other land was let on 364-day leases to six farmers. All the land under lease had belonged

FIGURE 21.4: AGRICULTURAL LAND IN GLENROTHES
NEW TOWN IN 1984

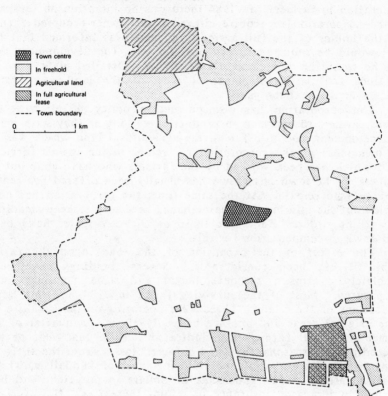

for many years to Glenrothes Development Corporation, the body responsible for the construction of the town.

Since the establishment of the town in 1948, it has been the policy of the corporation to indicate the extent of the area which is likely to be developed for as long a period as is possible into the future, and to acquire the necessary agricultural land within the town's boundary by compulsory purchase at an early stage. Thereafter, the land has been held first in full agricultural lets and then 364-day leases as the moment of development has approached.

Thus, farmers have in most cases been aware well in advance as to whether their land would be required for urban uses. However, there has been much less certainty about the short-term future. Some land has been held on an annual basis for many years, despite the fact that development of it was unlikely, while in other instances building has begun before even annual crops have been ready to be harvested. In these cases compensation has had to be paid by the corporation to farmers. In 1984 there was no intention on the part of the corporation to acquire either of the owner-occupied farms, but the holder of the full agricultural lease was informed that his land would be required in the medium term for development and that he would be compensated accordingly. Detailed plans were in existence for the development of most of the land on 364-day leases over the next ten years.

The corporation has also pursued a policy of allowing its tenant farmers to carry on in production as long as they wish prior to development, and to offer all the agricultural land which was in the ownership of the corporation for rental to the town's farmers. Land which has been worked by the farmers who have gone out of business as the town has grown has usually been offered for rental to those who remain. At the same time, the corporation has only carried out the minimum of maintenance necessary to keep steadings in working order. Rents for those on 364-day leases have been held down in compensation for this.

The effect of the expansion of the town upon the farms within it has been considerable. Several holdings have been completely overtaken by development and some steadings have disappeared. Most of the surviving farms in 1984 had lost large proportions of their land. Three were operating on only a third of their original areas and another had only 10 ha - a quarter of its former size. All farmers also indicated that in that year or the preceeding few seasons, they had suffered losses from the theft of crops or trespass and could point to instances of vandalism, which in some cases had cost thousands of dollars to put right and had resulted in increased insurance premiums thereafter. However, no farmer could assess in any but a very approximate manner the extent to which yields had been reduced or the overall level of costs raised, a finding which is consistent with that of Dent's (1981) study.

It is of interest to note that, in the face of these common circumstances, the tenant farmers of the new town have almost all adopted the same response. They have accepted whatever extra land the corporation has offered on short lease, even where it has been separate from their main holding or in small or awkwardly-shaped parcels, or adjacent to the built-up area, unfenced and therefore very exposed to interference. In some cases, they have also acquired land beyond the town boundaries to maintain the scale of their operations. Almost all have continued to employ good agricultural practices, such as the use of rotations and the treatment of fields after harvest against weeds and pests, even on land held on 364-day leases. There has been, however, a general unwillingness to spend money on fencing or to repair drains on such land or to plant winter-sown crops before lets for the next season have been confirmed. It would appear that those farming tenanted land on short lease have adopted a marginal-cost approach, whereas owner-occupied holdings and land on the full agricultural lease have been run with a view to the long term.

CONCLUSION

Four conclusions may be drawn from these findings. First, urban extension appears to have proceeded at a more rapid pace than the adjustment of land holding on farms around the edge of towns and cities in Scotland during the last twenty years. This has lead to a much slower rate of growth in farm size than elsewhere and has not been offset by intensification of land use. Second, farmers appear to be responding rationally in the face of imminent land loss by moving over to a marginal-cost basis for their operations. Third, the continued existence in business of holdings which have been very greatly reduced in size, and the use of exposed and awkward parcels of land, may indicate the extent to which marginal costs of farming in lowland Scotland fall below average costs at scales of output which are less than that at equilibrium. However, it probably also reflects the extent to which government-managed prices for farm products in the United Kingdom exceed the levels which are necessary if the average farm beyond the urban fringe is to make only normal profits. While a reduction in those prices might lead to the demise of many small farms in the urban fringe, it might also lead to the transfer of their land, at least in the short run, to holdings which are of sufficient size to take advantage of the recent rightward movement of average and marginal-cost curves in agriculture. This will be to the benefit of the whole industry. Last, the relatively low incidence of land idling in the urban fringe in Scotland may be taken to indicate that the problems of which so much is heard - urban interference with farming and the deliberate running down of land to encourage its re-zoning - are much less important than may have been thought. Also, as this paper has attempted to demonstrate, the processes of adjustment within the industry would appear to be able to cope at present with the costs and uncertainties of farming on the urban fringe, notwithstanding the conclusion about farm size above. It is unfortunate, in these circumstances, that recent decisions by the Secretary of State for Scotland which allow the re-zoning of agricultural land in the Edinburgh Green Belt for development, should have been justified precisely upon the urban-fringe, problem-location argument.

320

REFERENCES

Blair, A.M., 1980, "Urban Influences on Farming in Essex", Geoforum, 11, pp. 371-384.

Bryant, C.R., 1981, "Agriculture in an Urbanizing Environment: A Case Study from the Paris Region, 1968 to 1975", Canadian Geographer, 25, pp. 27-46.

Coppock, J.T., 1955, "The Relationship of Farm and Parish Boundaries - A Study in the Use of Agricultural Statistics", Geographical Studies, 2, pp. 12-26.

Dawson, A.H., 1982, "Unused Land on the Urban Fringe in Scotland". In A.B. Cruickshank (ed.), Where Town Meets Country. Aberdeen: University Press, pp. 97-106.

Dent, D., 1981, "Farming in the UK Urban Fringe", Farmers' Club Journal, 54, pp. 5-43.

Feaver, I.J., 1982, "Social Injustices to Farmers in the Urban Fringe, International Journal of Environmental Studies, 19, pp. 109-115.

Sinclair, R., 1967, "Von Thünen and Urban Sprawl", Annals of the American Association of Geographers, 57, pp. 72-87.

Thomson, K.J., 1981, Farming in the Fringe. Cheltenham: Countryside Commission.

PART 5
CONCLUSION

22

REVIEW AND PROSPECT
Chris Cocklin, Barry Smit
and Tom Johnston

The rural land resource provides a diversity of products and services. Some, like food, are essential to the maintenance of society, while others, like recreation, enhance the quality of life. Rural areas are also home to a significant proportion of the population, and they are where the environment is sometimes preserved in close to its natural state. Because rural areas are so diverse, it becomes very difficult to define "rural", except perhaps by resorting to such broad generalizations as "rural is that which is not urban" (Cloke, 1985). Unquestionably, though, the rural environment is of considerable importance because in one way or another it supports all of society.

Effective planning for rural areas has only recently emerged as a significant concern. In the developed world, the management of rural land has been traditionally of minor interest, with a prevailing view that the supply of land is virtually unlimited. When undertaken, planning was urban centred, and from this perspective rural land was evaluated primarily for its potential as a site for future urban development or as a supplier of goods and services for urban consumption. Not until the large conversions of land from rural, and particularly agricultural, uses were widely documented in the post-war period did concern begin to emerge for the more effective management of rural resources. This coincided with, and was a part of, the broader-based concern that arose throughout western society in the early 1960s for quality of the environment and conservation.

This collection of essays originates from a concern common to all of the authors: a recognized need to plan effectively for the use of the rural land resource. In order to provide the essential basis for such planning, several important research tasks must be undertaken.

323

In the first instance, the nature of land resource competition and its associated issues must be clearly understood. It was not so long ago that rural land-use change was not regarded as a problem. As the possibility of shortages of food and other products was foreseen, land competition emerged as an important concern. The nature of this competition is now better understood; theoretical frameworks exist by which to describe the processes in a general sense (Barlowe, 1972; Clawson, 1971; Found, 1971), and in many western countries the extent and rate of transferral is documented adequately. However, the issues surrounding this land transferral process are far from being resolved, although the lines of the debate are drawn well enough. At one end of the spectrum are those arguments based upon principles of economic efficiency and which suggest minimal regulatory intervention in the land market (Frankena and Scheffman, 1980; Stiglitz, 1979). This view holds that if shortages of agricultural land arise, then the market will adjust to ensure that sufficient resources are allocated to food production. Others have pointed to the existence of market failures, and argue that the pursuit of economic efficiency may result in food shortages for future generations (Briggs and Yurman, 1980; Plaut, 1980).

The issues themselves may be widely acknowledged, but the debates remain unresolved. Since the future is uncertain and the basic philosophies of interest groups are so different, conclusive answers are not likely to be found. Moreover, despite the emergence of a global economy, individual nations will probably tend to resolve resource issues at the domestic level. And within nations, many of the problems surface at a regional or local scale. Challenging opportunities exist, therefore, for analysts with an interest in rural resources to evaluate resource potentials and to assess possible options for future use.

The issue of agricultural land conversion has a long history in rural resource studies and has tended to dominate the literature. Land-use conflicts in the rural milieu are far more numerous, than those represented by the competition between urban demands and food production, however. Sites that are suitable for park development are often also well-suited to other land uses, which in the cases of mining, agriculture and forestry can often provide high economic returns to use. The purchase of land and its maintenance for recreation, however, can place a burden upon limited public funds. There may also be conflict between the preservation of the amenity value of farmland and changing systems of food production. As agricultural technology has changed, the visual character of the rural landscape also has changed, at the same time contributing to the loss of natural habitats.

Governments at several levels struggle to decide on the nature and degree of control which should be exercised over residential development in the countryside. There is continued debate over the management of extractive activities in rural areas. And there are widely differing views of appropriate conservation strategies for wetlands, wildlife habitats, and other natural areas. Also to be considered is the fact that rural land-use conflicts are likely to be intensified by environmental degradation and this raises further issues with respect to land resource utilization in the countryside.

A better understanding of the multifaceted nature of rural land conflicts is being developed. The papers in Part 2 of this book have provided some insight into the nature of the resource conflicts in both a general sense and with respect to some specific issues. The coverage is not comprehensive; conflicts also exist between agriculture and forestry, mining and agriculture, and between forestry and recreation, for example. In most cases, though, the issues are similar in that the resource allocation problem typically stems from the fact that parcels of land often have capability to support more than one activity for which there is a societal demand.

Equipped with better conceptualizations and understanding of land resource-use issues, analysis can be directed to the purpose of policy development. The development of appropriate data bases is essential to this task. Within the last ten years in particular, major technological advances have been made in the fields of information collection, storage and retrieval. The papers presented in Part 3 of this volume report on experiences in developing resource information systems. Such systems provide the opportunity to store vast quantities of data relevant to resource characteristics and use, and to retrieve this information in various formats.

In addition to general purpose information systems, efforts have also been directed towards the development of more focussed land evaluation systems. In these, biophysical data are combined with socio-economic information for the purposes of evaluating policy alternatives and for simulating the effects of various environmental, economic and social changes on resource use. Land evaluation systems provide access to extensive data bases and possess the capability to apply the stored information to specific policy questions. Somewhat similar capabilities are afforded by expert systems, which combine resource information with specified management decision rules.

Further improvements in such areas as remote sensing, communications and computer technology suggest excellent prospects for improving resource information systems. Better spatial and temporal coverage of the resource base will undoubtedly provide information previously unavailable. To have utility with respect to resource-use policy development, the stored information must be available in a form appropriate for the questions it is intended to address, and it is perhaps in this area that the greatest challenges will lie.

Access to information on the resource, while a necessary condition, is not sufficient for policy prescription. Appropriate frameworks for analysis must be developed in order that available information can be related to policy issues at hand. Contributors to Part 4 of this book offer insights into the development and application of methods within the context of rural land-use planning. Typically, the papers refer to the development and implementation of methods in response to specific land-use problems within rural areas. Although the methods have been developed for particular research problems, they are likely to find wider application, the possibilities for the generalization of the methodologies described in Part 4 being quite apparent.

With continued efforts in the field of methodology development, an array of appropriate techniques will be available to those involved in rural resource analysis and planning. Above all, appropriate methods must be developed to address the questions pertinent to the rural context. Through case studies, analysts should attempt to convince decision makers of the utility of these methods for the development of policy for rural resources. Access to, and application of, relevant information bases and suitable methods of analysis should promote better decisions instead of policy based on speculation and axiomatic deference to conventional wisdom.

This volume is not intended to represent a comprehensive coverage of the questions and issues relating to the use of rural land resources. Instead, it provides examples of recent developments and findings in the field of rural resource analysis. It also provides a framework for characterizing research tasks, and for showing how these tasks are associated with each other as well as with the process of public policy formulation.

This framework involves several stages. Initially land-use problems must be carefully identified and conceptualized. In the second stage, information is gathered and arranged in resource information systems. This provides an empirical base to assess the nature and extent of the problems. A third stage involves analysis of the relevant issues. The specific research questions will be guided by the issues of interest and the intended application. The analysis involves the identification of appropriate methods and their implementation, using resource information systems. Analysis contributes both to the empirical clarification of resource-use issues, as well as to public policy formulation.

The study of rural land resource problems remains in its infancy and the dominance of urban-centred planning is yet to be fully overcome. Continued efforts are required in the areas of problem definition, information systems development, and methodology. An increase in experience and knowledge should enhance the development of sound and coordinated policy with respect to the use of rural land, a resource of fundamental importance to society at large.

REFERENCES

Barlowe, R., 1972, Land Resource Economics: The Economics of Real Property. Englewood Cliffs: Prentice-Hall Inc.

Briggs, D. and E. Yurman, 1980, "Disappearing Farmland: A National Concern", Soil Conservation, 45, pp. 4-7.

Clawson, M., 1971, Suburban Land Conversion in the United States: An Economic and Governmental Process. Baltimore: Johns Hopkins.

Cloke, P.J., 1985, "Whither Rural Studies?", Journal of Rural Studies, 1 (1), pp. 1-9.

Found, W.C., 1971, A Theoretical Approach to Rural Land Use Patterns. Toronto: MacMillan.

Frankena, M.W. and D.T. Scheffman, 1980, Economic Analysis of Provincial Land Use Policies in Ontario. Toronto: University of Toronto Press.

Plaut, T., 1980, "Urban Expansion and the Loss of Farmland in the United States: Implications for the Future", American Journal of Agricultural Economics, 62 (3), pp. 537-542.

Stiglitz, J., 1979, "A Neoclassical Analysis of the Economics of Natural Resources". In V. Smith (ed.), Scarcity and Growth Reconsidered. Baltimore: Johns Hopkins, pp. 36-66.

ABOUT THE CONTRIBUTORS

NICOLAS ANTILLE is presently researching land use in le Valais. As a student in the geography program of the Swiss Federal Institute of Technology, he was involved with the work conducted by that institution on domestic energy in Kenya.

ALFRED BIRCH is Head of the Land Use Branch of Alberta Agriculture, Edmonton, Alberta, Canada. In this capacity he leads a small program of agricultural and natural resource policy research. Ongoing interests and planning projects include water management, land capability and use, soil conservation economics and automated resource data management.

MICHAEL BRKLACICH is with the Land Resource Research Centre, Agriculture Canada and is a Ph.D. candidate with the Department of Geography, University of Waterloo, Waterloo, Ontario, Canada. His research interests include evaluating prospects for sustainable food production in a changing environment and procedures for integrating biophysical and socio-economic approaches to resource assessment.

CHRIS COCKLIN is a Lecturer with the Department of Geography, University of Auckland, Auckland, New Zealand. He was a founding member of the Rural and Urban Fringe Study Group of the Canadian Association of Geographers. His research interests are in the areas of rural land-use analysis and planning, resource management and energy studies.

DOUGLAS COCKS is Senior Principal Research Scientist in the CSIRO Divison of Wildlife and Rangelands Research, Canberra, Australia. His research interests are in land-use planning and policy, and geographic information systems.

DONALD DAVIDSON is a Reader in the Department of Environmental Science, University of Stirling, Stirling, Scotland. His research interests are in the assessment of soils for land use, and the analysis of soils from archeological sites.

RICHARD DAVIS is Leader of the Knowledge Systems Group of the CSIRO Division of Water and Land Resources, Canberra, Australia. He is interested in applying advanced computer concepts to the management of the natural resource base with particular interests in artificial intelligence and geographic information systems.

ANDREW H. DAWSON is a Senior Lecturer at the University of St. Andrews, Fife, Scotland. He is an economic geographer with particular interests in the spatial impact of the management of the economy and Eastern Europe, especially Poland.

MARK FLAHERTY is an Assistant Professor with the Department of Geography at the University of Victoria, Victoria, British Columbia, Canada. His research interests are in land rating, land planning and international development.

MARIE-FRANCE GERMAIN is with the Methodology Division, Statistics Canada, Ottawa, Ontario, Canada.

HANS GILGEN is a Lecturer at the Geography Department of the Swiss Federal Institute of Technology. His background is in biogeography and mathematical modelling, and his writings range from historical studies of the roots of human ecology in geography to technical papers on geographical information systems.

TOM JOHNSTON is a SSHRC Doctoral Fellow and a Ph.D. candidate with the Department of Geography, University of Waterloo, Waterloo, Ontario, Canada. His research interests are in public policy analysis, and structural change in agriculture.

GARETH JONES is a Lecturer in Geography at the University of Strathclyde, Glasgow, Scotland. His research interests are in vegetation productivity and natural resource conservation.

LAURIE LUDLOW is a Research Associate with the Land Evaluation Group at the University of Guelph, Guelph, Ontario, Canada. Her research interests are in environmental resource management, specifically land-related planning issues and techniques for evaluation.

RAY MCBRIDE is an Assistant Professor with the Department of Land Resource Science, University of Guelph, Guelph, Ontario, Canada. His research interests include the development of methodologies for agricultural land rating systems, the characterization of soil degradation processes and the treatment of municipal wastewaters in agricultural and other ecosystems.

GEORGE MCCAW is with the Economic Programs and Government Finance Branch, Economic Development Division, Department of Finance, Ottawa, Ontario, Canada.

GEOFFREY MCDONALD is a Reader with the School of Environmental Studies, Griffith University, Brisbane, Australia. His research interests are in land-use planning, resource management, and impacts of resource development.

EDWARD W. MANNING is the Chief of the Land Use Analysis Division of Environment Canada, Ottawa, Ontario, Canada. He is the author of over 50 books and articles on topics concerning land resources, resource planning and program impact analysis.

IAN MOFFATT is with the Department of Environmental Science at the University of Stirling, Stirling, Scotland. His major research interests are in understanding the dynamics of environmental systems, carrying capacity and sustainable development.

RICHARD MUNTON is a Reader in the Department of Geography, University College London, London, England. His main research interests are in land-use planning and the restructuring of agriculture and its consequences for the rural environment.

PAUL NANNINGA is an Experimental Scientist with the Knowledge Systems Group of the CSIRO Division of Water and Land Resources, Canberra, Australia. As part of his research into artificial intelligence applications for natural resource planning and management he is writing an expert system for the managers of Kakadu National Park, Northern Territory, Australia. He also has an interest in research in neural circuitry.

UDO NEILSON is with Dendron Resources Surveys Ltd., Ottawa, Ontario, Canada.

M. DUANE NELLIS is an Associate Professor of Geography at Kansas State University, Manhattan, Kansas, United States. His current research focus is on the impact of irrigation development and associated groundwater depletion on the Kansas High Plains region.

JOHN T. PIERCE is an Associate Professor with the Department of Geography, Simon Fraser University, Burnaby, British Columbia, Canada. His research interests are in land resource issues and policies, and food production potential.

JOHN J. PIGRAM is a Senior Lecturer with the Department of Geography and Planning, University of New England, Armidale, New South Wales, Australia. His research interests are in outdoor recreation and access to rural environments, and water resource management and irrigation agriculture.

ANN POHL lives in Toronto, Ontario, Canada and was an urban planner with this city from 1976-1984. She helped found the Preservation of Agricultural Land Society, and the Ontario Coalition to Preserve Foodland.

ROY RICKSON is with the School of Environmental Studies at Griffith University in Brisbane, Australia.

ROBERT RYERSON is with the Canada Centre for Remote Sensing, Energy Mines and Resources, Ottawa, Ontario, Canada.

BARRY SMIT is a Professor with the Department of Geography, and the Director of the Land Evaluation Group, University of Guelph,

Guelph, Ontario, Canada. His research interest is in rural systems, and includes analyses of sensitivities of food production systems to environmental and socio-economic changes.

DIETER STEINER is a Professor in the Department of Geography at the Swiss Federal Institute of Technology. His work on remote sensing and quantitative methods is known internationally. Most recently he has been attempting to give rigourous and systematic underpinnings to human ecology as an approach.

PETER SULZER is presently working in Peru as a cartographer. As a student in the geography program of the Swiss Federal Institute of Technology, he was involved with the work conducted by that institution on domestic energy in Kenya.

H.A. VAN KLEEF is with the Institute for Land and Water Management Research, Wageningen, The Netherlands.

WILLEM VAN VUUREN is with the Department of Agricultural Economics and Business, University of Guelph, Guelph, Ontario, Canada. His research interests include rural resource development, preservation of wetlands, land tenure, and soil erosion.

ROSEMARY VILLANI is with the Canada Centre for Remote Sensing, Energy, Mines and Resources, Ottawa, Ontario, Canada.

DAN WILLIAMS was an Agroclimatologist with the Canadian Government from 1960-1985. Now retired, he lives in Coldwater, Ontario. His research interests include agroclimatic resources, Canadian prime farmland losses, environmental degradation and the interrelations of agroclimatic and socio-economic factors.

BEN WISNER is presently based at the Department of Human Ecology, Rutgers University, New Brunswick, New Jersey, United States, while consulting with ILO, UNESCO and the United Nations University's Food-Energy Nexus Program. He has worked on a range of human ecological problems in Africa including issues of access to fuel wood, water supply, food storage, nutritional assessment, and the changing situation of rural women.

INDEX